INDUSTRIAL RELATIONS RESEARCH ASSOCIATION SERIES

FEDERAL POLICIES AND WORKER STATUS SINCE THE THIRTIES

AUTHORS

Eileen Ahern

Irving Bernstein

Wilbur J. Cohen

Joseph P. Goldberg

James E. Jones, Jr.

Garth L. Mangum

D. Quinn Mills

Raymond Munts

Rudolph A. Oswald

Leo Teplow

EDITORIAL BOARD

Joseph P. Goldberg

Eileen Ahern

William Haber

Rudolph A. Oswald

i

First Edition

Library of Congress Catalog Card Number: 76-47838

PRICE $7.50

INDUSTRIAL RELATIONS RESEARCH ASSOCIATION SERIES

PROCEEDINGS OF THE ANNUAL WINTER MEETING (Spring Publication)
PROCEEDINGS OF THE ANNUAL SPRING MEETING (Fall Publication)
Annual Research Volume (Fall Publication)
  (MEMBERSHIP DIRECTORY HANDBOOK every sixth year in lieu of research volume)
IRRA NEWSLETTER (Published Quarterly)

Inquiries and other communications regarding membership, meetings, publications and the general affairs of the Association, as well as orders for publications, copyright requests, and notice of address changes, should be addressed to the IRRA publication office: Barbara D. Dennis and James L. Stern, Co-editors; Richard U. Miller, Secretary-Treasurer; Elizabeth S. Gulesserian, Executive Assistant.

INDUSTRIAL RELATIONS RESEARCH ASSOCIATION
7226 Social Science Building, University of Wisconsin
Madison, WI 53706 U.S.A. Telephone 608/262-2762

Kowa Graphics, Inc., 510 N. Hickory, Champaign, IL 61820

CONTENTS

PREFACE

To provide a cornerstone for this historical analysis of federal social and labor policies as they affected and continue to affect workers, Irving Bernstein evokes the social unrest of the Great Depression—when unemployment peaked at 25 percent of the labor force in the worst year, 1933, and never fell below 14 percent. He discusses the political climate of that time and presents an interesting account of those who shaped and administered New Deal social and labor policies. One was Frances Perkins, whom President Roosevelt appointed Secretary of Labor at the time he took office in March 1933. The program she proposed at the outset was effectuated within 12 years, an achievement that was possible because over a long period much thought had been given to the social problems of industrialization.

First some emergency measures had to be taken, on a trial-and-error basis: the Federal Emergency Relief Administration, the Works Progress Administration, and the Public Works Administration. Training was not a general objective under conditions of job scarcity, as Garth Mangum mentions in his chapter later in the volume, but constructive efforts were taken through the National Youth Administration and the Civilian Conservation Corps.

Roosevelt tried to stimulate business recovery through the National Industrial Recovery Act (NIRA) of 1933. The codes of fair competition provided for in that legislation had to contain minimum wage and hour standards and restrictions on child labor. Although the Supreme Court in 1935 held the NIRA unconstitutional, the Act demonstrated, as Rudolph Oswald points out, that compliance with labor standards could be secured on a national scale.

The precursor of general federal minimum wage-hour laws was the minimum prevailing standards requirement applying to government contractors. Since contracts had to go to the lowest bidder, Oswald comments, these laws—the Davis-Bacon Act of 1931 and the Walsh-Healey Act of 1936 (and later, the McNamara-O'Hara Act of 1965) —assured that the lowest bidder was not the one who paid his employees the least.

The Fair Labor Standards Act (FLSA) of 1938 was the only major labor legislation enacted in the late thirties when, as Bernstein describes, there was a swing back to conservatism. Oswald examines the revisions of this basic law up to the present and the difficulties that always accompany changes in it. The Equal Pay Act of 1963 amended the FLSA by prohibiting discrimination based on sex in the payment of wages for jobs requiring equal skill, effort, and responsibility, performed under similar working conditions.

In labor relations, also, there was a reservoir of experience that could be tapped when the crisis of the 1930s made change essential. Joseph Goldberg observes that principles had been emerging over a long period of management-labor relations in the United States.

Section 7 (a) of the NIRA required a guarantee of the right of workers to organize and bargain collectively, and it was used by unions in coal, steel, textile, garment, and other industries before the demise of the NIRA. The National Labor Relations (Wagner) Act of 1935 provided a longer-lasting statutory guarantee of these rights. The same policy applied to the railroads and airlines through amendments in 1934 and 1936 to the Railway Labor Act of 1926.

The trend toward conservatism resurfaced in the postwar years. In 1947 the Congress, responding to public sentiment that labor had become too powerful, passed the Labor Management Relations (Taft-Hartley) Act, amending the Wagner Act though not, Goldberg emphasizes, changing its basic principles. The LMRA recognized the right of workers to refrain from self-organization, defined certain activities as union unfair practices, and provided a procedure for national emergency disputes.

After the McClellan Committee hearings on corruption in a number of national and local unions, Congress in 1959 enacted the Labor Management Reporting and Disclosure (Landrum-Griffin) Act which regulates the internal affairs of unions and provides a "Bill of Rights" for union members.

Goldberg examines the adaptability of the LMRA to new issues and new sectors of workers and discusses policy and procedural problems of the National Labor Relations Board, often the focus of criticism by management, labor, and the public. He raises the question whether the LMRA and the NLRB have been diminished by requirements of Title VII, the Railway Labor Act, the FSLA, and others, and he recommends a study of the interaction of these statutes. James E. Jones, Jr., makes this point, too, in his chapter on fair employment practices.

Wilbur J. Cohen is one of the key figures Bernstein mentions as shaping New Deal social policies. Cohen's chapter provides in rich detail the history of the Social Security Act of 1935. "The Great Depression clearly revealed the increasing and severe human problems of dependent old age in an industrial, urban society," he writes. Social security enables people to plan ahead, and it helps employers, economic planners, and Congress to allocate resources to meet human needs in a responsible manner.

Signed by President Roosevelt on August 14, 1935, the measure had had wide public support despite some vigorous opposition. On May 24, 1937, the Supreme Court affirmed the constitutionality of the old-age benefits and unemployment insurance programs. Chairman of the first Advisory Council on Social Security was J. Douglas Brown. Among others in this important path-breaking group were Paul Douglas, William Haber, and Edwin E. Witte.

Cohen points to features of the Act that he believes account for its success, and he also discusses current criticism of certain aspects of social security and makes recommendations for change and further development.

The unemployment insurance system became law as Title III of the Social Security Act. Again, as Raymond Munts observes, the Great Depression had revealed the need. He reviews the history of efforts to cushion the effects of unemployment under union, employer, and joint plans, most of which collapsed in the 1930s. Numerous industry leaders supported the move for a government plan.

The unanticipated intensity of the 1970s' recession has had a severe impact on the financial structure of the federal-state unemployment insurance program. Munts examines the reasons for the "chronic underfinancing that characterizes many states." He reviews revisions made in unemployment insurance since 1935 and presents data on the questions: Are unemployment insurance laws more, or less, generous than they were 30 years ago? And, is the disparity between the states tending to widen or narrow?

In his discussion of policy questions, Munts examines the amount and duration of benefits, waiting weeks, work-qualifying requirements, disqualifications, and other factors. He also considers the impact of unemployment insurance on the labor market and the new issues that have developed with manpower policies and related matters of current concern. Mangum also addresses himself to these issues.

When World War II ended 12 years of labor market slack, the country had to meet the unprecedented production challenge without the background of a well-conceived policy. The war and its aftermath brought changes to which society is still reverberating. Technological developments were the main influence. Rising labor force participation of women (19 percent before the war, 27 percent in 1947, and 44 percent by 1975) was another major factor. High birth rates of the 1947–57 period predetermined youth employment problems from 1963 to sometime in the 1970s.

Reviewing postwar manpower programs, Mangum concludes that most of the people who went through them came out sufficiently better off in employment stability and income to justify the cost. Nevertheless, he finds that the programs fell short of the need and the commitment. A major defect is failure of most programs to take labor market realities into account; only the equal employment opportunity policies had a significant impact on the way labor markets work, Mangum points out.

Overall, his assessment is that not much progress has been made on policy development since the 1930s. Manpower policy has not had the fundamental thinking that preceded the Wagner Act and social security. This is what is needed, in his estimation—not new legislation. For the period 1975–2000, Mangum recommends that manpower policy be planned in full recognition of demographic, social, and economic trends, several of which are already apparent.

Concerning employment policy, Mangum finds the commitment in the Employment Act of 1946 "largely rhetorical." He writes, "Following the Korean conflict, unemployment trended persistently upward through a series of short, mild recessions. With each recession, unemployment rose higher, and with each recovery, left a higher residual of unemployed people."

With unemployment rates persisting around 8 percent in the recession of the 1970s, manpower policy questions are concerning many industry leaders at this time. Mangum also discusses the manpower implications of unemployment insurance policy.

When the production requirements of the war expanded the workforce enormously, only one in 20 defense workers was black, although blacks comprised 10 percent of the population. There was no more than 3 percent black participation in the skilled workforce of the construction industry. Unions reflected the discriminatory attitudes of the society.

A. Philip Randolph, leader of the Brotherhood of Sleeping Car Porters, organized a march on Washington for July 1, 1941. In response to this pressure, President Roosevelt issued Executive Order 8802, on June 25, 1941, establishing the Committee on Fair Employment Practices. Twenty years later, in 1961, President Kennedy issued Executive Order 10925 which required affirmative action and provided sanctions for noncompliance. As Jones points out, the Executive Order approach, applying only to government contractors, was very limited.

Congress finally provided statutory prohibition of discrimination in employment through Title VII of the Civil Rights Act of 1964, but, as Jones observes, the legislation did not follow either the NLRB or the FLSA models: The Equal Employment Opportunity Commission was not given enforcement powers, but this deficiency was repaired to some extent when Congress enacted the Equal Employment Opportunity Act of 1972, which also extended coverage of Title VII.

Jones analyzes enforcement policies of the Office of Federal Contract Compliance and court decisions involving Title VII and other statutes, including the impact of the LMRA on discrimination issues. He predicts, ". . . the clash of labor relations laws with equal employment laws is likely to involve us in the process of harmonizing these national policies for a long time into the future."

Pointing out that most cases to date have dealt with blue-collar employees, Jones anticipates increasing concern over at least two important issues in the next decade: To what extent can principles be transferred from the blue-collar sector to professional and technical groups? Will concepts developed on the job-relatedness of tests be used to challenge qualifications requirements imposed by licensing mechanisms and by employers, and the requirements of particular diplomas and degrees? Overall, Jones concludes that the transformation of fair employment practices should be dated only from 1965.

A new era of federal involvement in labor policy was ushered in by the comprehensive Occupational Safety and Health Act of 1970. Leo Teplow traces the history of state legislation as well as the safety and health requirements under Walsh-Healey and other federal laws enacted for particular situations, such as the Federal

Coal Mine Safety Act of 1952 and its subsequent revisions, and the Federal Metallic and Non-Metallic Mine Safety Act of 1966. He also discusses voluntary programs in industry, the development of consensus standards, and past and current attitudes of employers, unions, and the public.

"Almost every aspect of an occupational health standard now being developed by OSHA raises labor relations issues," writes Teplow. He examines other matters that have implications for collective bargaining, such as proposals for joint safety committees and the reasons for much management resistance to them, and he cites new directions being taken: (1) The 1970 agreements between the major rubber companies and the United Rubber Workers provide for joint committees to oversee extensive research programs conducted by two leading graduate schools of public health, designed to identify work-related causes of death or disease in that industry. (2) The United Steelworkers and the major companies in the steel producing industry have agreed upon extensive health and safety provisions ranging from joint committees to treatment of alcoholism. (3) The automobile industry has developed new collective bargaining solutions in agreements with the United Auto Workers. One of the features is company-paid and company-trained union safety representatives.

Teplow evaluates OSHA/1970, making recommendations for future substantive and administrative changes.

The United States has had wage policy programs in nine periods, beginning with the National War Labor Board of the first World War, down to the present Council on Wage and Price Stability. D. Quinn Mills discusses important differences among these agencies. Some had a statutory base; others, like the 1966 "Guideposts," did not. Some were tripartite, some had disputes-settlement mechanisms, some were administered mainly on a case-by-case approach, others issued comprehensive regulations. Mills's analysis of the standard to determine compensation increases is of particular interest today.

Few wage-price programs have had overt support from either management or labor, but some have had it from one or the other for brief periods. Mills warns that the government must get the cooperation of both management and labor, as either can make the program ineffective, or even bring about its demise.

The idea of partial or selective controls has not been much accepted, Mills says, except in a period of gradual decontrol or in the construction industry. The tripartite Construction Industry Stabilization Committee of 1971–74 was a major factor in bringing down the first year total compensation increase from 17 percent in 1970, to 11 percent in 1971, to 6.0 percent in 1972, and to 5.4 percent in 1973.

"In some instances, fringe benefits have become a virtually uncontrollable engine for inflationary pressures," Mills writes. He refutes the argument that insurance and pension plans cannot be inflationary because they do not add to purchasing power. Increases in nonwage compensation have other economic consequences: Price increases may be required because of high costs of insurance programs to employers; inflationary pressures may be exerted in the medical industry by increased health insurance programs; the impact of an increase in insurance costs on the total compensation of one group of workers may be transmitted to others and translated into either increased fringe benefits or higher wages.

Insurance plans of the 1970s, Mills states, cannot be regulated by methods used in past stabilization periods. He discusses this problem as well as noninsurance benefits such as paid holidays, vacations, overtime, and shift premiums. The relative importance of both types of fringes has been increasing in the total compensation package.

The editors are grateful to the outstanding people—both academicians and practitioners, the latter representing management, labor, or government—who wrote the various chapters for this volume. As noted, several of the authors had a role in the events they describe. The editors' purpose in preparing this review of the past is to contribute to an understanding of present problems in the various areas and to stimulate thought about how these problems might be solved in the future. In this spirit, the editors dedicate this volume to Nathaniel Goldfinger (1916–1976) in recognition of his encouragement of research on industrial relations problems and his leadership as President of the Industrial Relations Research Association in 1974.

The Editors:
JOSEPH P. GOLDBERG, *Chairman*
EILEEN AHERN
WILLIAM HABER
RUDOLPH A. OSWALD

CHAPTER 1

The New Deal and Federal Labor Policies

IRVING BERNSTEIN
University of California, Los Angeles

Frances Perkins has recounted an incident that is significant for this chapter and this volume. In late February 1933, while she was New York's Industrial Commissioner, she received a call to visit President-elect Franklin D. Roosevelt at his East 65th Street house in New York City. Since the matter was already a minor national issue, she anticipated his purpose. He would invite her to become Secretary of Labor in his New Deal cabinet.

"I've been thinking things over," Roosevelt said, "and I've decided I want you to be Secretary of Labor." Miss Perkins demurred. She pointed out that she was not from the labor movement and that the American Federation of Labor, which took a proprietary interest in the Labor Department, had endorsed Dan Tobin, the president of the Teamsters. Impressed with her competence and eager to be the first President to name a woman to the cabinet, Roosevelt brushed this argument aside. Here it is best to quote Miss Perkins.

> Since I seemed to be making little headway, I tried a new approach. I said that if I accepted the position of Secretary of Labor I should want to do a great deal. I outlined a program of labor legislation and economic improvement. None of it was radical. It had all been tried in certain states and foreign countries. But I thought that Roosevelt might consider it too ambitious to be undertaken when the United States was deep in depression and unemployment.
>
> In broad terms, I proposed immediate federal aid to the states for direct unemployment relief, an extensive program of public works, a study and an approach to the establishment by federal law of minimum wages, maximum hours, true unemployment and old-age insur-

1

ance, abolition of child labor, and the creation of a federal employment service.

The program received Roosevelt's hearty endorsement, and he told me he wanted me to carry it out.

On March 5, 1933, Frances Perkins was sworn in as Secretary of Labor.

Justice Harlan Fiske Stone considered Miss Perkins "the first real Secretary of Labor the country has ever had." He greatly admired her "capacity and wisdom." He might have added foresight. The program she proposed, and Roosevelt accepted, in a one-hour conversation on a February evening in 1933 was totally effectuated. The unemployment relief program became the Federal Emergency Relief Administration in 1933 and was converted into the Works Progress Administration in 1935. The Public Works Administration of 1933 undertook the main public construction activities and was supplemented by an FERA offshoot, the Civil Works Administration, and, later, by WPA. The National Recovery Administration of 1933 in its industry codes of "fair competition," among other things, regulated minimum wages, maximum hours, and child labor. The legislation was held unconstitutional in 1935 and was succeeded by the Fair Labor Standards Act of 1938, which was exclusively directed to wages, hours, and child labor. The Walsh-Healey Public Contracts Act of 1936 provided for minimum wages and maximum hours under federal contracts that exceeded $10,000 in value. The Social Security Act of 1935 established the general unemployment insurance and old-age pension systems of the United States. The Railroad Retirement Act of the same year provided for old-age and disability pensions for railway employees. The Wagner-Peyser Act of 1935 set up the U.S. Employment Service.

In her conversation with Roosevelt in February 1933, Miss Perkins failed to foresee one important area of New Deal labor policy, federal protection of the right of workers to organize and bargain collectively. It took ambiguous form at the outset in 1933 in Section 7 (a) of the National Industrial Recovery Act as a counterweight to industry's right under NRA codes to form trade associations to fix prices and allocate markets without regard to the antitrust laws. A fully articulated policy for industry in general emerged in the National Labor Relations Act of 1935. Amendments to the Railway Labor Act in 1934 and 1936 established essentially the same policy for the railroads and the airlines.

In sum, the New Deal period was the seminal era in the initiation and formulation of American labor policy. It is hardly a coincidence that of the eight substantive chapters in this volume, five deal with policies tracing their historic origins to the thirties. This raises two interesting questions. First, why was this period so significant? Second, why were the policies treated in the remaining chapters omitted?

There are, it seems to me, half a dozen answers to the question of the importance of the time. The first, and by far the most consequential, is the Great Depression itself, particularly its most obvious manifestation, massive joblessness on a scale unmatched in American history. While there were no contemporary systematic official statistics of unemployment, itself a small national scandal, the Bureau of Labor Statistics has estimated retrospectively for the whole year 1933 that 12,830,000 persons were out of work, 25.5 percent of the labor force. Robert R. Nathan, who worked up monthly estimates at the time, set the figure for the worst month, March 1933, at 29.2 percent. The BLS statistic for the best year of the period, 1937, was 14.3 percent. But this was only part of the problem. An unknown number, but clearly many workers, were on short time to spread the limited amount of available work. In the face of shrinking markets and in the absence of unions in most industries, employers cut wages. There were reports of children working for as little as a nickel an hour.

Unemployment produced profound social and emotional consequences. Immigration from abroad virtually ceased and the secular movement from farm to city slowed. Transiency took their place—jobless workers, often with their families, wandering aimlessly and gathering in junkpile Hoovervilles. The most dramatic illustration was the migration from the dust bowl of Okies, Arkies, and Mizoos to California. Homes and furniture were lost, the health of the poor declined, the family as an institution suffered. Perhaps most important, morale sagged. In the struggle for immediate survival, hope for the future evaporated.

Thus, the depression automatically thrust labor problems onto the center of the stage of national policy. While a minority disagreed, Roosevelt, backed by the great majority of the citizenry,

felt that it was of critical importance to develop policies to provide relief to the jobless, to stimulate business recovery and thereby
raise the level of private employment, to provide public jobs with
public works and also to improve the nation's capital stock, to
shore up wages and diminish child labor, to try to improve the
functioning of the labor-market machinery, and to develop long-
term programs of unemployment compensation and old-age pensions. In this context, as well, it seemed sensible to stimulate the
development of unionism and to encourage the spread of collective bargaining.

The second important factor was the political liberalization
of the country. This took place both at the federal as well as
at the state and local levels, though it is the former that is relevant here. The decade of the twenties had been relatively pros-
perous; business rode high in esteem, and the Republican Party
dominated both the Congress and the presidency. The tide began to turn with the congressional elections of 1930, when the
Democrats captured the House and narrowed the Republican
majority in the Senate to one, which was damaging to President
Hoover because the progressive Republicans voted against him
on key issues. One of those senators, in fact, George W. Norris
of Nebraska, was the principal author of the prolabor Norris-
LaGuardia Act of 1932. The decisive break occurred in 1932,
when Roosevelt defeated Hoover by over seven million votes and
won in the electoral college by 42 to 6 states. The Democrats
swept both houses of Congress by heavy majorities. This was
the political precondition for the legislation of the "Hundred
Days" of 1933, which included NRA, FERA, and PWA.

In defiance of the rule of American politics that the President's party suffers losses in off-year elections, Roosevelt's personal
popularity and public acceptance of the New Deal lifted the
Democrats to towering majorities in both the House and Senate
in 1934. The Seventy-Fourth Congress, which convened early the
next year, must have been the most liberal ever elected. It is
no coincidence that the Wagner Act, the Social Security Act, and
WPA were legislated in 1935. Despite the fact that Roosevelt
won an even greater victory in 1936 over Alf Landon, losing
only two states, than he had in 1932, this was the political watershed. The country would soon swing back toward conservatism,

and this was confirmed by Republican congressional gains two
years later. In fact, the only significant labor legislation enacted
in the late thirties was the Fair Labor Standards Act of 1938,
and it was passed because of exceptional Administration pressure
and after notable concessions, particularly on exemptions from
coverage.

Third, and also political, is leadership, about which several
points may be made. A historic difference between the dominant
American parties has been the concept of the presidency: The
Republicans have stressed a limited role for the occupant of the
White House, while the Democrats have offered vigorous leadership. Hoover, with his emphasis on private and local responsibility, his concern with a balanced budget, and his distaste
for federal programs, was squarely in the Republican tradition.
Roosevelt, by contrast, was the supreme exemplar of the Democratic concept of the presidency. He both believed in strong presidential leadership as a matter of principle and personally enjoyed it. FDR himself had much to do with the flood of progressive legislation. Though there is no space to go into the details,
perhaps the Social Security Act is the best illustration. Roosevelt
involved himself heavily in the drafting of this complex statute,
left his mark upon many of its major features, and regarded the
law as his most important domestic accomplishment.

Another point concerning political leadership is the domi-
nance of the New York crowd. There are four individuals who
played decisive roles in the development of the New Deal labor
policies—Roosevelt, Miss Perkins, Senator Robert F. Wagner, and
Harry L. Hopkins. Roosevelt and Wagner were native New York-
ers. Although Miss Perkins came from Massachusetts and Hopkins from Iowa, both had lived and worked in New York for
many years before they came to Washington in 1933. While the
chemistry is mysterious, the fact is too impressive to be explained
by coincidence alone. New York made a formidable contribution
to the nation in the New Deal labor policies.

Fourth, a major pressure group, organized labor, pushed politically for the passage of labor legislation. This was a rather
complicated process because (1) the American Federation of Labor in 1933 was numerically and economically very weak; (2)
the AFL was more interested in collective bargaining legislation

than in programs to promote employment and social welfare; (3) with the walkout of John L. Lewis and his industrial-union followers from the AFL in 1935, leading to the formation of what would be known as the Congress of Industrial Organizations, the labor movement split and the AFL and CIO adopted differing legislative policies; and (4) the New Dealers, notably Roosevelt and Miss Perkins, viewed labor policy more broadly to encompass the unorganized than did the union leaders. Nevertheless, this pressure group was an important source of support for much of this legislation. The AFL played a central role in the passage of both Section 7 (a) of NIRA and the Wagner Act. It also offered support to a number of the other laws, such as the Social Security and Wagner-Peyser Acts. The CIO was the main lobby behind the enactment of FLSA in 1938. Finally, one must note in this context the independent railway labor unions, which proved themselves exceptionally effective in gaining crucial amendments to the Railway Labor Act and the passage of the Railroad Retirement Act. The political power of labor, even when it was economically weak, was enhanced by the declining political influence of industry. Business, which had taken credit for the prosperity of the twenties, was now saddled with the blame for the depression of the thirties. The political scale tipped automatically in favor of labor.

The fifth reason for the burst of New Deal labor legislation was the contribution of intellectuals, which, again, was composed of several elements. It is said that a mature generation in power puts into effect the ideas it learned in its youth. Thus, there was an intimate connection between the Progressive Era and the New Deal. Roosevelt and Wagner had served in the New York legislature before World War I and had worked for the enactment of labor-reform laws at the state level. Frances Perkins was the lobbyist they dealt with for the National Consumers' League, seeking to regulate hours, wages, and child labor. FDR constantly invoked Theodore Roosevelt. Miss Perkins had studied with the unorthodox economist, Simon Patten, at the University of Pennsylvania and had worked with Jane Addams at Hull House in Chicago and Florence Kelley at the Consumers' League. Hopkins started work in 1912 at Christadora House on the lower East Side of Manhattan. Eleanor Roosevelt was active in the Women's Trade

Union League and was a friend of Florence Kelley and Lillian Wald of the Henry Street Settlement in New York.

There was, as well, the impact of the Wisconsin school. The Progressive movement had made its greatest gains in that state when Robert M. LaFollette was governor early in the century. He turned to the state university at Madison for advice—in the labor area, to the great institutional economist and reformer, John R. Commons. LaFollette's sons and Commons's students had a significant effect on national policies in the thirties. Bob, Jr., sat in his father's seat in the United States Senate and was second only to Wagner as the congressional leader on labor and social legislation. Governor Philip LaFollette called the Wisconsin legislature into special session in 1932 to enact the nation's first unemployment insurance law. Commons had drafted the original version in 1921; his student, Paul Raushenbush, had redrafted it in 1931; and another student, Assemblyman Harold M. Groves, introduced the bill.

The Wisconsin group had its greatest impact on the Social Security Act. This measure originated in the Administration rather than the Congress and was, of course, highly technical. In 1934 Roosevelt created the cabinet-level Committee on Economic Security with Miss Perkins as chairman. She put her Assistant Secretary of Labor, Arthur J. Altmeyer, in charge. He had taken his Ph.D. with Commons and had been his research assistant. Altmeyer persuaded Edwin E. Witte to become executive director of the Committee on Economic Security. Witte was another student of Commons and was chairman of the Economics Department at Madison. Witte took to Washington one of *his* students, Wilbur J. Cohen, among whose lesser contributions to social security in the United States is the authorship of the chapter on that topic in this volume. William M. Leiserson, who was influential in shaping collective-bargaining legislation and who served as chairman of the National Mediation Board and as a member of the National Labor Relations Board, had taken his doctorate with Commons. Lloyd K. Garrison, who was chairman of the pre-Wagner Act National Labor Relations Board, was on leave as dean of the University of Wisconsin Law School.

The final reason for the flowering of labor policies in the thirties, though probably the least important, was the widely-held view that the United States was a comparative laggard among industrialized nations in this area and that the time had come to catch up. Miss Perkins spent six weeks in England in 1931 studying unemployment insurance. Witte's technical committees had much to learn from European experiences with old-age pensions, unemployment compensation, and welfare policies. The importation of Keynesian full-employment economics and the Swedish example of its success had a significant influence in the late thirties, though Roosevelt himself remained unpersuaded.

These factors, I think, both explain the outburst of labor legislation in general in the thirties and the particular policies adopted, five of which form chapters in this volume—collective bargaining, social security, unemployment compensation, the FLSA, and, in the special context of the Great Depression, manpower policies. But in that decade the New Deal did not develop policies on three of the problems that are the subjects of chapters in this book—fair employment practices, safety and health, and the wage-price dilemma. The next question, therefore, is why the New Deal failed to deal with these matters.

The most complex and interesting of the three is why Roosevelt and his subordinates did so little in the thirties to try to overcome massive historic discrimination in the labor market, not only against blacks and women, but also against Catholics, Jews, southern and eastern Europeans, Latin Americans, Asians, and American Indians. In the heyday of the civil rights movement in the sixties, a school of young historians, whose memories did not go back to the thirties, denounced Roosevelt for this alleged failure while finding kind words for Mrs. Roosevelt and Secretary of the Interior Harold L. Ickes, who spoke out for Negro rights. My feeling is that, while there is some merit to the charge, it is basically an exercise in the common historical fallacy of rewriting the past in the terms of the present.

Before discussing the reasons for inaction, it is necessary to note the two accomplishments. Under Hopkins, the FERA adopted a rule that the test of eligibility for relief was the need of the jobless and their dependents and that there shall be "no discrimination because of race, religion, color, noncitizenship, political affiliation, or because of membership in any special or related group." This policy continued under WPA. The impact was

enormous. Millions of unemployed black people and their families became eligible for relief and took advantage of this non-
discriminatory rule. Hopkins, moreover, quietly made special funds
available in the South in order to raise the appallingly low standards that prevailed in that region. Further, as will be noted in
greater detail below, Roosevelt, albeit reluctantly, launched the
first fair employment practices program in the United States in
1941.

But more interesting is the question of why the New Deal
developed no such policy during the thirties. It seems to me
there are four basic reasons. The first is that black consciousness
had not yet developed significantly. The overwhelming majority
of Negroes, while resenting discrimination in the labor market
and virtually every other area of the society, simply accepted it
as a fact of life. While there were several organizations that
worked to overcome discrimination, notably the National Association for the Advancement of Colored People, the Urban League,
and the Brotherhood of Sleeping Car Porters, and although Walter
W. White of the NAACP and A. Philip Randolph of the Porters
were vigorous leaders, none spoke for more than a narrow sector
of the black community. The main issue of the time was not to
stop job discrimination but to end lynching. If the political effectiveness of Negroes was weak, that of women as a lobby was
virtually nonexistent. Second, the enactment of antidiscrimination legislation would have required the support of organized
labor. While the CIO, once it became established, gave its backing, the AFL did not. In fact, the AFL craft unions, particularly
in the building and railroad trades, were among the most discriminatory organizations in the United States. Third, the Democratic Party was a coalition of northern liberals and southern
conservatives, and many of the latter based their political careers
on keeping the black man "in his place." While FDR's instincts
were northern and liberal, as the leader of the Democratic Party
he was compelled politically to drive a two-horse team. One illustration will suffice. In 1935 the social security bill went before the Senate Finance Committee, which was heavily weighted
with southern conservatives. The backing of its chairman, Senator Pat Harrison of Mississippi, was crucial to its passage and
Roosevelt got it. Finally, there is a certain irrelevance to anti-

discrimination legislation in the context of the Great Depression. The precondition for fair employment practices is employment. Such a policy could have accomplished very little in the face of massive unemployment.

In mid-1941, Roosevelt acted. By now the war in Europe was almost two years old and, following the fall of France in June 1940, the United States had launched vast programs both to aid embattled Britain and to rearm itself. Employment took a sharp turn upwards and jobs were opening in defense industries. Randolph, with the support of other Negro organizations, demanded an FEPC program and organized the "first" march on Washington for July 1, which was expected to draw 50,000 persons. While Roosevelt tried to head it off, Randolph refused to cancel the march. Thus, on June 25, 1941, the President issued Executive Order No. 8802, which prohibited discrimination in employment in defense industries and created the Committee on Fair Employment Practices to enforce the order. This was the inception of the FEPC policy in the United States.

The failure of the New Deal to confront safety and health measures is readily explained by three factors: First, the only reasonably comprehensive system of social insurance already in effect prior to the New Deal was workmen's compensation, which had its origins in the Progressive Era with Wisconsin and Commons, again, the leaders. For constitutional and political reasons, the system, with minor exceptions, developed in the states. By the thirties most of the states had workmen's compensation programs, and everyone assumed that this was a state rather than a federal responsibility. The problem, therefore, was not to get legislation through Congress but to persuade the lagging states to establish systems. Second, while American industry in the thirties, generally speaking, must have been an unsafe place in which to work, there was no contemporary way of finding this out. It is only very recently that we have learned about the gross inadequacy of our statistics of industrial injury and industrial disease. Finally, and this is the same point made in other contexts, when a man desperately needs a job, he is not much concerned about the conditions under which it will be performed. That is, unemployment was a far more urgent problem than safety and health.

The reason for the failure of the New Deal to develop wage-price policies in the thirties is self-evident. They flow from conditions of substantially full employment and price inflation. In the decade in question, the economy was in exact reverse—very high unemployment and wage and price deflation. Only during World War II, when the economy turned around completely, did the Roosevelt Administration impose wage and price controls along with rationing.

In closing, I should like to return to the point which opened this chapter. In November 1944 Roosevelt was reelected to a fourth term as President of the United States. On December 1 Miss Perkins wrote him a long letter. She recalled their conversation almost 12 years earlier when they had agreed on a labor program that "has now been carried out and is embodied in legislation, administrative and social practice." She reviewed the achievements in detail and expressed pride in their accomplishment: "These social and economic reforms of the past twelve years will be regarded in the future as a turning point in our national life." She then offered her resignation as Secretary of Labor, suggesting that it take effect on Inauguration Day, January 20, 1945. Roosevelt responded on January 22. He wrote that many other things remained to be done and "your resignation is not one of them. It is hereby declined. Indeed, it is rejected and refused." On April 12 Roosevelt died in Warm Springs, Georgia. Now, in fact, Miss Perkins did resign as Secretary of Labor.

Note: The opening quotation is from Frances Perkins, *The Roosevelt I Knew* (New York: Viking, 1946), pp. 150-52. The Stone estimate of Miss Perkins is from Alpheus Thomas Mason, *Harlan Fiske Stone: Pillar of the Law* (New York: Viking, 1956), p. 408, n. The Perkins-Roosevelt correspondence of December 1, 1944 and January 22, 1945 is in the Roosevelt Papers at Hyde Park. For the rest I have relied upon my own works, both published and unpublished. The former are *The New Deal Collective Bargaining Policy* (Berkeley: University of California Press, 1950), *The Lean Years* (Boston: Houghton Mifflin, 1960), and *Turbulent Years* (Boston: Houghton Mifflin, 1970). Two unpublished works have also been helpful. One is a work in progress that will cover labor problems and policies, excepting unionism and collective bargaining, in the period 1933–1941. The other is a chapter, entitled "American Labor in Depression and War, 1933–1945," written for the Labor Department bicentennial history of American labor.

CHAPTER 2

The Law and Practice of Collective Bargaining

JOSEPH P. GOLDBERG
Bureau of Labor Statistics

A constitutional revolution was required to permit New Deal economic policies to cope with the problems of the Great Depression. The revolution had to encompass labor-management relationships to ensure that recovery would have the support of the laboring classes and their union organizations. The National Labor Relations Act of 1935 provided this phase of the economic and social transformation of the role of the federal government. The transformation in approaches to labor-management relationships was an emerging and hesitant compromising development in the New Deal years. While revolutionary in formulation and immediacy of application, in retrospect it is clear that it was an outgrowth of emerging labor-management relationships. The law and its administration were the product of a long history of institutional developments in the country.

The basic features of the National Labor Relations Act have remained unaltered by the amendments that were passed in 1947 and 1959. The original enactment and the first revision were associated with bitter battles with ideological overtones of maintaining appropriate balances between capital and labor in the broad political arena as well as in company and plant labor-management relationships. Recently, the issues have been more circumscribed, with attention focused primarily on the effective administration of the Act by the National Labor Relations Board.

The Act and its administration have reinforced the characteristic aspects of labor-management relationships that are regarded as unique to institutional relationships in the United States. These are decentralized bargaining relationships, ranging from industry-wide to individual-plant situations, for which detailed terms are set forth in specific contracts. The legal side of labor-management relationships in the United States is viewed as involving one of the most litigious systems in existence, yet the most effective collective bargaining arrangements can and do function without involvement, or with minimal involvement, in the legal system.

The basic and continuing attributes of the statute are that it establishes the principles of free choice of bargaining representatives of workers through fair elections and the opportunity to engage in collective bargaining. The machinery for effectuation is provided through the specialized National Labor Relations Board. The content of collective bargaining, and resultant contracts, is left to the parties.

The administration and judicial construction of the terms of the Act have necessarily ranged more widely as the climate of labor-management relationships has altered radically in the past few decades. Many relationships have been well established. But they have been confronted with changing economic conditions; altered competitive relationships, both domestic and international; new trends in technology and systems operations; and resultant immediate and long-term impacts on the composition of the work force. New issues have developed in labor-management relations. Pressures for organization have developed in new sectors.

The Act has continued to occupy a key role in these developments. The NLRB has sought to define the appropriate scope of bargaining, as new issues have come to occupy central roles. There are those who have viewed these and other developments as unwarranted influences on collective bargaining. The jurisdiction of the NLRB has been extended in recent years, by statute and by administrative determination, to the quasi-public U. S. Postal Service, employees of private colleges, and private hospital employees. The influence of the Act is evident in the developing state laws relating to public employees.

The Roots of Labor Law

The revolutionary nature of the National Labor Relations Act did not derive from the expression of novel principles. The basic principles of the Act had been set out in diverse, piecemeal, and developing fashion over a period of 50 years. These expressions, while significant, could hardly make their imprint in a society in which the dominant ideology was for maintenance of laissez-faire in governmental policies. The efforts at union organization were initially countered in the courts in the United States, as in the industrializing countries of Western Europe, with treatment of union organization and concerted activities as criminal activities. Even following the landmark decision in *Commonwealth* v. *Hunt* in 1842, there remained substantial difficulties for the nascent efforts at union organization. That decision found that union organizations and membership, and activities in support of them, were not unlawful combinations, if their purposes and activities were not unlawful. The criminal-conspiracy doctrine withered away only gradually, as judges reflecting the views and concerns of the pervasive propertied business interests continued to shape the law applicable to union organizations. As business organizations grew, efforts at union organization encompassed large groups of workers, with increasingly socially embittered relationships and strikes. The courts reacted, beginning in the 1880s, by enjoining strikes as concerted activities threatening property. The temporary restraining orders, issued at the application of employers, effectively forestalled union pressures. The use of injunctions became so widespread that "government by injunction" became a growing political issue after 1896.[1]

Court decisions were also instrumental in developing federal regulation before the Wagner Act. Although the intent of applicability of the Sherman Anti-Trust Act with regard to organized labor was open to question, the federal judiciary early considered that the "every combination" in restraint of trade proscribed by the Act included labor organizations. In this application, it was used not to preserve competition or to preclude monopoly power, but "as a vehicle for the judicial formulation of a policy towards strikes, boycotts, and picketing."[2] With the restrictive effects of court actions under the antitrust laws and court injunctions, the AFL presented "A Bill of Grievances" to the President and Congress in 1906 seeking relief. Continued efforts produced the Clayton Act in 1914. Supreme Court interpretations subsequently demonstrated that the legal position of labor had been substantially unchanged by the enactment.

---

[1] Felix Frankfurter and Nathan Greene, *The Labor Injunction* (New York: Macmillan, 1930), p. 1.

[2] Archibald Cox, *Law and the National Labor Policy* (Los Angeles: Institute of Industrial Relations, University of California, Los Angeles, 1960), p. 4. *Adair* v. *United States*, 208 U.S. 161 (1908), and *Coppage* v. *Kansas*, 236 U.S. 1 (1915).

The judicial bonds on the emergence of labor organizations were further exercised in decisions that declared unconstitutional the relatively limited instances of statutes improving the status of organized labor. These included a federal statute and several state statutes outlawing yellow-dog contracts.[3]

Congress was increasingly attentive to the state of labor-management relations in the final two decades of the last century, particularly with strikes involving violence on the railroads and in the coal fields. Out of these concerns congressional investigations, first into specific disputes and later into the general state of labor-management relations, demonstrated an evolution of views regarding the role of the labor movement and the importance of collective bargaining relationships.

Early reports criticized employers for unwillingness to deal with officials of a union organization to which their employees belonged. The U.S. Strike Commission in 1894 appointed by President Cleveland to investigate the Pullman strike, reflecting the quasi-public character of the railroad industry, made public findings that had broad applicability. It pointed to the greater advances in England in utilizing conciliation and arbitration to reduce the incidence of strikes. Citing the growth of corporate power and wealth during the previous half-century and its association with the remarkable development of the United States, the report went on to state that "it will not be surprising if the marvel of the next 50 years be the advancement of labor to a like position of power and responsibility." The Commission recommended the enactment of federal legislation for the railroad industry establishing a standing commission to investigate and conciliate serious disputes.[4]

The first official report specifically calling for "democracy in industry" was that of the U.S. Industrial Commission in 1902. This report reflected the growing understanding of the nature of collective bargaining, limited as it was as it then existed. The report placed emphasis on state legislation, calling both for organizational rights for workers and the right to work without union membership, for prohibiting black lists and use of company

---

[3] Sanford Cohen, *Labor Law* (Columbus, Ohio: C. E. Merrill Books, 1964), pp. 134–37.

[4] Milton Derber, *The American Ideal of Industrial Democracy, 1865–1965* (Urbana: University of Illinois Press, 1970), pp. 86–87.

police, and for judicial restraint in what was deemed an abuse of the use of injunctions in labor disputes, except to enforce contracts and prevent irreparable loss.[5]

The U.S. Commission on Industrial Relations in 1915 developed further the emerging role for union organization and collective bargaining. There was disagreement among the members of the Commission on the role of government intervention, but there was general support for several basic principles. These included reaffirmation of the right of workers to organize in trade unions to bargain collectively through their chosen representatives as well as reaffirmation of the parallel rights of employers. Employers should not discharge employees for union membership and workers should not use coercive measures to induce membership. There was a split on government intervention, with a minority proposing legislation to establish an administrative body to prosecute unfair practices involving refusal to permit employees to become members of labor organizations and refusal of employers to meet with the authorized representatives of their employees. The majority of the Commission opposed imposition of the duty to bargain as leading to compulsory arbitration under government auspices.[6]

The overriding needs of wartime production and manpower mobilization with entry into the first World War resulted in the establishment of the first National War Labor Board. The tripartite membership of the Board was an indication of the developing status of organized labor, at least under wartime conditions. The principles adopted by the National War Labor Board in seeking to bring about settlements through mediation and conciliation were those set forth as the consensus of the U.S. Industrial Commission two years earlier. However, while the rights of workers and employers to organize and to bargain collectively through chosen representatives were the governing policies, it was also agreed that the status quo would be maintained as regards the "union shop." Thus, the Board would not impose union recognition where it had not already been established. But this was not to stand in the way of the right of workers to organize in their own unions. In

---

[5] *Ibid.*

[6] Philip Ross, *The Government as a Source of Union Power: The Role of Public Policy in Collective Bargaining* (Providence: Brown University Press, 1965), p. 8.

any event, the policies assured workers the right to bargain collectively through their chosen representatives and required companies to recognize and deal with committees. Where necessary, the Board ordered the election of shop committees.[7] This was the first introduction through governmental avenues of the majority vote by employees, although not for the determination of the majority bargaining representative as under the Wagner Act.

The union gains in membership during the war years and the status accorded on government councils proved to be only as lasting as war and immediate postwar governmental needs required. The augury for postwar relations was provided by the collapse of President Wilson's postwar labor-management conference in October 1919 over inability to reach agreement on labor's right to collective bargaining. The following decade was one of declining union membership, from 5,048,000 in 1920 to 3,400,000 in 1929, as union penetration in the unorganized industrial sectors was retarded by the welfare capitalism of the twenties, along with postwar depression, several unsuccessful strikes, and the uneven effects of prosperity.

The role of law in labor-management relations remained basically unchanged from its turn-of-the-century impact, assuming a balance in theory between the worker's legal right to organize and bargain collectively and the employers' legal right to thwart freedom of association and collective bargaining. Reality differed greatly, however, for the means available to employers in maintaining the advantage against union organization included coercion or threats, discharge or refusal to hire, refusal to deal with the union or its officers, freedom to organize a company union, and employment of detectives to spy on employees. "Under such circumstances, to speak of labor's right to organize was clearly a misuse of terms," William Leiserson said of these practices in 1938. "All that the employees had was a right to organize if they could get away with it, and whether they could or not depended on the relative economic strength of the employers' and employees' organizations."[8]

---

[7] *The National War Labor Board*, Bureau of Labor Statistics, Bull. No. 287 (1922).

[8] Cited in Irving Bernstein, *The New Deal Collective Bargaining Policy* (Berkeley: University of California Press, 1950), p. 8.

Only in the railroad industry was there a continuing evolution of labor-management statutory provisions, which may be viewed in retrospect as paving the way for an affirmative national labor policy. The provision for mediation in the Erdman Act of 1898 continued in effect, while the provision imposing criminal penalties for the discharge of employees for union membership was held unconstitutional by the Supreme Court. Railroad labor unions and management sought a new approach through legislation, following experience with the weakness of the Railway Labor Board established in 1920, the unsuccessful shop crafts strike in 1922, and the growth of company-encouraged employee-representation plans. The new approach was embodied in the Railway Labor Act of 1926, which was the result of agreement between railway executives and union officials to shift from the emphasis in the previous law on settlement of disputes by a national board to one based on collective bargaining. The duty of both sides to conclude agreements and settle disputes was set forth, and provision for settling disputes was made through steps calling for mediation and emergency fact-finding boards appointed by the President, if needed. Significantly, the Act provided for the selection of representatives by labor and management, respectively, "without interference, influence or coercion" by the other. A Supreme Court decision in 1930, in effect overruling earlier decisions, upheld an injunction against establishment of an employee-representation plan by a railroad and the use of threats of discharge to coerce employees into giving up outside union membership and into joining the company union.[9]

The Wagner Act

It was only with the impact of the Great Depression that the determination of general labor policy by the courts was finally ended. New economic ideas were superseding the prevalent notions of laissez-faire. Unemployment, which grew to an estimated 16 million between 1929 and 1933, reflected the insecurity and uncertainty that permeated the entire economy and all walks of life. With a further decline of union membership to under three million, the position relative to the size of the labor force was barely

---

[9] *Texas and New Orleans Railroad Co.* v. *Brotherhood of Railway and Steamship Clerks*, 281 U.S. 548 (1930).

equivalent to that of the first decade of the century. The need to increase mass purchasing power to provide a stimulus to the economy and to strengthen worker organizations through unionism and collective bargaining came to the fore as significant ideas molding governmental policies.

The Norris-La Guardia Act of 1932 finally provided redress to judicial intervention. The Act's statement of national policy expressed the helplessness of the individual worker to "exercise actual liberty of contract, and to protect his freedom of labor" in the face of "prevailing economic conditions, developed with the aid of governmental authority for owners of property to organize in the corporate and other forms of ownership associations." To cope with such conditions, "it is necessary that he have full freedom of association, self organization, and designation of representatives of his own choosing, and that he shall be free from the interference, restraint or coercion of employers of labor, or their agents, in the designation of such representatives or in self-organization or in other concerted activities for the purposes of collective bargaining or other mutual aid or protection."[10]

The Norris-La Guardia Act has been viewed as establishing the first period of laissez-faire governmental policy permitting labor's organizing efforts to take hold. "The point of this Act is not what it does for organized labor but is what it permits organized labor to do for itself without interference." The Act deprived the federal courts of the power to enjoin the self-help activities of unions, such as strikes in labor disputes, joining unions, strike benefits, and various techniques used to publicize a dispute, including picketing and peaceful assembly. Circumstances under which injunctions could issue were carefully stated, restoring the traditional rules of equity courts as they had existed prior to the judicial looseness of application in labor disputes. Yellow-dog contracts were made unenforceable in the courts. The broad definition of labor disputes in the statute and of cases arising out of disputes finally recognized the right of unions to engage in "certain theretofore proscribed stranger activities of unions in fulfillment of their heartfelt need to organize entire industries, so that, by standardizing employment conditions throughout such industries, they could

---

[10] 46 U.S. Stat. 70.

eliminate the competitive hazard to already established standards in existing unionized units of such industries, presented by the undercutting effects of nonunion wage and labor standard differentials."[11]

This Act, and similar legislation enacted in a number of states, established a brief period of laissez-faire in labor-management relations. The intent was not to provide direct supports to unionism, but to permit a climate of legal equity in which unionism could utilize self-help devices to meet the economic strength of business. With the continued prevalence of opposition to union organization on the business side, this meant that tests of economic strength were the main recourse available to labor.

The principles subsequently embodied in the Wagner Act were well established by the time of its enactment. The New Deal years preceding 1935 were, in fact, further testing periods for these principles. This was less a matter of conscious planning than part of the adaptation to the shifting economic, political, and ideational balances of the early New Deal period.

President Franklin D. Roosevelt and his Secretary of Labor, Frances Perkins, when they came to office, were convinced of the need for establishing federal legislative standards in several social fields. There was no similar orientation toward any legislative program that would encourage union organization and collective bargaining. It was only as the drive for organization among the unorganized in the mass-production industries grew, as the business opposition to New Deal policies continued, as the political influence of the AFL unions was apparent, and as the Supreme Court issued decisions declaring New Deal activities unconstitutional, that there was support for a legislative policy of encouraging collective bargaining. The major moving force in this evolution was Senator Robert Wagner, supported by the members and staff of the boards that were established under Section 7 (a) of the National Industrial Recovery Act and under subsequent congressional resolutions and executive orders.[12] There was an extensive, albeit telescoped, experience from 1933 to 1935 that provided a further extensive legis-

---

[11] Charles O. Gregory, *Labor and the Law* (2d ed.; New York: Norton, 1961), p. 190.
[12] Frances Perkins, *The Roosevelt I Knew* (New York: Viking Press, 1946), p. 239; Bernstein, pp. 26–27.

lative history of the National Labor Relations Act of 1935, better known as the Wagner Act.

The initial step in the New Deal evolution on collective bargaining, was Section 7 (a) of the National Industrial Recovery Act of 1933. The Act's provisions for efforts at recovery through the self-regulation of industries through trade associations and exemption from the antitrust acts, were viewed as requiring counterbalancing rights for labor organizations. The AFL, gradually altering its policy of voluntarism, actively supported the inclusion of Section 7 (a), which would require the specification of the right of employees to organize and bargain collectively through representatives of their own choice, free of interference or coercion by employers, in every industry code of fair competition. Yellow-dog contracts and any requirement for joining company unions were prohibited; however, no machinery and enforcement provisions were provided.

Unions used the provision as a basis for organizing drives in the coal, textile, clothing, and steel industries. Many companies in the steel, auto, rubber, and chemical industries construed Section 7 (a) as permitting the organization of company unions, and membership in these grew even more than it did in trade unions from 1933 to 1934.[13] With conflicting interpretations and developments surrounding Section 7 (a), and with rising strike activity threatening the recovery program, President Roosevelt established a tripartite National Labor Board, with Senator Wagner as chairman.

The National Labor Board, lacking enforcement authority, sought to mediate and obtain agreement. It had early success in establishing a precedent-making formula to deal with a recognition strike at Pennsylvania hosiery mills. The settlement included a secret-ballot election by the Board to determine representation, with the employers agreeing to negotiate with the union if it won the majority, as was the case. However, the Board ran into increasing difficulties with later refusals at compliance by major companies. The final blow came when the automobile industry refused to bargain with the burgeoning United Automobile Workers' union. With its mediation efforts failing in this dispute, the Board was superseded by an Automobile Labor Board, appointed by President

---

[13] Harry A. Millis and Emily C. Brown, *From the Wagner Act to Taft-Hartley* (Chicago: University of Chicago Press, 1950), p. 22.

Roosevelt, which accepted company unions and conducted elections on the basis of proportional representation of the various organizations rather than exclusive representation by the union receiving a majority vote.[14]

Even before the demise of the Board, its chairman, Senator Wagner, realized the need to write the principles established by the Board into legislation in order to obtain the compliance that had not been forthcoming from much of industry. His bill, as initially drafted, was opposed by industry. With widespread strike activity, major revisions were made to obtain broad legislative support for action in this field. As revised, however, the bill failed to receive support from the AFL and continued to be opposed in industry.

A threatened steel strike, along with already widespread strike activity in the spring of 1934, including the San Francisco general strike, turned President Roosevelt's concerns to the need for congressional action despite the legislative impasse. The result was his decision to transmit a resolution to the Congress, which was adopted as Public Resolution 44 in June 1934, under which the President was authorized to establish a board or boards to investigate disputes arising under Section 7 (a). There was authorization to conduct representation elections, but the issue of majority rule as against proportional representation was not resolved. The President appointed an all-public National Labor Relations Board. This nonstatutory Board developed further the common law that was to form the basis for the Wagner Act and its administration. The principles it formulated included notably the affirmation of majority rule as the basis for effective collective bargaining. It was confronted with the same obstacle as was its predecessor, however—inability to enforce its decisions against employer noncompliance.

In early 1935 Senator Wagner once again introduced a revised bill for a permanent National Labor Relations Board. Now there was the additional uncertainty of a contrast between labor policy associated with the Section 7 (a) developments and the legislation passed in 1934 amending the Railway Labor Act. At a time when

---

[14] Lewis L. Lorwin and Arthur Wubnig, *Labor Relations Boards* (Washington: Brookings Institution, 1935), pp. 231–62, 268–72.

company unions were widely sponsored by the carriers, the railway unions had been successful in obtaining explicit and detailed limitations on the power of the carriers to interfere with, influence, or coerce employees in the selection of their union representation. With this addition to the substantial and varied background of two years of the New Deal, the forces for and against the proposed National Labor Relations Act once again turned out.

The author of the measure, the NLRB, the union movement, industrial relations experts, religious leaders, and a handful of businessmen appeared in support. The opposition comprised the business community in a virtually solid phalanx, the company unions, an academic official and the Communists. Secretary Perkins was the only Administration official to testify, ambivalently.[15]

Within a week after President Roosevelt's endorsement of the bill for congressional enactment, the Supreme Court unanimously ruled the NRA codes unconstitutional, holding that there had been an unconstitutional delegation of legislative power and that the interstate commerce authority had been exceeded. Despite uncertainties over the use of the interstate commerce authority in the Wagner bill, the President reiterated support of it. Wagner arranged for revisions in the bill to bolster the constitutional support, and it was finally passed, and signed by President Roosevelt on July 5, 1935. It has been suggested that the substantial constitutional uncertainties thus anticipated as confronting the Act folded up the opposition to its enactment.[16]

The Wagner Act of 1935 for the first time established clearly in law the principle of the legal right of employees to organize into strong unions for collective bargaining. While the specific principles of the Act had received expression over a protracted period and had been practiced particularly in the nonstatutory early New Deal boards, this was their first integrated expression as national policy, with provision for enforcing the limitations on the employer's right to interfere with worker choice in union organization and collective bargaining. It established a permanent

---

[15] Bernstein, p. 100.
[16] James A. Gross. *The Making of the National Labor Relations Board,* Vol. 1 (1974), pp. 144–45.

specialized body to administer the Act, albeit with remedial rather than punitive authority.

The basic principles were relatively simple, incorporating long-sought-after union objectives. Employees have the right to self-organization and to designate representatives of their own choosing for collective bargaining. Only unfair labor practices by employers were specified, including interference with, restraint, or coercion of employees in organizing or selecting representatives, and refusing to bargain collectively with such representatives. A National Labor Relations Board was established to settle questions of representation and to conduct elections for the determination of the majority bargaining representative. The Board also was empowered to prevent any person from engaging in any specified unfair labor practice. Like other independent administrative agencies, the Board was to investigate, to hold hearings, and to issue decisions and orders to cease and desist from such unfair labor practices, "and to take such affirmative action, including reinstatement of employees, with or without backpay, as will effectuate the policies of this Act." When legal enforcement procedures became necessary, the Board was empowered to petition a United States Circuit Court of Appeals for enforcement of an order in an unfair labor practices case. Any person aggrieved by such an order could also petition the circuit courts for review.

The Wagner Act was intended to take the question of the right to union organization and collective bargaining out of the arena of economic struggle between employers and unions. In light of the previous 50 years of experience with judicial intervention against concerted union actions, the sponsors of the Wagner Act consciously established the principles and mechanism for protecting the rights to union organization, collective bargaining, and union concerted action, and specified only employer unfair labor practices. It was not intended to deal with all aspects of labor-management relations or with strikes in general. It was intended to require collective bargaining, but left the substantive terms and conditions of employment entirely to private negotiations and recourse to strikes or lockouts.

Virtually from its inception, the Act and the Board were the focus of attacks. The administration of the Act functioned under a cloud of constitutional uncertainty. Charges of one-sidedness were directed at the Act and the Board by employers. The split between the AFL and CIO made it the target of labor criticism as the Board found itself in the middle of the controversy in determining appropriate units for the conduct of representation elections.

The uncertainties over the constitutionality of the Wagner Act were not dispelled until April 1937, in the midst of the controversy created by President Roosevelt's proposal to "pack" the Supreme Court to counteract the persistent and unyielding conservatism of the court majority. In the *Jones and Laughlin* case involving the Wagner Act, the new majority, by a 5 to 4 vote, upheld the constitutionality of the Act, finding that the activities involved in the case had a "close and substantial" relationship to interstate commerce, and that the Act's effect was to reduce industrial strife that obstructs or impedes commerce. In its opinion, the Court found that the Act did not impose arbitrary restraints on the employer's ability to conduct his business for, as it stated: "The Act does not compel agreements between employers and employees," and furthermore, "the Act does not interfere with the normal exercise of the right of the employer to select its employees or to discharge them." As to the criticism of the one-sided application of the Act, in subjecting the employer to supervision and restraint and leaving untouched abuses for which employees may be responsible, the opinion went on to state, "we are dealing with the power of Congress, not with a particular policy or with the extent to which that policy should go. We have frequently said that the legislative authority, exerted within its proper field, need not embrace all the evils in its reach. The Constitution does not forbid 'cautious advance, step by step' in dealing with the evils which are exhibited in activities within the range of legislative power. . . . The question in such cases is whether the legislative, in what it does prescribe, has gone beyond constitutional limits. . . ."[17]

The contribution of the Court's decision to union organization and collective bargaining was gradually apparent. There was a growing disposition by employers in appearances before the Board

---

[17] *National Labor Relations Board* v. *Jones & Laughlin Steel Corp.*, 301 U.S. 1 (1937).

to comply with the requirements of the law. But the criticism of the administration of the Act continued, and the persistence of long-established employer opposition to union organizations was apparent in the disastrous "Little Steel" strike in 1937. Other more pervasive elements altering the climate for union organization and collective bargaining came with improved economic conditions, and even more with the stimulus to organization and collective bargaining during the war years.

The Taft-Hartley Act

A no-strike, no-lockout agreement between union and management leaders shortly after the declaration of war was the basis for the establishment of the tripartite National War Labor Board to deal with disputes during the war. The stabilization of wages was added to its responsibilities within a few months. During the war, union membership increased by over one million members a year, from 10.2 million in 1941 to 14.4 million in 1946, aided by the maintenance-of-membership formula applied by the National War Labor Board in disputes over union security arrangements. By and large, agreements were negotiated and disputes settled without recourse to strikes. Their economic terms were subject to the approval of the Board in accordance with its stabilization criteria. Strikes did occur, and with coal-mine stoppages in 1943, the Congress passed the War Labor Disputes Act over the President's veto. It provided for 30-days' notice of a dispute which might interrupt war production and a strike ballot vote by the NLRB, and it authorized the President to seize and operate struck plants. The strike votes, expensive and disruptive to NLRB activities, increasingly indicated support of strike actions, although strike action actually followed in only a small minority of the vote situations.

Collective bargaining accompanying the wartime growth of union organization had been constrained by the requirements of the wartime disputes and stabilization policies. With the end of the war, there was uncertainty over production cutbacks, with fears of recession and unemployment as had occurred at the end of the first World War. Furthermore, with earnings reduced by cutbacks in work-hours and rising prices, the pressures for substantial increases were great. There was substantial and widespread strike activity in the reconversion period, which demonstrated the strength and lasting power of the unions, unlike the post-World War I reconversion period.

The effect was a substantial change in the attitude toward unions, which were now widely viewed as having achieved too much power. The continued criticism of the Wagner Act and the growth of unions since its enactment made revision of the Act the focus of attention. The views of a small minority of members of Congress who had consistently sought basic revision of the Wagner Act "became the predominantly accepted view of the Congress as a new Republican majority joined hands with diehard southern Democrats" in the 80th Congress in 1946. The outcome was a statute without "any systematic, nonpolitical study or investigation authorized or undertaken by Congress before it acted on many complex and technical matters about which it had relatively little accurate information."[18]

The final Act, passed over President Truman's veto, did not include a number of broadly restrictive proposals, including limitations on industry-wide bargaining and detailed regulation of union affairs. However, unlike its predecessor statute, which had little impact on existing labor laws, the Taft-Hartley Act extended the federal authority. The Act restated the basic purpose of the Wagner Act to encourage union organization and collective bargaining, but added the need to eliminate certain union practices as obstructing and burdening commerce and as requiring restraints like those previously placed on employers. While continuing to guarantee to employees the rights of organization and collective bargaining, it added the right of employees to refrain from such activity. Employer unfair labor practices were repeated from the Wagner Act, but agreement on the closed shop was banned. The newly specified union unfair labor practices included coercion of employees to organize and bargain collectively through representatives of their own choice, or of employers in the selection of representatives for collective bargaining purposes. Further, union unfair labor practices included union efforts to cause an employer under a union shop clause to discriminate against employees who were denied membership or expelled for reasons other than nonpayment

---

[18] Millis and Brown, p. 362.

of uniform dues and initiation fees; union refusal to bargain collectively; union engaging in secondary boycotts or jurisdictional disputes; union charges of excessive or discriminatory initiation fees; and union causing an employer to pay "in the nature of an exaction, for services which are not performed, or not to be performed"—that it, to engage in featherbedding.

The former discretion of the NLRB in determining appropriate bargaining units was limited by provisions requiring professional employees to decide by majority vote whether to be included in a combined unit with nonprofessional employees, plant security personnel could not be included in a bargaining unit with other employees, and foremen were excluded from the Act's coverage. A craft unit could not be ruled inappropriate by the Board, even though it had previously designated a broader unit, without support by a majority vote of the persons in the craft.

Distinctions were made in the Act with regard to procedures for treating certain categories of unfair labor practices. The Board, when issuing a complaint of an unfair labor practice to an employer or union, has the discretion to ask the court for a temporary injunction. As regards charges relating to secondary boycotts, the Board must give these priority over all other cases, with petitions for injunctive relief to the courts required if there are reasonable grounds for believing the charge to be true.

Although permitting agreement on the union shop, the Act made a major concession to the precedence of state laws. Section 14 (b) of the Act permitted more restrictive state laws—that is, prohibiting the requirement of union membership as a condition of employment—to be controlling. However, the federal law banning the closed shop took precedence over any more liberal provisions of the state law.

The Taft-Hartley Act addressed itself to strikes and disputes settlements in several ways. The statute for the first time set forth a national policy and procedure for disputes imperiling the nation's health or safety. Drawing on the experience with the Railway Labor Act, discretion was left with the President on the application of the procedures calling for delay of strike action under an 80-day injunction, with fact-finding and vote by the union membership on the employer's last offer. The Act also intervened in the bargaining process by requiring that 60 days prior to the expiration of a contract, either party desiring to change the terms must notify the other, with a notice to the Federal Mediation and Conciliation Service 30 days later of a dispute if agreement has not been consummated.

There are several other provisions of the Act which have significance for one reason or another. The provision that unions or employers could bring suits for violations of contracts, while appearing to be a restatement of doctrines already established by the courts, has come to have a substantial influence on the role of arbitration of disputes under the terms of contracts. The Act required unions to file financial and organizational information with the Secretary of Labor, and union officials to file non-Communist affidavits. These filings were conditions for union ability to use the machinery of the Act for representation petitions and unfair labor practice charge filings.

Archibald Cox has said that the Taft-Hartley Act was the "offspring of the unhappy union between the opponents of all collective bargaining and the critics of the abuse of union power."[19] The basic principles of the Wagner Act were carried forward, but a new psychological environment was induced by the many provisions of the Act going beyond mere "equalization" of the positions of employers and unions. A former chairman of the Board has written, "From the outset, the Board had been charged with promoting unions and collective bargaining. There were only employer unfair labor practices under the Wagner Act; inevitably the Board's work—however fairly and objectively performed—was perceived as pro-labor. This perception was shared by labor, management and the Board's own staff. But Taft-Hartley was unquestionably conceived as a series of restraints on unions, and in this sense, it was designed to favor management."[20] The consequences of policy shift from encouragement to balance were felt most by unorganized employees and weak unions.

The Landrum-Griffin Act

The unions' hope for early revision of the Taft-Hartley Act met with a stalemate which was only removed by a new combina-

---

[19] Cox, p. 15.
[20] Frank McCulloch and Tim Bornstein, *The National Labor Relations Board* (New York: Praeger, 1974), p. 57.

tion of circumstances, with legislative changes arrived at once again in an atmosphere of adversary positions, charges that unions were being further restricted, and failure to meet the imbalances of the Taft-Hartley Act. The exposure of corruption in a number of national and local unions by the McClellan Committee produced a surge of public opinion for internal union regulation that placed even those in the Congress friendly to labor unions on the side of legislative reform. The persistence of the view that collective bargaining had contributed to the upward creep of prices and the growing animosity over technological change and work rules issues added to the general view of union impediments to improved productivity. Out of this climate, there emerged in 1959 the Landrum-Griffin Act (Labor Management Reporting and Disclosure Act).

The expressed purpose of the Landrum-Griffin Act was the reform of labor unions, not any major revision of the Taft-Hartley Act. The initial entry of the Taft-Hartley Act into internal union matters was now broadened. The Landrum-Griffin Act reasserted the basic purposes of the national labor policy regarding employee organization and collective bargaining and their impact on the flow of commerce of the nation. It added the principle that "in order to accomplish a free flow of commerce, it is essential that labor organizations, employers, and their officials adhere to the highest standards of responsibility and ethical conduct in administering the affairs of their organizations, particularly as they affect labor-management relations."

The Act sets forth a Bill of Rights for members of labor organizations, guaranteeing equal rights in elections, rights of free speech and assembly, the right to vote on increases in dues and initiation fees, and protection against arbitrary disciplinary action. Reports are required to be filed with the Secretary of Labor providing, respectively, the finances and the operational aspects of the union. Employers are required to file reports concerning any payments they made to unions or to union officials and certain classes of payments to labor relations consultants.

Unions assuming trusteeships over subordinate bodies must file reports promptly with the Secretary of Labor, and then report semi-annually. The reasons for which trusteeships may be established are specified in the Act. Regulations are established for the conduct of elections. Set forth are the terms of office for national and local officials as well as election procedures. Additional provisions relate to the fiduciary responsibilities of union officials, bonding requirements, prohibition of office-holding by certain classes of felons and Communists, and limits on the amount of loans by labor organizations to any officer or employee. The Secretary of Labor is empowered to investigate possible violations of the Act.

A separate title of the Act contains a number of amendments to the Taft-Hartley Act. An additional union unfair labor practice was provided making recognitional or organizational picketing unlawful under certain circumstances. Loopholes in the secondary-boycott unfair labor practice provision were tightened. A provision was added making it an unfair labor practice for a labor organization and an employer to enter into an agreement whereby an employer ceased to handle any of the products of another employer, or so-called "hot cargo."

Other provisions covered special industry requirements and aimed at facilitating administration. Agreements in the construction industry relating to work done at the site, and in the apparel and clothing industries were exempted from the "hot cargo" unfair labor practice provision. Prehire agreements were permitted in the building and construction industry. The voting rights of economic strikers were extended for a period of 12 months after the start of a strike, even if they were not entitled to reinstatement. The Board was empowered to delegate to regional directors its power of determining the appropriate bargaining unit, of providing for hearings, and of determining questions of representation. The non-Communist oath and union-filing requirements under the Taft-Hartley Act were repealed.

Objective evaluators of the development of governmental regulations over internal union administrations view this legislation as an inevitable concomitant of the government's assignment of legal and functioning power to unions as statutory bargaining representatives, and as integral to the government's responsibility to prevent abuse of power. In the relatively infrequent cases in which unions are unable to reach the stage of orderly and formal democratic procedures under their own impetus, "civil law is superimposing on union law a scheme of constitutional guarantees."[21]

---

[21] Jack Barbash, *American Unions: Structure, Government and Politics* (New York: Random House, 1967). pp. 148–49.

Generally, the effects of the Landrum-Griffin Act have not in-
hibited the growth of unions, and the changes required in consti-
tutions and by-laws did not affect operations appreciably.[22]

Whither Labor-Management Policies?

Developments in the almost two decades since the Landrum-
Griffin Act suggest that revisions in labor-management relations
law as the focus for altering economic and political balances between labor and management have diminished as major issues. The
intense labor-management antagonisms in such disputes as those
in the railroad, steel, electrical manufacturing, and maritime industries in the fifties and early sixties have been replaced by labor-
management efforts, aided by various ad hoc measures, to achieve
joint approaches to the problems of technological change and job
security.[23] Public policies, both permanent and transitory, were
increasingly concerned with the results of collective bargaining, and
they affected labor-management relationships in varied ways. These
included the general stabilization program between 1971 and 1974,
following the earlier years of more informal guideposts, and new
legislation, namely Title VII of the Civil Rights Act, the Occupational Safety and Health Act, and the Employment Retirement and
Income Security Act. The rights and protections set forth in these
statutes had significant effects on established bargaining relationships.

These new developments go beyond the Labor Management
Relations Act, which basically provides the means to establish a
collective bargaining relationship. But the role of this Act, and
of the National Labor Relations Board under it, continues as a
basic foundation of the system of labor-management relations in
the United States. The Act continues to serve as a major means
for resolving representation disputes in situations where organization is just taking hold or in which new developments have occurred. The continued presence of a great majority of workers in
the country who are unorganized, together with the continued
growth of unfair labor practice charges before the NLRB, reveal

---

[22] Philip Taft, *The Rights of Union Members and the Government* (West-
port, Conn.: Greenwood Press, 1975), pp. 271–85.
[23] Joseph P. Goldberg, "Bargaining and Productivity in the Private Sector,"
in *Collective Bargaining and Productivity* (Madison, Wis.: Industrial Relations
Research Association, 1975), pp. 15–44.

the "extent of determined opposition to collective bargaining that still exists."[24] The continued influence of the Act has also been evident in the great organizational drives among public employees, with the Act serving as the model for many state laws and procedures covering public employee collective bargaining.

Efforts at reform of the Act remain among basic policy objectives of the AFL-CIO. There has been the unsuccessful 25-year effort to obtain full rights to peaceful job site picketing by construction workers. With so-called "right to work" laws in effect in 20 states, repeal of Section 14 (b) continues to be sought to eliminate the circumvention of national labor policy. The conservative position, on the other side, has been represented by proposals to remove unfair labor practice charges from NLRB jurisdiction and to assign them to the courts. However, the emphasis in recent years has increasingly been to look to the specific provisions of the Labor Management Relations Act and their administration as the means for enhancing the purposes of the Act. Where employers have accepted the results of representation elections and engaged in bona fide collective bargaining, the purposes of the statute have been achieved. Where employers use the review and appeals procedures, with awareness of the limited, remedial penalties, to delay and obstruct the Board's orders, the purposes of the Act are thwarted.

The congressional oversight hearings of 1975–76 on the administration of the Labor Management Relations Act devoted much attention to the effect of the long process involved in negotiating first contracts after elections or in dealing with unfair labor practice charges through review and appeals procedures of the Board and the courts, respectively, in recent years. With final court decision on a Board order coming two years after filing a charge of refusal to bargain, the initiating union loses its foothold among the employees who had voted for the union. That there is a real and growing problem has been cited by a former Board chairman in the doubling of unfair labor practice cases before the Board, from 15,800 in 1965 to 31,125 in 1975, as evidence of "a widespread, continuing defiance of the law."[25]

---

[24] Derek C. Bok, "Reflections on the Distinctive Character of American Labor Laws," *Harvard Law Review* (April 1971), p. 1400.
[25] Statement of Frank McCulloch, *Daily Labor Report*, Nov. 18, 1975.

Union spokesman supported proposals that would restore to the Board the power to hold prehearing elections where there are no substantial legal questions, and to hold elections at set periods in every case, with unresolved legal questions to be raised through appropriate election charges. Such changes would give the Board's administrative law judges greater decisional authority in unfair labor practice cases, subject to discretionary review by the Board. Board decisions would be made self-enforcing where petitions to review were not filed in 30 days and no objections were filed within 15 days after notice of filing of the Board's order in the court.

Unions also supported amendments which would go beyond the present mere provision of restitution of back pay for employees who are illegally discharged, and which would satisfy the need for more effective remedies where employers have refused to bargain over first contracts with newly certified unions and have engaged in protracted litigation, with the possible ultimate loss of the union's position as well as legally entitled union benefits. They called for broad rule-making by the NLRB on substantive matters of the law as well as on administrative procedures.[26]

Employer spokesmen opposed the proposals outlined above. As regards remedial actions, they stressed the "equitable and remedial, rather than punitive, approach inherent in the Act to the remedy of unfair labor practices." The Chamber of Commerce expressed support for measures that would divest the NLRB of its jurisdiction to hear and decide unfair labor practice cases by assigning these cases to federal district courts, leaving to the Board only the responsibility for certifying collective bargaining representatives.[27]

The present chairman of the Board expressed her support of the proposals for greater delegation of authority to administrative law judges and for making the Board orders self-enforcing. She stressed that the Board disposes of over 90 percent of its unfair labor practice charges in less than 50 days, and that over 80 percent of representation cases are concluded by elections based on in-

---

[26] See statements of Elliott Bredhoff, Jacob Sheinkman, and Andrew Biemiller in *Daily Labor Report*, May 3 and 4, 1976.

[27] Statement of U.S. Chamber of Commerce on Labor Law Reform before House Labor Subcommittee on Labor-Management Relations, *Daily Labor Report*, Feb. 17, 1976.

formal agreement between the parties within about 40 days after the filing of the petition. But to cope with those relatively few instances of undue delay, she expressed support for action by Congress on the procedural proposals to aid the Board. On these, she cited the support of representatives of labor and indicated that she had talked "to chief executive officers of large corporations who favor this delegation," while the Chamber of Commerce and the National Association of Manufacturers still had to be persuaded.[28]

The Board also stated that the National Labor Relations Act does provide the Board with broad remedial powers, with the Supreme Court holding that Board-prescribed remedies will not be disturbed unless there is a showing that the order "is a patent attempt to achieve ends other than those which can fairly be said to effectuate the policies of the Act. The Board's authority is solely remedial—for the purpose of rectifying harm done to workers—and deterrence alone is an improper basis for a remedy." Although the Board has been able to devise a number of extraordinary measures in most violations not involving a refusal to bargain to deal with "repeat and/or flagrant offenders," it cited the Supreme Court decision in the *H. K. Porter* case, involving a refusal to bargain, as indicating that congressional action was required to remove the limitations on its remedial authority. In the *H. K. Porter* case, the Supreme Court held that the basic premise of the Act, that of private bargaining without government compulsion, would be violated by the Board order to an employer to agree to a checkoff of union dues clause, even though the refusal to accept the clause had been in bad faith. This holding led the Board subsequently, in the *Ex-Cell-O Corp.* case involving the employer's unlawful refusal to negotiate with the union representative, to conclude that it lacked authority to provide a "make whole" remedy—to order the employer to reimburse the employees for contract benefits they might have obtained.

The Board described the extraordinary measures it has devised and applied to deal with such "repeat and/or flagrant offenders" in cases involving other unfair labor practices. Thus, in the case of *J. P. Stevens and Co.*, the company was directed to mail notices to the employees' homes that it would not violate the Act in the

---

[28] Statement of Betty Southard Murphy, *Daily Labor Report*, May 5, 1976.

respects found, to read the notice on company time and at a convening of employees, and to provide the union with access opportunity to company bulletin boards, and with names and addresses of employees. In the *Tiidee Products, Inc.* case, the Board ordered the company to pay the litigation expenses of the union and the Board. The court of appeals modified the Board orders, deleting reimbursement of Board litigation expenses and limiting liability for the union's litigation expenses to those incurred in the initial proceedings before the Board.[29]

The continued influence of the Labor Management Relations Act has been demonstrated in the extension of its application. This has been accomplished with adaptation to the specific situations covered. Thus, the Postal Reorganization Act of 1970 authorized collective bargaining in the newly established U.S. Postal Service on wages and working conditions under the general laws applying to private industry, while providing for binding arbitration in the event of negotiation impasses. The NLRB was assigned jurisdiction over unit determinations, union recognition, and adjudication of unfair labor practice charges in the Postal Service.

The growth of organization among employees of state colleges and universities and their coverage by state public employee statutes was accompanied by NLRB reassertion in 1970 of jurisdiction over private institutions of higher learning, with resultant Board decisions on appropriate units of professional employees among teaching staffs of colleges and universities. This reversal of a decision made 20 years earlier was based on recognition of the extensive noncommercial interests of large universities and their income-producing results, increasing federal support, the increase in union organization and disputes, and the limits of state legislation applicable to such institutions.[30]

The similar growth of organization and disputes among the 1.5 million employees of private nonprofit hospitals required congressional action in 1974 to repeal the exemption for such institutions, included in the Taft-Hartley Act, and to give them the same rights and protection enjoyed by 1.2 million employees of proprietary hospitals. In recognition of the public interest in the maintenance

---

[29] NLRB responses to questions posed by House Labor Subcommittee on Labor-Management Relations, *Daily Labor Report*, June 12, 1975.
[30] *Cornell University*, 183 NLRB No. 41, 75 LRRM 1269 (1970).

of continuity of health services, a new provision was added making it an unfair labor practice for a union to strike or picket a health-care institution without first giving 10-days' notice. Additional special-notice periods involving initial contracts and contract terminations for health-care institutions were set. Intended to give the parties time to conclude agreements, these provisions were supplemented with a special conciliation procedure for this industry. The Director of the Federal and Mediation Service was authorized to establish impartial boards of inquiry to report and make recommendations to the parties within 15 days of appointment where a threatened or actual strike or walkout would substantially interrupt the delivery of health care in the locality involved.

The continued viability of the principles and procedures of the Labor Management Relations Act is evident in their more recent application to employees who are excluded from coverage under the Act. The troubled agricultural relations situation in California, exacerbated by rival unionism, appeared to have been provided a means for resolution with the enactment of the California Agricultural Labor Relations Act of 1975. For the first time, provision was made for the conduct of secret-ballot elections in bargaining units of agricultural workers, with the elections conducted by the Agricultural Labor Relations Board. Unfair labor practices of employers and labor organizations were set forth in the law. After elections affecting more than 50,000 farm workers were conducted, opponents of the intent of the Act to protect farm worker organization and collective bargaining succeeded in cutting off funds for the board.

The institutionalization of the principles and machinery established in law by the Wagner Act has been most notable as one aspect of the organizational explosion among public employees. The 5.3 million members of public employee unions and associations of federal, state, and local employees in 1974 represent almost a three-fold growth since 1960. This has been the result of concern over lagging economic conditions and the impact of working conditions on the attainment of professional goals, as well as the contrast with the rights of collective bargaining and procedures available to workers in private industry under the National Labor Relations Act. The National Labor Relations Act has become the primary source of experience for the arrangements established for public employees to participate in organizations to represent them. The election procedures for majority determinations and unfair labor practices provisions are set forth in the federal executive orders and are apparent in the statutes or administrative regulations of the more than 40 states that have either comprehensive or limited coverage of state and/or local employees. Most of these state arrangements require, while others permit, collective bargaining, with only seven states with no bargaining laws or laws prohibiting bargaining. The diversity in coverage and practice among the states has made for continued consideration of federal labor policy for public employees, whether through the NLRB or a specialized agency for public employee coverage, together with standards for state legislation in collective bargaining for public employees.

The disputes-settling policies under United States law need only be treated summarily in this context. These policies are generally founded on the primacy of agreement through private collective bargaining, with recourse to arbitration only where the parties agree. The federal law is set out in the Taft-Hartley and Railway Labor Acts. The provision of national emergency strike procedures under the Taft-Hartley Act has resulted in its use in 34 disputes since 1947. Its use as one of a number of alternatives available in major disputes appears to have been established at present. The Railway Labor Act's dispute-settling procedures received much criticism and proposals for revision for a decade after the work-rules issue and declining employment created a continuing series of crises, with several requiring ad hoc arbitration by congressional action. Recently, however, labor-management relations on the railroads have improved, aided in part by the merger of several unions. The states may provide a body of experience with varied arrangements relating to strike authorization, fact-finding, and arbitration. While public employee strikes are widely prohibited, a few states permit public employee strikes under specified conditions. Binding arbitration of police and firefighter disputes, enacted with union support, is practiced extensively.[31]

---

[31] Arvid Anderson, "Bargaining Issues in the Public Sector: More in '74," in *Proceedings of the New York University 27th Annual Conference on Labor* (1975), p. 86; James L. Stern and others, *Final Offer Arbitration: The Effects on Public Safety Employee Bargaining* (Lexington, Mass.: D. C. Heath and Co., 1975).

The basic labor-management relations policy in the United States remains that defined in the Wagner Act. The measure of the success of that Act and its evolution is the success of collective bargaining through organizations freely chosen by employees. The NLRB has been substantially successful in treading the fine line between lubricating the industrial relations system without intruding in the substance of collective bargaining. There have been areas where warnings have been issued, as in the Board's designation of mandatory and nonmandatory subjects of bargaining, supported by judicial decisions, with mandatory subjects increasing greatly, including such matters as pensions and subcontracting.[32] But, on balance, these decisions appear to have been geared to actual developments and appear to have aided collective bargaining. Similarly, the Board has followed Supreme Court decisions which have given primacy to contractual agreements to arbitrate grievances, and has effectively established a federal policy on grievance arbitration.[33] To the extent that these formulations involve substantive matters, they appear to have affected collective bargaining minimally, while aiding the effective functioning of collective bargaining.

The role of the Wagner Act is a continuing and expanding one. There remain substantial areas where the Act is still hardly felt, notably in the case of agricultural workers and in industries and areas where employers continue to resist union organization and collective bargaining. Recent developments in the public employee field particularly demonstrate that requirements derived from the Act are essential to establishing meaningful labor-management relationships in our legal and social climate. It has been suggested that perhaps the Act and the NLRB have been diminished by the growing need to relate these to the requirements of a broad unitary labor system covering the Civil Rights Act (Title VII), the Railway Labor Act, and also the wage and hour laws, the Labor Management Reporting and Disclosure Act, and others.[34] One can raise serious questions regarding the impact of a unitary system on

---

[32] See, for example, Committee for Economic Development, *The Public Interest in National Labor Policy* (1961), p. 82.

[33] H. H. Wellington, *Labor and the Legal Process* (New Haven: Yale University Press, 1968), p. 100.

[34] Charles J. Morris, "The National Labor Relations Board: Its Future," *Labor Law Journal* 26 (June 1975), pp. 334–44.

the collective bargaining system, which is the mainspring of our law of labor-management relations. There is real need, however, for study of the interaction of the several statutes, policies, and judicial decisions with collective bargaining processes and developments. Particular attention would be given to the manner in which the parties have adjusted to these expanding legislative requirements.[35] The need is to ensure a continued, adaptive, and enlarging role for collective bargaining.

---

[35] See the description of the successful results of the union-initiated proposals for industry-wide negotiations "to reform seniority provisions to bring them into compliance with Title VII, and to achieve a goal the union has long sought in bargaining, when Title VII and government enforcement were not on the horizon." Elliott Bredhoff, "New Methods of Bargaining and Dispute Settlement," in *Proceedings of the New York University 27th Annual Conference on Labor* (1974), pp. 17–20.

CHAPTER 3

The Evolution and Growth of Social Security

WILBUR J. COHEN

University of Michigan

Historical Development

The story of the evolution and growth of the social security system in the United States is one of the most notable and successful examples of incremental and practical development in social legislation in our nation's 200-year history.

Its roots can be traced to the establishment of the poor law in England in 1601. This Elizabethan statute taxed all householders of a parish for relief of the destitute among them and thus established the principle of secular public responsibility for the care of the indigent. English poor-law legislation was later brought to America by early colonists; eventually, various social-welfare services were provided by local volunteer groups, religious associations, and local communities to deal with the problems of beggars, the mentally ill, orphans, abandoned or neglected children, the blind, unwed mothers, and others. As the nation expanded, however, exclusive local responsibility for the indigent became increasingly difficult, especially when an urban-industrial society superseded the farm–small-town economy.

The general concept of social welfare has an even longer history, however. The functions generally considered social-welfare activities have evolved over several thousand years through responsibilities handled first by the family and tribe, later by religious institutions, local communities, and county, state, and federal governments. Combined with these arrangements have been the volunteer activities of individuals, groups, and organizations designed to meet emergency and continuing social-welfare needs. At one time—and still true in some cultures—the method of dealing with retirement and old age involved rearing sons whose responsibility included the care of the elderly as a moral duty. Religious institutions have also had a role in the development of social-welfare services in many cultures. The Judeo-Christian ethic pervades social-welfare programs and philosophy not only in the United States but also in other western countries. The biblical concepts of the golden rule and "thy brother's keeper" have both been significant in the establishment of private and public programs to alleviate suffering and poverty and to provide services to those in need.

As social policy developed in the United States, the comparative roles of the state and federal governments became a controversial issue. Article I, section 8, of the U.S. Constitution confers on Congress the power ". . . To lay and collect Taxes, Duties, Imposts and Excises, to pay the Debts and provide for the common Defense and general Welfare of the United States." Whether this provision gives Congress the power to enact social-welfare legislation was for years highly debatable. A historic decision was made in 1854 when President Franklin Pierce vetoed legislation, passed by Congress, which provided for federal aid to states in the form of land for the construction of facilities for the care and treatment of the insane. Pierce felt that the legislation would establish a precedent in the care of the indigent that would eventually lead to federal participation in measures for the care of other indigents and thus "transfer to the Federal Government the charge of the poor in all the States." He indicated his belief that the responsibility for social welfare belongs exclusively to state government.

President Pierce's view was reinforced by succeeding Presidents and Congresses and by general public agreement until the massive distress of the Great Depression of 1929 and the 1930s revealed a need for assistance far greater than localities and states could provide. Social-welfare services thus remained mainly a local responsibility until this century. State responsibility for providing financial help to the needy developed gradually; it was not until the 1930s that all states had departments of social welfare with statewide responsibility for the operation of such programs.

Concern about an obligation to the poor, however, became a dominant issue in the United States and in Britain as industrialization and urbanization expanded in the 1800s. In Britain, the poor law of 1834 improved the administrative machinery of the relief system, but it also expressed a philosophy, with which many disagreed, that poverty was a result of human failing and mismanagement. Increasing criticism of the law led to an investigation by a royal commission established in 1905 which recommended changes in policy and administration; a minority report of the commissioners—published in 1909 by Sidney and Beatrice Webb—sought to eliminate the repressive practices engendered by the poor law and the implied humiliation attached to poverty. The minority report recommended the creation of categorical programs by a "breakup of the poor law." A number of economists and social reformers in the United States adopted these concepts, which later became the basis for U.S. social-welfare policy.

Other developments that had a critical impact on the character of social welfare in America were the establishment in the 1880s of social insurance in Germany and the enactment in 1911 of the first social-insurance program in Britain.

Small First Steps

Although the economic depression of 1929–1933 was the immediate cause of the enactment of the 1935 Social Security Act, economists such as Professors Henry Seager and John R. Commons and reformers such as I. M. Rubinow, John B. Andrews, and Abraham Epstein had been advocating similar measures for more than two decades, and many small steps toward social welfare were taken before the big leap forward was made.

The movement for legislation to provide cash benefits and medical care for injured workmen began in the first decade of the 20th century. The first program of social insurance in the United States was the state workmen's compensation laws (now called worker's compensation), which provided some cash payments and reimbursement for medical costs for disabilities or deaths arising out of or in the course of employment. These state programs established certain statutory rights, superseding the common-law rights of employees and defenses of the employer, in order to protect families and society from the uncertainties of the law and judicial interpretations. The workmen's compensation system was the first income-guarantee program established by legislation in the United States for any large group of employees outside of those for whom the government had a special responsibility, such as war veterans. In 1908 the federal government established a similar program for federal employees, and a large number of states enacted such programs in the early part of the 20th century. However, it was not until 1948 that the last state, Mississippi, adopted a workmen's compensation program.

In the early part of the century, there was also a demand for state "mother's pension" laws to provide a payment to families in which the breadwinner had died or was killed and had left dependent children. And immediately before World War I there was a strong drive for the enactment of state health-insurance laws, a drive which collapsed during the war and postwar period of the 1920s, largely because of the opposition of the American Medical Association and the apathy which came from the relative affluence of the times. Immediately after World War I, however, a campaign began for the passage of state old-age-pension laws; the Fraternal Order of Eagles and Abraham Epstein took a leading role in the campaign. At the same time, the need for state unemployment-insurance laws was also strongly voiced. Under the leadership of Professor John R. Commons of the University of Wisconsin and several of his colleagues and students, Wisconsin enacted the first state unemployment-"reserves" law in 1931.

All this agitation for social-welfare laws and the consequent legislation in states such as New York and Wisconsin served as the training ground for the men and women—Frances Perkins, Arthur J. Altmeyer, Edwin Witte, J. Douglas Brown, and others—who were to become the leaders in formulating the Social Security Act of 1935.

Why wasn't a social security program—aid to the unemployed, the aged, and dependent children—passed during the 1920s when it was obviously needed so desperately? As Senator Robert F. Wagner noted, the Presidents of that decade, Harding, Coolidge, and Hoover, were sincere believers in the "dogma of self-reliance and individual thrift," even for those who were too old or too young to work and therefore in no position to save for the future. A system of compulsory contributions against time of need—the cornerstone and the strength of the present social security program—was viewed by some as "un-American." Their administrations were supported in this philosophy by the nation's chambers of commerce and manufacturing associations, both of which advocated individual responsibility for meeting the risks of old age, unemployment, and ill health. These groups were also joined in their opposition by the American Federation of Labor (AFL),.

which did not officially change its position and support social insurance until 1932.

Federal aid to encourage state unemployment-insurance and state old-age-assistance plans became a key issue in Congress in 1934 and might well have become law in that year. President Roosevelt decided, however—on the advice of Frances Perkins and Harry Hopkins—to seize the historic moment to provide a wider range of programs and alternatives.

The Great Depression

As a change in attitude toward the poor gradually took place in this country in the early part of the century, there occurred a slow, uneven, but steady development in the welfare programs provided for those in need. But it was the depression of 1929 and succeeding years that gave the impetus which led to the greatest change in attitude and eventually to the enactment of the Social Security Act of 1935.

The Great Depression clearly revealed the increasing and severe human problems of dependent old age in an industrial, urban society. The security of life provided by an agricultural society was gone. The consequent dependence of the elderly on the earnings of their adult children was reliable only as long as those earnings continued. But with widespread unemployment and the layoff of a working son—together with the loss of savings through bank failures—many formerly self-reliant old people became dependent on relief. By 1934, the plight of the elderly created a public demand for action. Among other campaigns for drastic remedies to treat the insecurity of the aged was the Townsend movement. Begun in California, the movement proposed for all people over 60 a monthly pension of $200, to be financed from the proceeds of a stimulated business activity caused by their expenditures—certainly, an oversimplification of the function of money in a complex economy. Supporters of the plan sent millions of postcards to their representatives in Congress, exerting an extraordinary appeal on Congress for some kind of action.

The winter of 1932–1933 was a particularly bad time for most Americans. On his inauguration in March 1933, President Franklin D. Roosevelt began a number of emergency programs to stimulate business recovery and to alleviate poverty and distress among the thousands of unemployed. He believed it was a time for quick action and immediate results. On June 8, 1934, the President sent to Congress a special message indicating that in January of the following year he would offer proposals intended to avoid in the future the insecurity that economic collapse had made evident. It was, he said, a time for the enactment of positive and systematic programs to prevent poverty. Drastic emergency measures were necessary in a period of crisis, but the President hoped that constructive measures to protect people against the perils of unemployment, old age, and illness would also be passed by Congress.

Full Speed Ahead

It was against this background that in June 1934 President Roosevelt established by Executive Order a Committee on Economic Security to produce the constructive proposals for the prevention of economic insecurity. Frances Perkins, Secretary of Labor, was chairman of the committee; other members were Henry Morgenthau, Jr., Secretary of the Treasury; Homer Cummings, Attorney General; Henry Wallace, Secretary of Agriculture; and Harry Hopkins, Federal Emergency Relief Administrator. Professor Edwin E. Witte was appointed executive director. As with other high-level committees, the major planning effort was assigned to a staff of specialists, among them J. Douglas Brown, Arthur J. Altmeyer, Barbara Nachtrieb Armstrong, Murray W. Latimer, and Otto C. Richter. An advisory committee, under the chairmanship of Frank Graham, then president of the University of North Carolina and later senator from North Carolina, was appointed to represent the points of view of labor, employers, and the general public.

The old-age-security group of the total staff of the Committee on Economic Security was small compared to the group assigned to unemployment and health insurance because public interest in plans to protect the elderly was not as great as that in programs to protect the unemployed—a consequence of the desperate conditions a year or two earlier when some 13 million Americans were unemployed. Also, because state programs for unemployment insurance had already been established in Wisconsin and Ohio, the idea of unemployment insurance had become more widely accepted; old-age insurance, however, remained a doubtful concept. The old-age-security group firmly believed, however, that a national contributory social-insurance program was necessary to meet the needs of steadily increasing numbers of elderly people. From the first, it was the group's conviction that any old-age-insurance plan in the United States should be national, compulsory, and contributory and should provide benefits to workers 65 and over as a matter of right. The chief concern was whether the federal government had the constitutional authority to impose such a system. In 1934, there was very little in the long history of American constitutional law to justify optimism.

Aside from determining a constitutional basis for a national, compulsory old-age-insurance program, the most difficult problem faced by the group was deciding upon a workable plan for financing the system. To pay even modest benefits to those already nearing retirement required the assumption by the system of a heavy accrued liability; although current contributions would be adequate to meet the early benefits, the question was: How far should this accrued liability be recognized by the gradual building of reserves to meet it when younger contributors are eligible for benefits? A full reserve was considered essential for private, individual insurance, but in social insurance, the group was convinced that a full reserve was not only unnecessary but would place an impossible burden on the national economy. In place of a full reserve, it was decided that a government contribution to the system would be necessary; the provision for an eventual government subsidy seemed the only way of paying modest benefits in the early years and, at the same time, of avoiding a large, invested reserve. But the amount of benefits proposed was less important than the establishment of the principle of old-age benefits as a matter of right and related to past contributions to a national system. Later, after the constitutionality issue had been determined favorably, there was opportunity to study the complex financial, actuarial, and benefit aspects of the system, and the Social Security Advisory Council of 1937–1938 could take advantage of the acceptance of the program to provide for more adequate benefits.

A significant development which occurred during consideration of the Committee on Economic Security's proposals was the issuance of a statement by President Roosvelt on November 14, 1934, indicating that he might defer consideration of the old-age-insurance proposal to some future date, after it had been more fully thought out. After much debate and discussion, however, any doubts that the President had were resolved, and an old-age-insurance proposal was included in the legislation submitted by him to Congress in 1935—although it was not called "insurance" then for fear the U.S. Supreme Court might hold that the enactment of an insurance plan was unconstitutional.

The work of the committee—the drafting of the report, the drafting of the bill, and their submission to Congress—was accomplished in a period of six months, a remarkable achievement.

The Incremental Approach

The key strategy formulated by the great social security pioneers—Frances Perkins, Arthur J. Altmeyer, Edwin E. Witte, J. Douglas Brown, Harry Hopkins, and President Roosevelt—was that the American people would be willing to make improvements in a broad, sound program, but only on a step-by-step basis. This group believed the "millennialist" approach should be avoided—that is, the requesting of large-scale changes which would be more than the economy could digest at one time or than a limited number of human beings could administer effectively. This policy of incremental improvements has through the early years of the system (1939–1968) allowed changes in the system to be inaugurated successfully with appropriate planning, widespread acceptance by the individuals affected, participatory involvement of groups with special concerns, and a gradual adaptation of costs by the economy.

Despite the fact that the Congress in 1933 and 1934, and possibly in 1935, might have been willing to enact more comprehensive and radical programs, the six principal policy formulators were aware of the difficulties involved in effectuating untried plans which, however good they might appear on paper, had to be put into operation in the 3,000 counties of the nation, each with diverse traditions, attitudes, and values. Their rejection of the millennialist approach in favor of an incremental one was a wise and correct choice for the establishment of such far-reaching programs.

But with every incremental change there has been criticism from fellow citizens who view with alarm a governmental role in providing income or services to men, women, and children. Even today, when further proposals for additional improvements in social security, national health insurance, or welfare are discussed, there are those who claim that the cost will lead to bankruptcy, or people's incentive to work will be undermined, or the proposal will "kill the goose that lays the golden egg," and the problem should be left to the private sector to handle or to individual responsibility. These recurrent issues must be reexamined periodically in the changing context of economic, social, and political developments.

Administrative Efficiency and Feasibility

A major component in the strategy developed by Arthur Altmeyer was that the social security program should undertake responsibilities only when there was a reasonable expectation that added tasks could be administered with an acceptable degree of efficiency. Altmeyer postponed action on coverage of farm hands, farmers, domestic-service employees, and the self-employed until feasible methods of collecting contributions from these groups could be worked out. He also postponed action on disability insurance until practicable means of making the diagnosis and determinations of disability were assured.

Altmeyer had been a student of Professor Commons at the University of Wisconsin. Commons, an advocate and evaluator of labor legislation, deeply influenced his students by the repetition of his view that: "If you ever have a choice between a very good law which will be badly administered and a not-so-good law which will be very well administered, always choose the latter." A broad-gauged activist in the mold of the great political economists of the first two decades of this century, Commons contrasts sharply with the theoretical orientation of the macroeconomists and the mathematical formulations of the econometricians of today. Good administration was not simply a small part of his labor legislation courses, it was a major part. He constantly stressed its importance and taught his students that in the United States environment, effective administration was the key to incremental improvement in social legislation.

A Human Service Philosophy

The philosophy enunciated by Altmeyer and John G. Winant, the first chairman of the Social Security Board, and put into effect so ably by John J. Corson as assistant executive director of the Social Security Board, was that the old-age-insurance program should give service to individuals—compassionate, kindly, helpful service. It was to be a humane service that responded to human needs and difficulties; the agency was not to be operated on an adversary basis, but rather as an organzation concerned with the interests of the beneficiary. This spirit of public service has permeated other parts of the program—such as survivors, disability, and health insurance—and to the staff in the local, regional, and central offices. The philosophy of service has been accompanied with the development of a public information system designed to inform individuals of their rights and responsibilities and to explain the program in terms citizens could understand—even when the explanation annoyed conservative economists because it simplified complex concepts into ideas which the average person could understand and to which he or she could respond.

The Economic Security Bill

Congress Debates

The historic report of the Committee on Economic Security was transmitted to Congress on January 17, 1935, and the Economic Security bill was introduced in both the House of Representatives and the Senate on the same day. Robert L. Doughton, chairman of the House Committee on Ways and Means, and David Lewis, a member of the committee, introduced the bill in the House. Senator Robert F. Wagner, Sr., introduced it in the Senate.

The bill that President Roosevelt transmitted to the Congress was an omnibus measure consisting of a number of different programs; the two most popular provisions related to federal grants for old-age assistance and federal measures to stimulate states to enact state unemployment-insurance laws. The provisions for establishing a national system of old-age benefits were the least known and the most controversial aspects of the proposed bill, partly because of doubts about the constitutionality of such a system and also because of the financial questions raised by such a large-scale and long-range plan.

Thomas H. Eliot, one of the lawyers responsible for drafting the original social security legislation, is credited with the strategic idea of arranging the bill so that the first title dealt with federal grants for old-age assistance. The concept of old-age assistance was generally popular and well accepted by the public; it had, in fact, been discussed in Congress in previous years and was one of the major reasons why social security legislation was so well received. Many of the state and local old-age-assistance programs were by 1934 in virtual bankruptcy or inoperative; the proposal to provide federal grants to the aged was therefore widely heralded by governors, mayors, and members of Congress, as well as by the older people who were on relief rolls.

In retrospect, passage of the 1935 law now seems an inevitable consequence of the depression, industrialization, and urbanization. But in 1935 President Roosevelt called in members of the Congress to urge them to act promptly. Senator Jennings Randolph, one of the participants in the meeting, recalls that the President said, "We must act now. We will make mistakes. But if we don't act now we may not have the opportunity to make mistakes." Roosevelt might have been able to obtain a broader and more comprehensive program in 1935, but his advisers were apprehensive about their ability to implement the variety of new programs they were advocating.

In order to expedite the passage of the legislation, the Roosevelt Administration made an unusual request, to which Congress acceded—namely, that both the House and Senate committees conduct public hearings simultaneously. This rare procedure has almost never been followed since then, primarily because the U.S. Constitution gives the House of Representatives the power to initiate tax laws. Because social security legislation is based in part on the taxing power, the Senate will not consider such legislation until the House has acted upon it. On a number of occasions, in fact, it has taken two years for any far-reaching amendments to the Social Security Act to pass both houses of the Congress.

Aside from being opposed by a small hard-core of conservative members of Congress, one aspect of federal aid to the states was opposed by southern Democrats who were hypersensitive then, as they are now, to what they viewed as an intrusion of the federal government into states' rights. One provision dropped from the original legislation, for example, was the requirement that state old-age-assistance programs must meet a minimum federal standard of "health and decency." Senator Harry F. Byrd, Sr., chairman of the Senate Committee on Finance, discovered that phrase in the bill and denounced it as an invasion of states' rights; the federal government, in his view, had no right to tell the states what was "healthy and decent." Senator Byrd was a powerful man, so the phrase was stricken, and thus for nearly 40 years there has been a wide and varied set of standards and payments by the states in the welfare programs.

Another famous southerner was Senator Huey Long of Louisiana, who had his own social-welfare program—called "share the wealth" and "every man a king," so named because its aim was to redress the inequalities in income and wealth. Senator Long was determined to push his program for all it was worth in the hope that he might be a serious dark-horse presidential candidate in 1936 against President Roosevelt. By holding a one-man filibuster on the last night of the Senate session of Congress in 1935 in opposition to farm legislation that President Roosevelt had endorsed, he managed temporarily to deprive the social security program of initial funding until February 1936.

On the other hand, had it not been for the strong support of two conservative southerners, Senator Pat Harrison of Mississippi and Representative Robert Doughton of North Carolina, the chairmen of the Senate and House committees, respectively, in charge of handling the legislation, the federal old-age-insurance provisions would never have become law. Another factor in the passage of the legislation was the support of William Green, president of the American Federation of Labor, and several key industry executives, such as Marion B. Folsom of Eastman Kodak, all of whom supported both the old-age-insurance and unemployment-insurance provisions. Insurance companies were publicly silent about these programs during the 1935 legislative debate, although several actuaries from private insurance companies had aided in the formulation of the 1935 plan.

The opposition to the legislation in the House of Representatives was led by the seven Republican members of the Commit-

tee on Ways and Means whose minority views were expressed as
follows:

> The federal government has no power to impose this
> system upon private industry. . . . [This system] would
> not in any way contribute to the relief of present econ-
> omic conditions, and might in fact retard economic re-
> covery.
> These titles impose a crushing burden upon industry
> and upon labor. They establish a bureaucracy in the field
> of insurance in competition with private business. They
> destroy old-age retirement systems set up by private in-
> dustries, which in most instances provide more liberal
> benefits. . . .

In spite of opposition, however, congressional approval was
won in a little over six months of congressional consideration,
and the bill was passed—after undergoing revision and change—
as the Social Security Act.

Signed into Law

On August 14, 1935, the Social Security Act was signed into
law by President Roosevelt. Looking on in the cabinet room of
the White House were Senator Robert Wagner, Secretary of Labor Frances Perkins, and members of the House Committee on
Ways and Means and the Senate Committee on Finance. Roosevelt clearly realized the significance of the new law because he
noted that the act "was a cornerstone in a structure which is
being built but is by no means complete."

The Social Security Act established a federal old-age-benefits
program; a federal-state program of public assistance for the aged,
blind, and dependent children; and a federal-state program for
unemployment compensation, maternity care, crippled children's
services, child-welfare services, public-health services, and voca-
tional-rehabilitation services. From these beginnings, the social
security system has grown in dimension and scope in ways that
no one could have imagined in 1935.

To those who participated in its planning, the most notable
outcome has been the extent to which these fundamental concepts have guided the development of one of the largest under-
takings in social engineering in the world. The system remains

today basically national, compulsory, and contributory. Benefits are a matter of right; coverage is nearly universal; contributions are a percentage of wages, with equal shares paid by employer and employee; a pay-as-you-go system of financing is combined with a limited contingency reserve invested in federal securities. It is the largest and most effective public program to prevent dependency and poverty. Without it the number of poor people in this country would increase from 25 million to 35–40 million. Besides preventing dependency and poverty, the program allows individuals a greater freedom of choice when certain hazards develop. It enables them to plan ahead, and it helps employers, economic planners, and the Congress to allocate resources to meet human needs in a responsible and effective manner.

The Dissenters

Given the severity of the economic depression in which this country found itself as social security legislation was being developed in 1934, few members of Congress—even if ideologically opposed to social security—could afford to oppose it publicly. Help for old people, half of whom were by then probably insolvent, was the kind of cause that ranked with mother, country, and flag in its automatic patriotic appeal. Open opposition came only from persons such as Congressman Robert F. Rich of Pennsylvania, who called Roosevelt a "socialist" for advocating social reforms, and from Congressman Hamilton Fish of New York, who suggested that the day might come when Roosevelt would have to be impeached for violating the Constitution.

Soon after the Social Security Act was passed, various groups and individuals opposed to it prepared to rally support for basic changes in the program before it could take effect on January 1, 1937, when the payroll tax was to begin. These people were especially eager to make capital of their opposition to the program in the presidential election year of 1936. The GOP candidate for president, Alf Landon, though a fairly progressive Republican, embraced the anti-social-security campaign which was fostered by the Republican National Committee. The attack was simple: The government, if left in the hands of the Democrats, would take away part of the workers' already meager paychecks and might never give it back.

In the last fortnight of the campaign, some factories distributed notices in their employees' payroll envelopes that carried the frightening message, "You're sentenced to a weekly pay reduction for all your working life. You'll have to serve the sentence unless you help reverse it November 3." The Republican National Committee also developed propaganda literature, designed to make it appear as though it had been sent officially by the Social Security Board in Washington, that attempted to alarm the American worker about the payroll taxes. Some of the propaganda attacks were developed as inserts in payroll envelopes of workers the week before the election. One of the inserts read as follows:

> Effective January, 1937, we are compelled by a Roosevelt "New Deal" law to make a 1 percent deduction from your wages and turn it over to the Government. Finally, this may go as high as 4 percent. You might get this money back but only if Congress decides to make the appropriation for the purpose. There is NO guarantee. Decide before November 3—election day—whether or not you wish to take these chances.

As the campaign progressed, Landon became increasingly enthusiastic about the anti-social-security crusade. In a campaign speech in Milwaukee on September 27, 1936, he made the fatal mistake of attacking old-age insurance as a "cruel hoax" and "a fraud on the working man." "We must," he said "repeal the present compulsory insurance plan." By the end of his campaign he was portraying the social security program as an example of federal oppression. And in one of his last major speeches, given in St. Louis, he conjured this image: "Imagine the field opened to federal snooping. Are the employees being registered for social security numbers going to be fingerprinted? Are their photographs going to be kept on file in a Washington office? Or are they going to have identification tags put around their necks?"

Others expanded this imagery and warned of an actual metal dog-tag that workers would be required to wear around their necks. The chairman of the Republican National Committee charged that the only humanity Roosevelt would show would be to have the dog tags made of stainless steel so they would not discolor the workers' skin. Hearst newspapers, which backed Landon, carried page-one stories with headlines such as. "Do You Want a Tag and a Number in the Name of False Security?" On the day before the election, the Hearst papers printed a picture of a man with a social security numbered tag around his neck and a faked application form, a purported "reproduction of the form of application" for social security "which starts cutting wages" and for which "you will have a record in the files in Washington."

But all these attacks were based on a misjudgment of the American voter. The attackers had thought that the average man would rebel against the so-called "pay cut" which would occur because of the new social security payroll taxes, but the reaction of the workers was that if employers were suddenly so solicitous of their welfare, there must be something good about old-age insurance. As a result, there was little defection by the working man to Landon, and he was overwhelmingly defeated at the polls, thus providing clear endorsement by the voters of the Roosevelt social security program. This electoral support was later to have an important impact in convincing the Supreme Court of the importance of interpreting the law as constitutional.

U.S. Supreme Court Approval

The next major hurdle for social security was U.S. Supreme Court affirmation of the constitutionality of both the old-age-benefits program and the unemployment-compensation program. The government's position was brilliantly argued by a young lawyer named Charles Wyzanski, who later became, and still is, a federal district judge in Boston. He spoke before the Court without a note for reference and handled himself with great assurance.

But an even more memorable event than the argument of the case for social security was the handing down by the Supreme Court of its decision upholding the constitutionality of the major provision of the act. On Monday, May 24, 1937, John G. Winant, a former Republican governor of New Hampshire who had been the chairman of the Social Security Board, Arthur Altmeyer, who became chairman when Winant resigned in indignation at Landon's attack on social security, and others involved in the preparation and administration of social security legislation heard Justice Cardozo read the majority decision of the Court. Commenting on old-age insurance, Cardozo said:

Needs that were narrow or parochial a century ago may be interwoven in our day with the well-being of the Nation. What is crucial or urgent changes with the times . . . Congress did not improvise a judgment when it found that the award of old age benefits would be conducive to the general welfare. . . . The number of persons in the United States 65 years of age and over is increasing proportionately as well as absolutely. What is even more important, the number of such persons unable to take care of themselves is growing at a threatening pace. . . . The problem is plainly national in area and dimension.

Shortly after the decision was handed down, Altmeyer approved a memo to the staff of the Social Security Board which stated that because of the decision the old-age-benefits program could now be called "old-age insurance" and the unemployment program, "unemployment insurance." The American public was—and still is—insurance-minded and opposed to terms like "welfare," "the dole," and "handouts." Although many of those who still disagree with the level of benefits or methods of financing social security claim the system is not insurance, they are clearly wrong because the program meets the criteria for insurance established by insurance experts and organizations.

In the same month as the Supreme Court's decision, the first Advisory Council on Social Security was appointed; named chairman of the Council was Professor J. Douglas Brown, a labor economist from Princeton University. It was this Advisory Council of 1937–1938 which developed, in cooperation with the staff of the Social Security Board, the basic pattern of benefits now incorporated in the system. Among others who were members of this important path-breaking group were Professors Paul Douglas, William Haber, and Edwin E. Witte, all of whom had been teaching social security courses as a part of the labor legislation field.

Roosevelt the Innovator

Although Roosevelt's social security program was a significant break with the past, the assistance and help it offered were by any standard moderate indeed to the average American. The President clearly hoped the program would eventually be expanded to provide more adequate coverage. On one occasion, he said to Frances Perkins, "I see no reason why every child, from the day he is born, shouldn't be a member of the social security system. . . . I don't see why not. Cradle to the grave—from the cradle to the grave they ought to be in a social insurance system."

In spite of the modest assistance the program offered, an innovative President was ready and able to take advantage of a unique political situation favorable to social action and push through the necessary legislation quickly.

Public Acceptance

The term "social security" has been used in this country to identify the broad range of programs covered under the Social Security Act. In popular parlance, however, it has come to be particularly identified with the Old Age Insurance Program (now Old Age, Survivors, Disability, and Health Insurance—OASDHI). The lives of each of the 215 million people now living in the United States are affected directly or indirectly by the overall program. As of 1976, more than 100 million people have worked sufficient time in employment covered by the Social Security Act (Title II) to be insured for benefits, and over 32 million individuals regularly receive such benefits each month (OASDI). Several million persons receive Medicare benefits each year (Title XVIII). In addition, several million persons received weekly unemployment-insurance benefits in 1975–76 (Title III); some 11 million receive welfare checks each month under Title IV (AFDC); another 4 million aged, blind, and disabled persons receive supplemental security income under Title XVI (SSI); nearly 25 million received aid from Medicaid in 1975 under Title XIX; and millions of others receive social services (Title XX) and child-welfare services (Title IV) and have their medical bills paid for through the maternal and child health and crippled children's provisions of social security (Title V).

Through the years since 1935, social security has thus become an accepted part of the American way of life. In 1975 over $100 billion was paid in benefits under all the various provisions in the Social Security Act. Together with other federal, state, and private pension and social welfare programs, the total amount presently disbursed approximates $200 billion annually—a significant volume of purchasing power which has set a floor under consumer income and has helped moderate the adverse economic impact of the current recession on families and on the economy.

The widespread public acceptance of the program can be attributed in large part to its contributory earnings-related social-insurance philosophy. This significant aspect of social security—which emphasizes the work ethic and individual and social responsibility—appeals to both liberals and conservatives, Democrats and Republicans, and to most individuals among labor and employer groups at all socioeconomic levels. The federal statutory right to earned benefits without recourse to welfare or resource restrictions strongly appeals to minority groups as well as those in the majority. The low cost of administering the cash benefits of the program (only about 2 percent of benefits) has made social security both a unique and acceptable feature of our society.

Changes Made Since 1935

The social security program has been amended and extended by the Congress in major respects some 15 times since its enactment in 1935; although some setbacks have occasionally occurred, substantial progress has been made in improving the original legislation. It has been one of the most exhaustively and continuously studied—both within and outside government—of any program ever enacted by Congress. On five occasions from 1938 to 1971, it has been reviewed by the advisory councils established under the auspices of Congress and composed of economists, other social scientists, and leaders of both labor and business. The conclusions and recommendations of these councils have been influential in creating the improvements that have been made in the system since its inception.

The Social Security Act of 1935 provided for only two social insurance programs: old-age insurance and unemployment insurance. Since then, additional protection has been added, and the program has been expanded to protect the entire family. Nearly all Americans now have a personal stake in the system, relying on it to safeguard themselves and their families against economic catastrophe when earnings cease because of old age, disability, or death.

In 1939, survivors insurance was added to provide monthly life-insurance payments to the widow and dependent children of a deceased worker. The face value in 1976 of this life insurance is approximately 1 trillion dollars, nearly equivalent to the total of all private life insurance in the United States. In addition, some 800,000 young people at any one time are able to finish high school and go to college even though the family breadwinner has died, become disabled, or has retired; they can do so because monthly payments are now made to dependents up to age 22 if they are attending school. Social security has thus become one of the largest student-aid programs in the nation.

In 1950 and 1954, old-age and survivors insurance was broadened, and in 1956, disability insurance was added to the program. Over 1.3 million disabled workers are receiving disability benefits in 1976, and an additional 1 million persons receive payments as the dependents of such employees. The law also currently provides medical-insurance protection to some 22 million aged persons and several million disabled persons because of the enactment of Medicare in 1965 and its application to the disabled under age 65 in 1973. A new cost-of-living escalator was added to the law in 1972; at the same time there was an automatic increase in the maximum earnings base and retirement test in relation to wages. The cost-of-living escalator guarantees higher future benefits for all beneficiaries. In 1974, existing state programs of financial assistance for the aged, blind, and disabled were replaced by a new income supplement (SSI) to be administered by the Social Security Administration and financed from general revenues.

Because of these incremental improvements in the program, nine out of ten workers are now covered under social security, including members of the armed forces, the self-employed, farmers and farm workers, domestic help, and nearly everyone except certain government employees who are protected by separate systems. Over 90 percent of all people 65 and over are eligible under the program; 95 out of 100 mothers and children in the country are entitled to monthly benefits in the event of the death of the main breadwinner in the family; and 85 out of every 100 workers are entitled to disability-insurance benefits in the event of total permanent disability.

The Social Security Act was clearly one of the most far-reaching pieces of social legislation ever enacted by Congress. Its passage and the improvements made in it since that time have marked the end of a long struggle for protecting and increasing the human rights of the aged, unemployed, and dependent children.

Social security has become far more than a retirement program. It is also the largest life-insurance program, the largest disability-insurance program, the largest health-insurance program in the nation.

Looking Ahead

Despite social security's remarkable achievements, however, there are many proposals for future change and reform. Successful proposals for change will have to meet public acceptability and be in accord with our traditions and values. But at the same time it is essential to recognize that some change in the system is inevitable. We must be receptive to new ideas that make good sense.

Looking ahead, the number of persons ages 65 and over will grow from the present 22 million to about 30 million by the year 2000 and to probably 50 million by the year 2030. We must begin to consider how to prepare our society for a much greater proportion of older people—perhaps as much as 15 percent of the total population. The long-run implications of these projections will require imaginative consideration and solution. The next Advisory Council on Social Security should consider longer range problems, offer recommendations for action by the President and the Congress, and outline the options which should be considered.

There are also important short-run changes needing prompt attention. The most immediate is congressional action to increase the maximum earnings base ($15,300 in 1976) for contributions and benefits. Under the existing law, which provides for the automatic increase in the maximum earnings base in relation to increases in wages, this figure is estimated to be about $17,000 in 1977. A step-by-step increase to about $30,000 within the next five to ten years would result in sufficient additional income to cover expected expenditures in the near future and to rebuild the reserve fund. It is essential that Congress enact legislation to prevent public anxiety about the future financing of the system.

The most far-reaching legislation needed is the enactment of a national health-insurance plan as part of the social security system. Proponents of public-sector responsibility in a national health-insurance plan believe that only through the public sector can equity to all participating individuals be assured. Equity in this context will provide greater assurance of similar treatment of individuals in similar circumstances with respect to financing costs, access to the delivery system, adjudication of grievances, and other key matters. Private plans cannot meet all these requirements, no matter how generous.

A number of changes should be made in the social security system to remove inequities in the law against women and to make the system more responsive to their needs. For example, the level of retirement benefits is linked to the individual's record of earnings from employment. For purposes of computation, the five lowest earning years are disregarded; earnings for the remaining working years are averaged, and the benefit level is linked to the result. This method of averaging earnings works to the disadvantage of women whose work records are erratic or marginal. Many women work for several years, then have children and leave the labor force to raise their families, returning to a career later when their children are in school or grown. Their years of zero-earnings are averaged with the salaried years, severely reducing the level of benefits in retirement. This inequity can be removed if only the five or ten highest earning years are considered for purposes of computing benefits. Such a change would have a major impact on the financial security of many older women.

An improvement that would have even greater impact on women is an amendment in the law to recognize household employment as covered employment under the system. Homemakers, whether male or female, make a contribution to the national economy, just as do those working for pay. If household work were defined as covered employment, a woman would not have to be married or engaged in a career to receive social security protection; she would have protection in her own right. A homemaker would, of course, have to pay a premium to receive protection.

Another significant advance in social security that would affect women and families would be a cash maternity benefit—giving women an amount equal to eight weeks' salary for the period.

The provisions incorporated in the 1939 amendments to provide benefits to wives, widows, and dependent parents have been of important value in promoting family security. Since that time, however, the proportion of women in the paid labor market has increased. The basic law should be reexamined in the light of these changed conditions and the existing discrimination against divorced women and married women who work for substantial periods of time.

For many older and disabled people, the current recession has created problems that could be ameliorated by two benefit improvements: Individuals ages 55 and over who are totally disabled for their regular work should be entitled to benefits, and those persons between the ages of 60 and 62 should be entitled to draw their social security benefits at actuarially reduced amounts.

It is imperative that the social security program be administered without regard to partisan political influence; to assure its nonpartisan administration, the program should be placed under a board, as was the case from 1935 to 1946 with the terms of office of board members rotated to assure their political independence but with confirmation by the Senate to assure accountability.

A high priority for national policy should be a further reduction in the number of persons in poverty. A program of full employment is essential in order that all other social programs operate effectively and efficiently. But in the interim, the present welfare system must be improved by providing a national floor for aid to families with dependent children (AFDC) and by authorizing the same kind of automatic device to relate these payments to the increase in the cost of living, as in OASDHI and SSI.

For the long term, the United States must decide how to distribute the benefits of its future economic growth. Not all our increased wealth should be spent on new highways; a good share of it should be invested in the elderly, the blind and disabled, and women and children as well as in education. Congress should take the lead in reexamining national priorities by appointing a commission to study and make recommendations on incremental procedures to improve domestic welfare.

The Critics

A great deal of opposition to the payroll tax—and to other features of social security—has been engendered recently by the new brand of elitist economists, both conservative and liberal, including Professor Milton Friedman of the University of Chicago, and by newspaper columnists and magazine writers. They make the argument that the payroll tax is a "regressive" tax and the system is unfair for lower paid and middle-income blue-collar workers.

Social security contributions are regressive, these critics contend, because the wealthy pay a smaller percent of their earned income than do the poor, in contrast to the general income tax under which the wealthy pay a higher percentage. If social security collections were taxes for the general support of government, this charge would be unanswerable; one cannot imagine that Congress would have imposed these levies or have allowed them to remain on the law books except as part of a social-insurance system. The charge illustrates, however, the fallacy of examining the two parts of social security in isolation from each other—an approach that distorts the issues and loads the argument. The issue is not whether social security taxes are regressive but whether the social security system, taking into account both benefits and contributions, is subject to this charge. There are no convincing data which indicate the system as a whole is regressive.

The benefit formula in OASDI is designed so as to give a larger return for each dollar of contributions to the low-wage earner than to the high. Although there are other factors to be considered, some favoring the poor and some not, the net effect of the system is to transfer some income from the more affluent to the less affluent. It is legitimate to argue that the system should be made more progressive—for instance by the introduction of a government contribution derived from general revenues—but it is not legitimate to argue that the total system is regressive.

Another criticism that has gained prominence as the amount of contributions has been increased is that, regardless of the liberality of future returns, the present burden is more than those in low- and moderate-income brackets ought to bear out of current earnings. Critics often point out that many of these people pay more in social security contributions than they do in income taxes. The fact is, however, that many persons pay more for any number of things, such as automobiles and housing, than they pay in income taxes; there is nothing inherently inequitable in charging them more for the important protections of social security than they are charged for the general support of government.

The resolution of these various financing issues lies in the enactment of a comprehensive national social-insurance program, including cash benefits and medical coverage, which will be financed on a tripartite basis with contributions from employers, employees, and general revenues of the federal government.

The provision in the OASDI program most frequently under attack—primarily from conservatives—is the test of retirement This test has been a bone of contention for many years, with support at various times for its abandonment or for the automatic payment of benefits upon attainment of age 65. The retirement test is the mechanism used to determine if a loss of income has occurred because of retirement, its effect being reduction or suspension of benefits for those periods in which earnings are above stated amounts. These amounts will be increased in the future by automatic adjustment provisions in the present law in order to keep pace with rising earnings, and, of course, as in the past, they may be further increased by amendments to the law. The present structure of the test is probably as fair a method as can be devised if retirement is not to be abandoned altogether as a condition of eligibility.

There are those who believe that the condition of eligibility is unfair because it deprives people of benefits for continuing to work after age 65 and because it stands in the way of those on the benefit roll who wish to supplement their social security income as much as they can. Supporters of the retirement test point out that its abolition would cost the equivalent of a .34 percent increase in the combined employer-employee contribution rate and would benefit less than one-tenth of those over age 65 who are otherwise eligible for benefits. They ask whether funds in this amount are not better used either to supplement the incomes of those who still have substantial earning power or be apportioned among the nine-tenths who do not or cannot earn enough to bring them within the ambit of the retirement test. Although arguments like these have persisted through the years, they have no bearing on the soundness or durability of the social security system. Congress has repeatedly considered the issue and concluded that adaptation of the test to fit rising levels of earning is preferable to its repeal.

Another attack on the retirement test, however, has destructive implications: the contention that if benefits are withheld because of earnings, they should also be withheld because of the receipt of private pension payments, dividends, interest, or other unearned income. Such a change would deprive the program of one of its major strengths—its encouragement of people in their working years to supplement their social security protection through savings and private pension plans.

Occasionally critics reveal their ignorance of the way in which Congress decided to finance social security by charging that the system is financially unsound—even bankrupt. They arrive at this erroneous conclusion because there is not sufficient money in the social security fund to pay off all its obligations for the indefinite future. If this criterion were applied to most private pension plans in the United States, they, too, would be considered "bankrupt." By this criterion, the Federal Civil Service Retirement Fund is bankrupt, and nearly all state and local public employee retirement systems are bankrupt.

On the advice of leading economists, insurance and banking experts, and public representatives, Congress decided that social security should be financed on a pay-as-you-go basis because a governmental social security plan does not need to be on a full-reserve basis. Some $40 billion in U.S. government bonds presently back up the system; these bonds are guaranteed as to principal and interest by the federal government, and they have the same value as government bonds held by banks, private insurance companies, and individuals.

The ultimate question posed by current attacks on the system is whether the American people should continue to support contributory social insurance that is designed to prevent poverty from occurring or should place basic reliance on measures to re--

lieve poverty after it has become a fact. Necessary as relief programs are, they rank a poor second to prevention.

The Right to Appeal

An important feature of the social security system is its provision for an orderly and available appeals and hearings procedure for reviewing and revising decisions with which an individual does not agree. If, for example, a claimant disagrees with any decision of a social security official, he may request an administrative review of that decision by another official. Forms for the review are available in local social security offices. A lawyer is not needed in the administrative-review process, although one may be used if the individual so wishes. If the claimant is not satisfied with the administrative review, he may then appeal to the federal courts. He will, however, need a lawyer for this procedure. If he does not have a lawyer or cannot afford one, the local legal aid or legal services office can be of service.

It is important to emphasize that an individual's rights to social security are protected by law, the federal courts, and the Constitution of the United States.

A Sound and Flexible Structure

The social security program is a sound structure which can evolve and adapt to changing needs. It is an institution created with care and intelligence. It has succeeded because its founders had the foresight to create a framework sufficiently strong and flexible to stand the test of time. The United States has both the economic resources and the administrative capacity to continue to improve it incrementally in relation to our national priorities and productivity.

Remarkable progress has been made since the original act was passed in 1935, but President Roosevelt's comments are still pertinent: The structure of social security is still being built and is by no means complete. The next decade should produce still further improvements in the program.

CHAPTER 4

Policy Development in Unemployment Insurance

RAYMOND MUNTS
University of Wisconsin

The History of Unemployment Insurance Shapes Its Policies

Union and Management Experiment to Alleviate Effects of Unemployment[1]

The earliest union efforts to cushion the effects of unemployment for their members (c. 1830s) were part of benevolent programs of self-help. They took the form of crisis contributions by working members for their unemployed brethren and can be best understood as a form of worker philanthropy under trade-union auspices. This private relief played an important role in helping workers through periodic depressions, but the programs usually disappeared in good times. Even when contributions were regularized to persist over the business cycle, the plans suffered from actuarial inadequacy and casual administration. In 1931, only three national unions and some eight locals had plans in operation than had been established prior to the Great Depression.[2]

The first joint union-management plans were started in 1894 in the wallpaper industry, but not until the 1920s did the big burst in joint plans come about—in the needle trades and the hat, hosiery, and lace industries. Three of the plans guaranteed a certain amount of work and the other 12 paid benefits during periods of unemployment. Some plans were fully employer-financed; others also

---

[1] This section and the next draw heavily on the accounts in William Haber and Merrill G. Murray, *Unemployment Insurance in the American Economy* (Homewood, Ill.: Richard D. Irwin, 1966), and Daniel Nelson, *Unemployment Insurance, The American Experience 1915–1935* (Madison: University of Wisconsin Press, 1969).

[2] U.S. Department of Labor, *Unemployment Benefit Plans in the United States and Unemployment Insurance in Foreign Countries*, BLS Bull. No. 544 (Washington: U.S. Government Printing Office, July 1931).

had some employee contributions.[3] By 1933, half of these plans had been discontinued—casualties of the depression.[4]

Many issues about negotiated unemployment insurance were already apparent in these early union efforts. Although some people thought that unemployment insurance programs should be the duty of government rather than a subject for bargaining, Samuel Gompers's preference for the private approach prevailed. However, much disagreement remained on the issue of employee contributions. Even fully employer-paid plans were subject to the castigations of militant leftist leaders, who regarded them as a kind of capitalist "Bandaid" and did not wish to be put in a position of great dependence on employers.[5]

In the early period, it was company-sponsored plans, more than the union or joint plans, that caught the public's fancy. Between 1917 and 1933, 19 industry plans were established that included protection for about 80,000 employees in 38 firms. Some were benefit plans, some were savings plans, and others were employment-guarantee plans.[6] The view was widespread that "the problem of unemployment was essentially one of business and business management and must be met by business statesmanship."[7] Louis D. Brandeis, a severe critic of inefficient business management, argued that the employer rather than the union leader held the key to the solution of the unemployment problem. "Society and industry," he maintained, "need only the necessary incentive to secure a great reduction of irregularity of employment. In a scientifically managed business, irregularity tends to disappear."[8] The leaders of

[3] The largest plans were those of the Amalgamated Clothing Workers in Chicago, New York, and Rochester (33,000 participants) and the American Federation of Full-Fashioned Hosiery Workers (15,000 participants).

[4] U.S. Department of Labor, *Unemployment Benefit Plans.* . . .

[5] At the 1922 ILGWU convention, the delegates were told such funds would "put the workers in a position of greater dependence upon the employers." In a discussion of joint plans of any kind at the 1924 convention, a leftist leader said with disdain, "Now we are in the life insurance business and later we are going to build houses and railroads. Our problem is organizing the shop." But by 1928 when the Communists were no longer in control, the convention urged that unemployment funds be part of every agreement. See Raymond Munts, "Welfare History of the I.L.G.W.U.," *Labor History*, vol. 9, Special Supp. (Spring 1968) , pp. 87–88.

[6] Best known among the guaranteed employment plans was Procter and Gamble's; among the benefit plans, that of the Rochester group of firms; among the individual plans, that of J. I. Case in Wisconsin.

[7] Judge Elbert H. Gary, as quoted in Nelson, *Unemployment Insurance*, p. 12.

[8] In Nelson, *Unemployment Insurance.*

business who established the unemployment plans in the 1920s regarded themselves as "scientific" managers. Only when plans to alleviate the effects of unemployment failed to spread to all industry and the country was convulsed by the Great Depression did some of them abandon the private approach and become proponents of an obligatory unemployment-benefits law.[9]

Legislative Proposals: The Effort to Americanize Unemployment Insurance

Although a number of European countries had legislated unemployment programs in the form of government assistance to union plans (the Ghent system), it was not until enactment of the British unemployment law that interest in the idea was kindled in the United States.[10] Bills were introduced in Massachusetts (1916), New York (1921), and Wisconsin (1921). The first two were copies of the British approach with tripartite financing (employers, employees, and government), while the Wisconsin bill was based on an insurance scheme that was to be financed exclusively by employers and that introduced the concept of experience-rating. The prime author of the Wisconsin bill, Professor John R. Commons, had been impressed with the stimulus given accident prevention by the variable premium rates in Wisconsin's workmen's compensation law, and he sought to apply the same principle to prevention of unemployment. During the 1920s, bills embodying the Wisconsin approach were introduced in Connecticut, Minnesota, and Pennsylvania.

But the unemployment insurance concept was to be shelved for a variety of reasons. The interest that had been kindled by the British and later the German laws, as well as by the recession of 1914–1915, disappeared with the ascendancy of political conservatism that followed the first World War. The American Association for Labor Legislation, which had been instrumental in calling attention to the European developments, began to concentrate more

---

[9] Among such men were Marion B. Folsom, treasurer of the Eastman Kodak Company; Gerard Swope, president of General Electric; Morris Leeds, president of Leeds & Northrup; Sam Lewisohn, vice president of Miami Copper Company; Walter C. Teagle, president of the Standard Oil Company of New Jersey.

[10] Among the early students of unemployment insurance were Henry R. Seager, Charles R. Henderson, William M. Leiserson, Louis Brandeis, John R. Commons, Isaac M. Rubinow, and John B. Andrews.

on the area of health insurance. The public was caught up in the "new emphasis" of business on scientific management, which, among other things, was supposed to do away with unemployment by social "engineering." Over all was the pall of Gomper's opposition, which had discouraged unemployment insurance proponents since 1916. "Such laws," he said, "are not advocated for the good of the workers. They are advocated by persons who know nothing of the hopes and aspirations of labor which desires opportunities for work, not compulsory unemployment insurance."[11] As summarized by Philip Taft, Gompers's opposition stemmed largely from fear of government—a fear supported by the long experience of the AFL with the executive and judicial branches during labor disputes.[12]

The Depression Brings Federal Intervention

The Great Depression changed everything. It showed the large numbers of persons whose jobs were at risk; it exposed the precariousness of private plans; it demonstrated the inability of the states to legislate on their own; and it changed the national AFL position. But a difficult political and constitutional issue was posed: How far should the federal government go in specifying the design of unemployment insurance laws?

The predepression view had been expressed in a Senate committee report in 1929: "Insurance plans against unemployment should be confined to the industry itself as much as possible. There is no necessity and no place for Federal interference in such efforts at this time. If any public insurance scheme is considered, it should be left to the State legislatures to study the problem."[13] Indeed, there was a rash of bills introduced in state legislatures from 1931 to 1934, but only one passed two houses—that in Wisconsin—and it passed conditionally; it would not become effective if more than 200,000 workers should come under voluntary plans in the state. Even in a political climate of crisis, states could not overcome a natural reluctance to disadvantage their own industrial develop-

---

[11] As quoted by Philip Taft, *The A.F. of L. in the Time of Gompers* (New York: Harper, 1957), p. 365.

[12] Taft, p. 365 ff.

[13] U.S. Senate, *Causes of Unemployment*, Rep. No. 2072, 70th Cong., 2d Sess. (Washington: U.S. Government Printing Office, Feb. 28, 1929), p. xv, as quoted by Haber and Murray, p. 71.

ment by imposing taxes on business. As Franklin Roosevelt, then the governor of New York State, expressed it: "All must act, or there will be no action."[14]

Early in the depression years, the AFL was still suspicious and favored preventive efforts rather than insurance benefits. In 1930, its president, William Green, expressed the view that unemployment insurance was "paternalistic. It is one system of the dole which demoralizes ambition, stultifies initiative and blights hope . . . . [T]he real cure is employment."[15] Preventive efforts preferred by the AFL included a national employment service, shorter workdays, and stabilization of employment. But by 1932 the pressure within was too great, and the AFL Executive Council instructed Green to draw up legislation on unemployment insurance. Several experts were consulted, including Felix Frankfurter of Harvard who was convinced that a federal plan would be unconstitutional because of the states' responsibility for regulation of manufacture and industry. The report to the convention that year urged the "passage of unemployment insurance legislation in each separate state, and the supplementing of each state legislation by federal enactments; such, for instance, as bills covering employees engaged in interstate commerce or employed in federal territories."[16]

In Congress, leadership was provided by Senator Robert F. Wagner of New York, who introduced a bill to get around the constitutionality question. It provided for a federal excise tax on employers, but if a state law contained the specified benefit standards, the employer could then receive a 100 percent offset on his federal tax. In effect, he would pay the state rather than the federal tax. This was a device suggested by Justice Brandeis after the Supreme Court upheld the Federal Estate Tax Act of 1926, which had used the offset approach to prevent states from undercutting each other through low inheritance taxes. This tax device was incorporated in the Wagner-Lewis bill, but because Franklin Roosevelt, now

---

[14] The reluctance of states to step out alone explains the resolutions of the Maine, Minnesota, Montana, and Wisconsin legislatures in 1933 urging Congress to enact unemployment insurance legislation.

[15] Not all top AFL leaders or even all members of the Executive Council agreed with Green; Vice President Wharton and Dan Tobin did not. See Taft, pp. 29–40.

[16] Taft, pp. 29–40.

President, was not yet sure what structure he wanted, he announced that he needed time to study the whole question of economic-security programs. The Wagner-Lewis bill was shelved. However, it is interesting in retrospect to note that this bill provided benefit standards that were not included in the Social Security Act the following year and remain an unrealized objective of organized labor.

The Economic Security Committee appointed by Roosevelt had three options for structuring unemployment insurance: a purely federal system, which was rejected on constitutional grounds; a tax-credit plan, such as the Wagner-Lewis bill; or a subsidy plan. Roosevelt expressed himself in favor of a cooperative federal-state system; thus, the committee's choice was limited to the latter two alternatives. Although there was considerable support for the subsidy approach, including that of the AFL, the committee's final decision was for a tax credit, as in the Wagner-Lewis bill, but with the fewest possible standards.

Arthur Altmeyer has explained that the committee's decision was based on two grounds:[17] First, since the tax-offset plan, unlike the subsidy plan, would require states to enact their own laws, there was more likelihood of retaining some residual results if the Supreme Court struck down the federal action. Second, because there were difficult policy questions that would have to be addressed in formulating standards, the committee preferred to put maximum responsibility for writing them on the states. Among the policy questions needing answers were the amount and duration of weekly benefits, whether protections should be provided for seasonal and partial unemployment, whether there should be employee contributions, and whether there should be employer experience-rating. Reading Altmeyer's account, one get the impression that while constitutionality constrained the choices, the decision was heavily influenced by a practical desire not to endanger the bill's passage by loading it with two decades of controversy. In short, the strategy was to avoid substantive policy questions. Although the constitutionality question was settled by a chastized Supreme Court in a decision that would have permitted any of the alternatives consid-

[17] Arthur J. Altmeyer, *The Formative Years of Social Security* (Madison: University of Wisconsin Press, 1966), pp. 18 ff.

ered by the Economic Security Committee,[18] many of the benefit and financing issues remain unresolved to this day.

Labor was to become a major supporter of the social security system of the United States, but one would not have predicted this at the outset. According to Witte,[19] of the four union leaders appointed to the Advisory Council,[20] only Green and Ohl participated in the meetings. The five employer members attended all meetings. After the bill had been introduced and hearings scheduled, William Green testified, making a long statement with so many suggestions for improving the bill that it was construed by some newspapers as an attack.

During the hearings, Green, speaking for the AFL, criticized the bill in a way that was to prove prophetic. He pointed out that the weak role assigned the federal government would jeopardize the quality of the program:[21]

> It leaves to the states almost complete freedom of action in the adoption of unemployment insurance laws. There are no standards set for the state laws to follow. Each state is free to determine the waiting period to be imposed, the amount of benefit which shall be paid, the length of time benefits shall continue, the wage earning group which shall be included under the act, the type of funds which shall be set up, and the manner in which such funds shall be administered.

Green then recommended the subsidy approach with standards.

However, when the struggle began in the Senate and continued between the Senate and House conferees over the final form of the social security legislation, "the American Federation of Labor did everything it could to insure passage of the bill."[22] The provisions for an unemployment insurance system became law as Title III of the Social Security Act of 1935.

---

[18] *Steward Machine Co.* v. *Davis*, 301 U.S. 548 (1937).

[19] Edwin E. Witte, *The Development of the Social Security Act* (Madison: University of Wisconsin Press, 1962), p. 54.

[20] William Green; George M. Harrison, president of the Brotherhood of Railway and Steamship Clerks; Paul Scharrenberg, secretary-treasurer of the California State Federation of Labor; and Henry Ohl, Jr., president of the Wisconsin State Federation of Labor.

[21] Taft, p. 282.

[22] Altmeyer, p. 33.

Labor's Role in Unemployment Insurance Since 1935

As enacted, Title III of the Social Security Act was an adaptation of foreign experience as modified by American preference for unemployment prevention first and benefits second. The vehicle for achieving the desired result was experience-rating.

At first, experience-rating had been struck out of the proposal in the House as inconsistent with the objective of reducing interstate cost differentials in order to put the states on an equal competitive level in their economic development. But experience-rating was restored by the Senate and was later to result in a reduction of revenues for the program substantially less than the standard 3 percent of payrolls.

The significance of this action lies in conjunction with another peculiarity of the American approach—the absence of any indication from the national government about the quality of benefits. With no minimum benefit standards and a built-in propensity for underfinancing, it was going to prove very difficult to develop an adequate benefit structure.

Labor was to have another source of difficulty in its legislative work—that of finding allies. In other areas of social security, such as old-age insurance and later Medicare, there were groups with which to work because social-welfare organizations had common interests with labor. But in unemployment insurance, labor frequently had to work alone, and usually in direct opposition to the interests of the employer-taxpayers and their organizations.

Finally, labor had difficulty because the state emphasis in the program decentralized legislative efforts and put a heavy burden on the weak resources of state central bodies.

To deal with these new legislative dimensions, Green took two steps. He urged state central bodies to study the administration of the state laws to protect the rights of labor (particularly the application of disqualifications), and he appointed a three-member committee on social insurance to keep abreast of developments and to recommend improvements. In 1944, this committee was increased from three to nine members, and Nelson Cruikshank was appointed director of AFL social insurance activities. The committee met twice a year, and between meetings all matters affecting social security were cleared with the committee by Cruikshank and his staff.[23]

The CIO also developed a social security committee and a research and legislative staff. The AFL and CIO committees worked in close harmony on social security issues in the following years, and, as a result, the AFL-CIO merger brought no great policy changes. In 1957, the social insurance department of the AFL-CIO staffed a program for coordinating state central body legislative work on unemployment insurance and workmen's compensation.

Labor's objectives during the period from 1938 to 1975 were, in general, to achieve a substantial replacement of wage loss due to involuntary unemployment. In the earlier years, the hope persisted that a single fund at the national level could be developed, but the pattern of mild postwar recessions never forced an overhaul of the prevailing system. Although second-best in labor's view, inserting national benefit standards for state laws to observe became the practical objective.

The need for standards was demonstrated over and over again as inflation and rising wage levels during the 1940s and 1960s made obsolete the weekly benefit amounts. Much of labor's efforts at the state level was a kind of treadmill exercise of constantly calling for the updating of benefits in an effort to keep up with rising wage levels, to the point where jobless benefits got to be known as $2 or $4 laws—the amount of increase passed in each legislative session. But the periodic adjustments were rarely sufficient to maintain, let alone improve, the wage-replacement rates.

It was the decline in the average weekly wage-replacement rate from about 43 percent to 32 percent by 1951 that gave rise to the demand for negotiated supplemental unemployment benefits. Seen from a historical perspective, the supplemental unemployment benefits proposals were a return to the Gompersian philosophy that companies should set aside reserves to conserve the wage earner's investment in the industry.[24] The supplemental unemployment

[23] Taft, p. 282.

[24] Green, in 1931 when he was still opposing unemployment insurance, argued that an application of the reserve principle to labor would assure workers either stable employment or income over the business cycle. "By allotting some of the income to a wage reserve, wages could be taken care of in business depression in the same way as dividends and interest. We believe that the practice of wage reserves can be established in much the same way as were other re-

TABLE 1
Benefit Experience, 1974, and High State–Low State Range

Average benefit amount, all states	$64.25
High state: District of Columbia	$83.83
Low state: Louisiana	$40.82
Average benefit as ratio to average weekly wage, all states	.364
High state: Hawaii	.446
Low state: Alaska	.237
Average actual duration, all states	12.7 weeks
High state: District of Columbia	19.1 weeks
Low states: New Hampshire and North Carolina	7.5 weeks
Average duration for exhaustees, all states	22.4 weeks
High state: Pennsylvania	30.0 weeks
Low state: Indiana	14.9 weeks
Average exhaustion ratio, all states	.31
High state: Florida	.48
Low state: New Hampshire	.04

benefit movement succeeded in those industries where companies wanted to retain access to a trained labor force following periods of high unemployment. To some extent, however, it also drew unions and companies away from efforts to improve unemployment insurance legislation.

Changes in Unemployment Insurance

In 1937, when unemployment insurance programs were being rapidly enacted in most states, legislators had no time to study the subject in detail and, therefore, they usually followed the recommendations of the Social Security Board. It was inevitable that, with time, the nature of these programs would become increasingly disparate. At the present time, there are separate plans for every state and the District of Columbia,[25] each with its own underwriting and administration, its own experience-rating plan, and its own benefit policy. The ranges in benefits are summarized in Table 1. Clearly, any generalizations about changes in unemployment insurance over the years must be scrutinized for the considerable diversity that has evolved.

---

serves. There is involved the development of intangible rights, the acceptance of the right of a wage earner to his job, the obligation of industry to conserve and advance the investment the wage earner makes in the industry." Taft, p. 32.

[25] There is also a program for railroad workers, one for federal government employees, and one for ex-servicemen. These last two are administered by the states as agents for the federal government, and for our purposes will be subsumed under the federal-state system.

Reasons for Change

Since the Committee on Economic Security recommended coverage of nearly all wage and salary workers, it was a source of considerable disappointment that Congress opted instead for limited coverage. One important reason for changes in the laws since then has been to fill out the original design.

Other changes have been necessary because of the shifting elements in the economic climate in which unemployment functions, particularly the upward movement in average wages and salaries. Rising earnings levels have brought about frequent adjustments in maximum weekly amounts and also in base-year earnings requirements.

Also, changes were necessary when prior predictions proved to be inaccurate. The original actuarial estimates indicated that 3 percent of the payroll would finance only up to 16 weeks of benefits for the unemployed. Experience over the years has shown that the cost of unemployment insurance was overestimated. Therefore, it has been possible to extend the duration of benefits and still stay within the cost range originally contemplated.

Public criticism brought about changes in the disqualification provisions, which have been stiffened considerably in definition, administration, and length of penalties. Finally, the desire to experiment with new concepts has produced changes; examples are allowances for dependents and so-called "triggered" extended benefits.

Coverage

Instead of the broad coverage recommended by the Committee on Economic Security, Congress chose to exempt certain groups— employees of businesses hiring fewer than eight persons, all employees of government and of nonprofit organizations, and agricultural and domestic workers.

Although coverage was later extended to federal civilian employees, members of the armed services, and employees of some small firms, it was the Social Security Amendments of 1970 that achieved the most significant increase in coverage since the inception of the program. By that time, 21 states had already extended coverage to employees of firms smaller than the federal law required, but other states seemed hard pressed to follow the example. It was frequently alleged that legislators in the latter states were reluctant to act because many of them were lawyers who employed secretaries and thus would be affected. The 1970 Amendments required all states to extend the tax to employers of one or more persons or employers with payrolls of more than $1500 in a calendar quarter.

The 1970 Amendments also required states to cover certain non-profit educational, hospital, and charitable organizations that employed four or more persons during a 20-week period. Unlike profit-making employers, these nonprofit organizations are not subject to the federal tax; instead, each organization may choose either to reimburse the state for unemployment insurance payments attributable to its employees or to pay a state tax. Employees of state hospitals and institutions of higher education were first covered in 1972.

Seventeen states have exceeded the federal requirements and extended to these nonprofit organizations the same size-of-firm coverage criteria that apply to all other employers. These state amendments still leave uncovered employees of churches or church-related organizations and employees of elementary and secondary schools.

Since 1948, the proportion of wage and salary workers in covered employment has risen from 76 to 88 percent. Remaining unprotected are 12 million wage and salary workers, almost all of whom are in state and local government employment (8.1 million), agriculture (1.4 million), and private household employment (1.7 million).

The issues posed if coverage were to be extended to these groups are primarily cost and feasibility. There has been very little disagreement that in principle it is desirable to make unemployment insurance universally applicable to wage and salary earners. Only four states have extended some coverage to farm workers and four have had some experience with coverage of household employees.

Weekly Benefit Amount

Instead of adopting a weekly benefit in the form of a flat cash amount, as in Britain, on the recommendation of the Social Security Board the states chose to relate the benefit to 50 percent of the claimant's wage loss. In some cases the amount was tempered with allowance for dependents or "weighted benefits" for lower wage earners. There was little justification for the 50 percent reimbursement except that it was the one that had been applied in Wisconsin.[26] Even less justification lay behind the Board's recommendation for the maximum benefit, but most of the states adopted the $15 maximum. This was about three-fourths of the mean wage in 1937 and meant that three out of four covered workers could get an individual benefit of half their wage loss.

Not much more was done about raising the maximums until the inflationary impact of World War II forced a reconsideration of wage loss and benefit levels. During and since the war, maximums have been adjusted upward many times (see Table 2), but rarely fast enough to keep a constant portion of the work force assured of reimbursement of half their wage-loss.

The large losses in benefits relative to wages occurred during the 1939–1953 period; the ratio was fairly well maintained between 1953 and 1960. Gains since 1960 are due primarily to three factors: the application of the flexible or sliding maximum, the record of the 1960s with its relatively low unemployment and climbing reserves, and the threatened federal intervention in the form of benefit standards.

The sliding maximum was first used in Wisconsin in 1959. Under that system, the legislature sets the desired ratio of the maximum to average weekly wages, while the actual dollar amount of the maximum is determined administratively once or twice a year, based on the average weekly wages in covered employment. By 1963, 11 states had adopted the formula, and by 1975, 32 states were using the sliding maximum. In many of these states, the

---

[26] Paul Raushenbush has explained the Wisconsin use of the half-of-wages approach as follows: "No one claimed, in 1930–31, so far as I recall, that U.S. weekly benefits should be high enough to cover every jobless worker's 'cost-of-living' or 'non-deferable expenses.' They would help of course; but maybe saving or even 'relief' might have to supplement U.C. in some cases. More basically, we were sure that 50 percent benefits would be more acceptable to the public than a higher percentage of wages. The public, and legislators—both then and now—feel that a W.C. claimant should draw a good deal more than a U.C. claimant. That's partly because most folks are far more sympathetic to an injured worker than to a physically-able jobless worker. But that feeling is probably mainly due to the common notion or conviction that benefits for a jobless worker should not be high enough to encourage 'malingering.'" From letter to Saul J. Blaustein, December 1970.

TABLE 2

Changes in Maximum Weekly Benefit Amount, by Number of States

	December 1939	December 1953	December 1961	December 1968	December 1972	July 1975
Maximum weekly benefit amount (MWBA)						
$10.01–$20	51					
$20.01–$30			7			
$30.01–$40			30	7		
$40.01–$50			12	23	3	
$50.01–$60			2	16	14	2
$60.00–$70				6	17	2
$70.01–$80					10	6
$80.01–$90					6	19
$90.01–$100					1	13
$100.01–$110					1	10
Over $110.01						10
MWBA as percent of average weekly wage						
20–29		2	2	1	2	
30–39		17	10	10	3	3
40–49	2	29	29	21	19	6
50	15	2	5	15	9	11
50.9–59			4	3	10	15
60–69	17	1	1	2	8	17
70–79	7					
80–89	7					
90–99	3					
Percent benefit payments at maximum	26	59	46	46	44	42

Note: The benefit amounts do not include dependents' allowances. The table includes the District of Columbia and Puerto Rico tabulations when available.

maximums are still quite low.[27] Looking at all states with and without sliding maximums, only 30 percent of all covered workers are in states with maximums at 60 percent of average weekly wages or above.

In the beginning, only the District of Columbia provided additional benefits for dependents, but as inflation eroded the benefit value and states were slow to raise maximums, the dependents' allowance emerged as an issue. Because they believed that unem-

---

[27] Nine states set their sliding maximum at 66 2/3 percent of the average weekly wage; six at .60 percent, and the rest (17) range from 57.5 percent to 50 percent.

ployment insurance was withering on the vine and new initiatives were needed, the CIO leadership attempted to develop pressures for the introduction of dependents' benefits in state laws. By 1955, only 11 states had added them. Since then, three states have added dependents' allowances, but three others have dropped them. Numerous studies have shown that benefits for dependents help achieve the support objectives of the program; yet legislatures continue to resist on the ground that unemployment benefits are wage insurance.

Weekly benefit amounts have risen on the average from $10.56 in 1940 to about $65 in 1975, but if the movement in wages over that period are considered, it can be seen that benefits were a smaller proportion of average wages in 1975 than they were in 1940 (see Table 3). Again and again, labor has had to trade some feature of benefits for higher weekly maximums in order to maintain the rate of wage replacement. Wider use of the flexible maximum will add an important element of stability to the benefit side of the unemployment insurance program.

TABLE 3
Changes in Average Benefit Amount, by Number of States

	1940	1950	1960	1970	1972	1975 est.
Average benefit amounts (ABA)						
Under $10	30					
$10.01–$20	21	28				
$20.01–$30		23	25	1		
$30.01–$40			25	12	3	1
$40.01–$50			1	22	17	1
$50.01–$60				16	24	13
$60.01–$70				1	7	19
$70.01–$80						16
Over $80.01						2
U.S. average amount	$10.56	$20.76	$32.87	$50.31	$55.82	$65.34
ABA as percent of average weekly wage						
Under 40	29	47	46	45	39	24
40–40.9	20	4	6	7	13	27
Over 50	2					1
U.S. average percent	39.1	34.4	35.2	35.7	35.9	36.0

Note: The table includes the District of Columbia and Puerto Rico tabulations when available.

TABLE 4

Distribution of States by Maximum Potential Weeks of Benefits for Total Unemployment, Classified by Variable and Uniform Duration

	Total	Maximum Number of Weeks									
		12	13–15	16	17–19	20	21–25	26	27–30	31–35	36–39
Dec. 31, 1937											
Total	51	4	13	29	1	4					
Uniform	1			1							
Variable	50	4	13	28	1	4					
Aug. 1, 1941											
Total	45		9	24	6	6					
Uniform	14		3	8	1	2					
Variable	31		6	16	5	4					
Jan. 1, 1950											
Total	51	1		5	2	21	9	13			
Uniform	15	1		2		6	3	1			
Variable	36			3	2	15	6	12			
Dec. 31, 1960											
Total	52	1				2	7	33	5	2	2
Uniform	13	1					4	7	1		
Variable	39					2	3	26	4	2	2
July 6, 1969											
Total	52	1						41	6	2	2
Uniform	8	1						7			
Variable	44							34	6	2	2
Dec. 1, 1973											
Total	52					1		42	6	2	1
Uniform	9					1		7	1		
Variable	43							35	5	2	1
Dec. 1, 1975											
Total	52					1		42	6	2	1
Uniform	8					1		6	1		
Variable	44							36	5	2	1

Duration

Basing its judgment on the amount of unemployment from 1922 to 1930, the Committee on Economic Security decided in 1935 that it would be risky to provide more than 16 weeks of benefits based on a 3 percent tax of payrolls. All but five states followed this advice and limited benefits to 16 weeks or less. Because of the record of high exhaustion rates accompanied by accumulating reserves, in 1942 the Social Security Board recommended an increase in duration of benefits to at least 20 weeks, and in 1944 the Director of War Mobilization recommended a *uniform* duration for all claimants of 26 weeks. This remained a national objective until 1955. Most states eventually accepted the 26-week duration, but only for those workers with substantial work records; the durations for others were variable but less than 26 weeks (see Table 4).

Uniform vs. variable duration remains an issue to this day. Uniform duration, in which every claimant is entitled to the same number of weeks of benefits, is consistent with the support objectives of the program by concentrating attention on the reemployment prospects of workers. Variable duration, in which potential weeks are a function of an individual's previous work record, is urged on the ground that entitlement should vary with the amount of contribution made on behalf of the worker; it also permits a shorter period of entitlement for those with only a marginal attachment to the labor force. At no time have more than 15 states followed the uniform principle, and today the number is down to nine.

The 26 weeks, or six months, of benefits as a maximum was discussed extensively for so many years that it became a kind of a sound barrier that was not penetrated until the recessions of 1958 and 1960–1961 when high exhaustion rates forced another look at the duration issue (Table 5). Nine states responded by extending the maximum duration beyond 26 weeks—some up to 39 weeks. Twenty-two states enacted temporary extensions, either with federal advances under the Temporary Unemployment Compensation Act of 1958 or on their own initiative (five states).

The recession of the late 1950s was widely attributed to structural changes in the economy, such as automation and industry relocation. In 1960, Congress enacted the Temporary Extended

TABLE 5

Exhaustions as Percent of First Payments, U.S. Average
and State Range, 1940–1975

Year	U.S. Average	Range[a]		
1940	50.6	24.7–75.6		
1941	45.6	20.8–67.7		
1942	34.9	12.7–52.2		
1943	25.2	2.6–43.1		
1944	20.2	7.0–51.2		
1945	18.1	3.4–79.6		
1946	38.7	12.1–73.8		
1947	30.7	11.8–65.6		
1948	27.5	8.3–59.2		
1949	29.1	15.8–54.7		
1950	30.5	20.7–58.9		
1951	20.4	12.4–94.4		
1952	20.3	12.3–44.2		
1953	20.8	8.6–41.7		
1954	26.8	15.1–52.3		
1955	26.1	12.9–51.8		
1956	21.5	11.1–49.8		
1957	22.7	12.0–41.1		
1958	31.0	12.2–46.6		
1959	29.6	7.4–47.2		
1960	26.1	9.0–45.5		
1961	30.4	18.3–48.2	N.H. = 12.9	
1962	27.4	16.3–45.5	N.H. = 12.6;	P.R. = 64.6
1963	25.3	11.4–41.3	N.H. = 10.5;	P.R. = 60.3
1964	23.8	15.8–39.4	N.H. = 8.8;	P.R. = 48.5
1965	21.5	13.0–36.1	N.H. = 4.1;	P.R. = 51.3
1966	18.0	8.7–33.9	N.H. = 2.3;	P.R. = 48.5
1967	19.3	9.8–32.0	N.H. = 1.3;	P.R. = 61.1
1968	19.6	10.2–35.0	N.H. = 1.3;	P.R. = 58.9
1969	19.8	9.6–41.2	N.H. = 0.6;	P.R. = 51.4
1970	24.4	13.2–41.2	N.H. = 4.3;	P.R. = 48.2
1971	30.5	14.2–49.0	N.H. = 10.0;	P.R. = 51.0
1972	28.9	15.7–45.1	N.H. = 5.0;	P.R. = 56.5
1973	28.5	13.2–45.3	N.H. = 2.7;	P.R. = 53.9
1974	31.1	16.1–48.0	N.H. = 4.0;	P.R. = 54.4
1975	37.8	22.2–59.2	N.H. = 10.7;	P.R. = 67.0

[a] New Hampshire, from 1961 to 1975, and Puerto Rico, from 1962 to 1975, were significantly at the extremes beyond the range of other state exhaustion rates. They are excluded from the range and are listed separately.

Unemployment Act, which authorized the extension of 13 more weeks of benefits to exhaustees—to 39 weeks in all. Unlike under the 1958 Act, the additional weeks of benefits were to be fully financed by the federal government. The 1960 Act established a watershed: The states now assumed responsibility for the cost of normal unemployment and the federal government the cost of long-term unemployment.

During the 1960s, it was widely agreed that while temporary extensions were one way of handling recession unemployment, it took too long for legislative bodies to respond to changing economic conditions. There was some experimenting among the states with temporary extensions triggered automatically by specified unemployment and exhaustion rates. The search for suitable automatic triggers culminated in the extended-benefit provisions of the Employment Security Amendments of 1970.

As previously noted, the 1970 law broadened coverage; it also provided a permanent program of extended benefits for persons exhausting their regular state benefits during periods of high unemployment. The weekly amount of the extended benefit is the same as a regular benefit; payment of extended benefits continues either half again as long as the individual's regular benefits, or 13 weeks, but no longer than a total of 39 weeks (regular plus extended). Designated unemployment rates, both nationally (all states together) and state by state, trigger the beginning and cessation of extended benefits.[28] The federal government reimburses the states for half the cost of the extended benefits.

Waiting Weeks

Related to the concept of duration is the issue of the so-called "waiting weeks" at the beginning of a period of unemployment before benefit payments can begin. At first, these no-benefit weeks were necessary to allow time for the processing of claims, but this administrative justification has been eliminated by modern record-

---

[28] The program is "triggered in" during periods of high unemployment at either the state or national level. Nationally, the "on" indicator is reached when the seasonally adjusted rate of insured unemployment equals or exceeds 4.5 percent in each of the three most recent months, and the "off" indicator occurs when the unemployment rate drops below 4.5 percent in each of the three consecutive months.

The state indicator is "on" for any individual state when the state's insured unemployment rate averages 4 percent for any 13 consecutive-week period and is 20 percent higher than the average rate for the corresponding 13-week period in each of the two preceding years. The state extended-benefit period ends when either of these conditions is not met.

An extended-benefit period begins with the third week after a week for which there was a national "on" indicator or a state "on" indicator, whichever occurs first. The period ends with the third week after the first week for which there are both national and state "off" indicators. However, an extended-benefit period must last for not less than 13 consecutive weeks and cannot be started again on the basis of a state indicator for another 13 weeks.

keeping. Some people continue to advocate retention of the waiting period as a way to hold down program costs, since every claimant is affected.

Precisely because so many are affected by these uncompensated weeks, steady pressure has developed over the years to reduce or even eliminate the waiting weeks.[29] Initially, 30 states required a two-week waiting period, 19 required three weeks, and two as many as four weeks. Some states also required waiting weeks for additional periods of unemployment during a benefit year. The trend to reduce this uncompensated time began in the early years of the program and continued until, by 1975, twelve states required no waiting period and the rest required only one week. Three states specify a longer period for partial unemployment benefits, and 10 states provide that the waiting period may become compensable retroactively if unemployment continues for a specified period—usually four or more weeks, depending on the state.

Work-Qualifying Requirements

Only those persons who are attached to the labor force, both currently and in the recent past, are entitled to unemployment compensation. A claimant must show evidence of a work history in a relatively recent period, such as the last year or 18 months (termed the base period).

The underlying rationale for this requirement is somewhat muddy. One reason given is that by producing a record of recent work for which contributions toward unemployment benefits have been made, the unemployed individual demonstrates that he is "insured" under the system and is entitled to benefits.[30] Another explanation is that a record of recent work is a necessary part of the work test, adding to the presumption that the applicant is work-oriented. For whatever reason, all states made benefit eligibility conditional on previous work.

---

[29] One might think there was a persuasive argument for keeping the waiting weeks and using the savings to extend the benefit and help the long-term unemployed. This has not figured as an acceptable policy trade-off because of the original gross overestimates of program costs.

[30] Support for this view lies in the fact that no state has ever experimented with giving benefits to new entrants to the labor force on the grounds that their benefits have not been funded. For discharged veterans, the cost is paid by the federal government.

Originally, it was agreed that the best measure of previous work was a specified minimum number of weeks of work. However, in order to simplify administration, most states adopted indirect ways of measuring this; for example, some specified a multiple of the weekly benefit amount or simply a total amount of earnings during the base period. Because flaws became apparent in these substitute measures, they have had to be changed frequently.

Another reason for changes in the qualifying requirements is that they are now used for a purpose other than that intended. In the past, a number of states specified that seasonal employment (for example, canning, fishing) was excluded from coverage, but all states have now switched to using the earnings-qualifying requirement for such cases. Now a *distribution* of work over the base year is required, the simplest examples being that the claimant have earnings in more than one quarter of the base year or that his earnings in the base year be some multiple of high-quarter earnings. Both of these distribution requirements are widely used in addition to the quantitative measures of base-year employment. The effect of the various requirements is that between 14 and 20 weeks of work in the base year are needed to establish eligibility for unemployment benefits, although some states, especially those that require a claimant to qualify on several tests, are more restrictive. Conversely, other states are excessively inclusive because they have failed to update their requirements in terms of current wage levels.

Disqualifications

The objective of unemployment insurance benefits is to provide cash support to those persons who are involuntarily out of work. The question is how "involuntary" is defined. Its meaning is found in the disqualification provisions.

The four main causes for disqualification are:[31] (1) being unable to work or unavailable for work (32 percent of total disqualifications); (2) leaving work voluntarily or leaving "without good cause" (30 percent); (3) discharge for misconduct (9 percent); and (4) refusal of suitable work (3 percent). The relative frequencies are for 1969 and have held fairly stable in years of normal unemployment.

---

[31] The distributions by cause vary somewhat with the rate of unemployment.

TABLE 6

Unemployment Insurance Disqualification Rates for 1950s and 1960s
Arrayed by Insured Unemployment Rates

	1950s			1960s	
Year	Insured Unemploy- ment Rate	UI Dis- qualifica- tion Rate[a]	Year	Insured Unemploy- ment Rate	UI Dis- qualifica- tion Rate[a]
1958	6.6	14.0	1961	5.7	17.5
1954	5.3	17.1	1960	4.7	18.5
1959	4.3	18.0	1962	4.3	21.1
1950[b]	3.9	18.0	1963	4.3	22.7
1957	3.7	18.5	1964	3.7	23.5
1955	3.4	20.2	1970	3.4	23.2
1956	3.1	19.5	1965	2.9	25.7
1952	2.9	19.0	1967	2.4	26.4
1951	2.8	19.3	1968	2.2	26.6
1953	2.7	21.1	1966	2.2	27.2
			1969	2.1	26.7

Source: Based on data published by the U.S. Department of Labor in *The Labor Market and Employment Security* (Statistical Supplement through 1963) and *Unemployment Insurance Statistics* thereafter.
[a] Number of disqualifications imposed per 1,000 claimant contracts.
[b] Insured unemployment and disqualification rates are for April–December 1950.

The remaining 26 percent of disqualifications are attributable to (5) involvement in a labor dispute, (6) fraudulent misrepresentation to obtain benefits, (7) special groups, such as persons attending school or pregnant women, and (8) receipt of wage-related income, such as pensions or dismissal pay. These eight causes accounted for a total of 1,700,000 disqualifications in 1969.

Using the base of "per 1000 claimant contacts" for all disqualifications, Leonard Adams has arranged the data according to levels of insured unemployment for the 1950s and 1960s (Table 6).[32] The table figures demonstrate clearly the higher rates of disqualifications in the 1960s at equivalent levels of unemployment. In general, it appears that between 1950 and 1970, the work test had become more stringent and was being applied more vigorously than before.

This tightening in definitions paralleled an increase in penalties applied. Pressure was particularly strong during the years that federal benefit standards were being considered in Congress. Critical

---

[32] Leonard P. Adams, *Public Attitudes Toward Unemployment Insurance* (Washington: W. E. Upjohn Institute for Employment Research, 1971), Table 5, p. 73.

TABLE 7
Number of States[a] with Specified Types of Disqualification Provisions
Selected Years

Disqualification Provision	1960	1970	1973	1975
Leaving work voluntarily				
Good cause restricted[b]	20	26	27	27
Benefits postponed:				
Fixed number of weeks	15	13	16	14
Variable number of weeks	21	17	19	18
Duration of unemployment	17	28	32	34
Benefits reduced or cancelled	17	19	17	17
Discharge for misconduct				
Benefits postponed:				
Fixed number of weeks	16	20	17	16
Variable number of weeks	27	24	23	23
Duration of unemployment	10	15	20	20
Benefits reduced or cancelled	17	25	17	17
Refusal of suitable work				
Benefits postponed:				
Fixed number of weeks	14	17	19	16
Variable number of weeks	23	17	19	20
Duration of unemployment	15	23	17	19
Benefits reduced or cancelled	16	15	13	13
Other				
Benefits denied:				
Unemployment due to pregnancy	35	38	30	23
Unemployment due to marital obligations	21	23	15	15

Source: Comparison of State Unemployment Insurance Laws (Washington: U.S. Department of Labor, Manpower Administration). See tables in chapter on "Eligibility for Benefits and Disqualification from Benefits."
[a] Some states are counted more than once because variations in their laws provide for different disqualifications depending on circumstances.
[b] "Good cause" is restricted to the work situation—that is, attributable to the employer or involving fault on the part of the employer.

articles appeared between 1960 and 1966, emphasizing the leniency in eligibility requirements and disqualification provisions. The articles alleged that the program was being abused by claimants who did not want to work or had lost jobs through their own fault. The result was that many states changed from a disqualification period of four or five weeks to total disqualification for the full period of one's unemployment (Table 7).

The trend toward severe penalties was curbed somewhat with the passage of the Employment Security Amendments of 1970, which specify that state laws cannot cancel benefit rights entirely for any reason other than discharge for misconduct connected with work, fraud in connection with a claim for benefits, or receipt of disqualifying income.

Recently, disqualifications for pregnancy and marital or domestic obligations have been receiving increased attention. The pregnancy issue has been the subject of constitutionality suits, a reflection of the growing awareness of discriminatory legislation. The number of states that specifically disqualify a woman during pregnancy has been reduced from 38 to 23. During the same period, the number of state laws denying benefits to individuals (both men and women) who leave work to preserve a marital relationship also decreased—from 22 to 15.

Evaluation of Benefit Changes

This review of specific revisions in unemployment compensation legislation would be incomplete without the addition of a more general evaluation of changes in benefits. Some provisions have been liberalized, some made more restrictive. What is the net result of these changes in terms of general support for the unemployed? Are unemployment laws more or less generous than they were 30 years ago? And what about differences among states? Is the disparity tending to widen or narrow?

Change in Mix of Benefits

When all types of benefit provisions are considered together, four kinds of changes or shifts in the principles of compensation can be identified: (1) a broadened coverage; (2) a reduction in the weekly rate of compensation relative to wage-loss; (3) an increase in the duration of compensation, that is, in the number of compensable weeks allowed; and (4) more rigor and strictness in applying insurability and disqualification provisions. Of these, only broadened coverage appears to apply in about equal measure across all states and does not involve any trade-offs or offsetting adjustments in other areas.

In the discussion that follows, reference to coverage will be omitted and the focus will be on trade-offs and shifting emphases on duration, weekly benefits, insurability, and administration. The purpose is to look at the program from the standpoint of an unemployed worker, and to ask whether over the years, the program has really improved or whether only the kind of protection provided has changed.

This analysis can be started in a simplified form. To the unemployed worker who had established his right to benefits, the two important factors are how much he gets per week and for how many weeks does he get it. Thus, for qualified workers, the measures of value of benefits are "average benefits relative to average wages" and the "average potential duration." In other words, what portion of lost weekly wages will be replaced and how long will payments continue if he needs them? At this stage of the analysis we omit concern about insurability and administration factors.

From 1938 until 1951, the weekly benefit amounts declined relative to wage levels and have since improved only slightly from the low point.[33] As a consequence, weekly benefits have not yet recovered the role they had at the beginning.

For duration of benefits, the situation has been the reverse. From 1941 until 1960, the average potential duration improved rapidly. Since then, emphasis has been on temporary extensions, while the regular duration provisions have been liberalized only slightly. The trend over the whole period has been toward longer entitlement.

The National Trend in Liberalization

We see that the net movement of weekly benefit amount is in one direction and of duration in the other. What if they are combined into a measure "average potential benefits relative to average weekly wages"? The combined trend suggests a net liberalization of 62 percent upward over the life of the program.

However, this overlooks the tighter eligibility definitions and penalties we have observed, and says nothing about changes in

---

[33] There are two different ways of looking at national experience with unemployment benefits: the program approach and the state-policy approach. The program approach weighs each according to how many covered workers are in the state or what proportion of the total experience that state represents. The state-policy approach has no weighting for the size of the state. For example, there is a difference between the national average weekly benefit amount and the average of the state weekly benefit amounts. The Department of Labor uses the program perspective in reporting national trends, but in this paper the state-policy perspective is used throughout.

administration that may affect the probability of qualifying for compensation. If it were more difficult to qualify in 1972 than in 1938, then from the viewpoint of all unemployed workers the liberalization would be something less than the 62 percent observed.

For this purpose it is necessary to develop an overall index that takes account of all the dimensions of benefits that may affect the unemployed. The construction of the index is treated elsewhere.[34] The mean of all states since 1938 is shown in Figure 1. The net liberalization appears to be more nearly in the amount of 39 percent after all adjustments (except for coverage) are made. This estimate is preferred to the one above because it takes account of the trade-offs between benefits and insurability that have occurred since about 1958.

It is important to reiterate that in plotting these trends the program is being analyzed only in terms of its value as wage insurance and of its benefits as a fractional replacement of wage-loss. Of course, in strict dollar terms benefits have risen many times over—in large part because wages themselves have also risen. Against a backdrop of price and wage inflation, it takes a lot of effort just to stand still. Organized labor has made great efforts to improve unemployment insurance, and without this effort benefits would have become hopelessly outmoded; but much of this legislative work must be seen as a necessary treadmill activity. Nevertheless there is a net improvement detectible in the program from 1939 to 1972 of the order of 40 percent.

The Increase in Interstate Variation

An ostensible reason for federal intervention in the enactment of unemployment insurance was the reluctance of the states to impose payroll taxes, an understandable position for them to take in the context of interstate competition for industrial capital. This reason for including unemployment insurance in the Social Security Act was undercut by another decision—to allow experience-

---

[34] The method of constructing the index and its use in analyzing trends and variation is described in a separate paper that is available from the author on request. Essentially, it uses the cost rate developed by actuaries to predict annual benefit payments and standardizes them by assuming a 4.5 percent covered employment rate in every state for every year. This "standardized benefit ratio" serves to measure the value of benefits for covered workers. It holds both unemployment and the size of the program constant, so it is useful for cross-section as well as historical analysis of state programs.

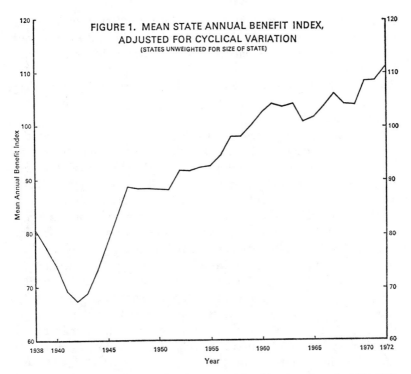

FIGURE 1. MEAN STATE ANNUAL BENEFIT INDEX, ADJUSTED FOR CYCLICAL VARIATION
(STATES UNWEIGHTED FOR SIZE OF STATE)

Note: Mean state annual benefit index (unweighted by size of state), 1938–1972, adjusted for cyclical variation:

Year	Mean Annual Benefit Index	Year	Mean Annual Benefit Index	Year	Mean Annual Benefit Index
1938	80.7	1950	88.4	1962	103.9
1939	77.4	1951	88.3	1963	104.3
1940	74.0	1952	91.8	1964	101.0
1941	69.3	1953	91.8	1965	101.9
1942	67.5	1954	92.3	1966	103.9
1943	69.0	1955	92.8	1967	106.1
1944	73.1	1956	94.7	1968	104.2
1945	78.4	1957	98.1	1969	104.1
1946	83.6	1958	99.2	1970	108.5
1947	88.9	1959	100.3	1971	108.7
1948	88.5	1960	102.7	1972	111.2
1949	88.5	1961	104.1		

rating. It would seem that by introducing a factor encouraging tax-rate variation, experience-rating would conflict with the overall objective of achieving equal competitive advantages for the states. This suggests a question that can be answered empirically: Has experience-rating actually brought about more variation among the states in benefits and costs than the varying levels of unemployment would lead one to expect?

This is frequently alleged, but it is difficult to prove because the trade-offs in benefit provisions make the state programs difficult to compare and because, for any given year, there are varying unemployment rates among the states. Fortunately, the benefit index referred to above is a tool that can be used to overcome these difficulties. Since the benefit index is also an estimated cost rate for a hypothetical level of unemployment, the necessary comparisons were made. The following are the findings:

The first unemployment insurance laws were very similar in their provisions, but by 1950 there was enough dissimilarity that the cost rate for equal levels of unemployment varied enormously. Alaska and Hawaii are excluded from the computations because they were not in the program at the earlier date and their inclusion would magnify the extremes in the later comparison. The actual range can be seen from the 1972 figures. The benefit index (or estimated cost rate for 4.5 percent unemployment) varied from 156 (Hawaii), 152 (District of Columbia), and 147 (Vermont), to 79 (Indiana), 75 (Oklahoma), and 68 (Alaska).[35]

Not only has the range or difference between extremes increased, but the entire dispersion has also increased. The standard deviation has risen from 13.4 in 1950 to 16.4 in 1972. Again, Alaska and Hawaii are excluded so as not to magnify the picture.

The benefits in the most liberal states in 1950 were almost twice as costly as those in the least generous states for the same levels of unemployment. Further, this disparity has increased slightly since 1950 until the costs of benefits in the high-level states are now more than twice those in low-benefit states.

---

[35] The index figures here may be interpreted to mean that if unemployment had been 4.5 percent in each state in 1972, this much (in hundredths of a cent) would have been paid out for each dollar of wages and salaries in covered employment.

The Persistence of State Preferences

In the years since 1947, those states high on the benefit index list are likely to have stayed there and those low on the list are even more likely to have remained near the bottom. Continuously near the top during the whole period have been Hawaii, Vermont, Maryland, and Utah. Others prominently toward the top, at least since 1965, are the District of Columbia, Wisconsin, Rhode Island, New Hampshire, and North Dakota.

On the other hand, near the bottom in 1972 and during most of the period since 1947 are Virginia, Texas, Alabama, Louisiana, Georgia, West Virginia, Florida, Indiana, Oklahoma, and Alaska. There appears to be a notable consistency in the ranking of states according to the benefit index. (It should be remembered that the index that produces this generalization is based on *benefits relative to wage* and therefore does not adversely reflect on low-wage states as such.)

The persistence of these divergent state attitudes toward benefits has helped bring broader support to labor's objective of federal benefit standards as the only way to achieve some degree of equitable treatment for the unemployed across the nation.

Recent Policy Issues

Some policy issues still beset unemployment insurance because of imprecise objectives or compromises in structure that date from the beginning. In this category are underfinancing, state-by-state reserve systems, and the use that has been made of experience-rating. Other controversies exist because of such new thrusts as national manpower policy and the national policy to reduce poverty, both of which affect unemployment insurance and have required a rethinking of its role.

National Manpower Policy

A fairly new aspect of the environment in which unemployment insurance now operates is national manpower policy, which did not exist in wartime prior to 1960. Manpower policy has pursued such various objectives as creating more job opportunities for the unskilled, raising the income of hard-core disadvantaged workers by upgrading their skills and improving their work habits, and reducing structural unemployment and inflationary pressures through retraining programs to increase the number of workers with skills that are in short supply in the labor market. The objectives and forms of manpower programs vary with administrations and economic conditions. Because of similarities in purposes of manpower programs and unemployment insurance, these programs must necessarily be related or complementary.

In forging the relationships, however, neither the manpower arm nor the unemployment insurance arm can be subordinated because their roles are different. Manpower programs are concerned with efficiency in the development, allocation, and use of human resources. Unemployment insurance, which is concerned with a quality of life—that is, surcease from the scramble of the labor market—is an idea based on deep-seated moral premises. People comprise the work force of society, but they are also the ultimate justification for that society. Therefore, the forces of supply and demand by themselves are not permitted to dominate our livelihood.

For these reasons, unemployment benefits should not be discontinued if the jobless worker refuses training opportunities, at least during the normal duration of the benefit period. Otherwise, there would be a denial of the worker's earned right to benefits. Any time during the receipt of regular state benefits, the claimant and not the unemployment insurance authorities should have the right to make the decision about training or relocation.

But because unemployment insurance is a holding operation and benefits cannot be continued indefinitely, a different approach is justified for the long-term unemployed under nonrecession conditions. In such instances, the worker's willingness to take active steps toward readjustment might be an appropriate condition for continuation of income-support payments.

The issues are old ones—avoidance of work disincentives on the one hand and provision of adequate support on the other. If it could be shown that benefits do, in fact, subsidize a more effective job-search, which might be possible where quality manpower services were applied in a tight labor market, then the conflict in objectives could be reduced.

There are sources of work disincentives in the unemployment insurance program other than the weekly amount and duration of benefits, and needless ones at that; prime examples are the partial benefit schedules and retroactive waiting weeks.

Elimination of Poverty

When the abolition of poverty was made a national goal in the 1960s, most of the proposals were for "opportunity" rather than income-maintenance programs. A few changes were made in old-age insurance to the advantage of low-income persons, but in general the social-insurance programs remained as they were. In considering unemployment insurance in this context, a difficult question is posed: How much should unemployment insurance be tailored to the "equity" considerations of wage insurance, and how much to the "adequacy" criteria of poverty alleviation?

Although unemployment benefits are related to wages, unemployment programs make four kinds of concessions to low-income workers: (1) there are maximum benefit amounts, the presumption being that higher paid workers are better able than are lower paid workers to tighten their belts and that they may have some savings to draw upon during periods of unemployment; (2) similarly, nine states compromise the half-of-wage-loss principle by providing that lower paid workers shall receive a larger fraction of their lost wages in benefits; (3) eleven states adjust the benefit amount according to family size; and (4) nine states provide uniform duration so that persons with low earnings in their base year can draw more in total benefits than can low earners in other states.

Despite these compromises in the interest of the poor, it is estimated that in normal years no more than one-fifth of all unemployment insurance payments go to poor households, and 16 percent of all households receiving payments are poor households.[36] This estimate, of course, says nothing about the dynamic role of benefits in preventing all recipient families from entering a cycle of demoralization and joblessness. But the fact remains that a great many beneficiaries are not poor and a great many poor are not beneficiaries. Unemployment insurance is not for those who have obligations that prevent them from being in the labor market, nor

---

[36] Ben Gillingham, *Cash Transfers: How Much Do They Help the Poor,* Special Report Series (Madison: Institute for Research on Poverty, University of Wisconsin, January 1971).

is it sufficient for those with earnings far below their minimum needs. A strategy for abolishing poverty must work through broadly based programs directed toward families with the lowest incomes.

What are the possible relationships between broad-based income-maintenance plans and unemployment insurance? The first decision to be made is whether unemployment insurance (and other social security systems) should be replaced by the new plan or whether the new plan should be integrated with the old. A strategy that involved substituting a new income-maintenance plan for existing programs would have trouble gaining support. For example, a proposal to abolish unemployment insurance in the interest, say, of a negative income tax or demogrant must take account of the very fundamental character of unemployment insurance as a social contract between capital and labor, and it would have to recognize that at a stage in the growth of modern industrial societies, an exchange was made—the unfettered movement of capital for a sharing of the burden of unemployment. Such an "agreement" with wage earners could not be abrogated lightly.

The substitution question may be put in different ways, but it boils down to whether wage earners as a group would lose or gain as a result of the change, and determining gain or loss involves attempting to measure the intangible value of being insured—that is, protected—as well as the economic return to wage earners as beneficiaries.

The alternative is to integrate an income-maintenance plan with existing social-insurance programs. Here it makes an enormous difference what type of plan is to be integrated—whether it should be an income-tested type such as a guaranteed income or negative income tax, or demogrants such as flat benefits for the aged, children's allowances, or income-tax credits. Actually, integration with a demogrant would serve to relieve unemployment insurance in its difficult policy areas of long-term unemployment and wage-qualifying requirements, and would free it to perform its wage-insurance mission more effectively.

Until income-maintenance plans are again under consideration, unemployment insurance can be improved toward wage insurance, manpower, and antipoverty objectives. Standards should be set to assure the effectiveness of the maximum benefits and to prevent the grosser kinds of limitations on duration of benefits. Work disincentives associated with partial benefit schedules and retroactive waiting weeks should be eliminated, and effective labor-market services should be offered. For greater impact on low-income persons, coverage could be extended to agricultural and domestic workers, and dependents' benefits could be enacted to provide a flat amount per dependent. If written in this form, they could be easily removed should Congress enact an income maintenance plan in which family size was a factor in deciding the amount of payments.

Underfinancing and Fiscal Integrity

The 1970s recession has had a severe impact on the financial structure of the unemployment insurance program. As in 1975, benefit payments in 1976 will be about twice the income expected from payroll taxes, and more than half the states have exhausted their reserves. By the end of 1975, 15 states were in a deficit position and had to borrow over $1 billion. By the end of 1976, an estimated 28 states will need to borrow about $4.5 billion in order to continue the flow of benefits.

Part of the difficulty lies in the fact that the intensity of the recession was unexpected, in light of experiences since World War II. In addition, many states entered the 1970s with low reserves after a number of high-employment years during which they could have built up their funds. The tax rates and reserve levels of states that had to borrow during 1975 are shown in Table 8 and indicate in every case a tax yield well below the 2.7 percent of payroll originally contemplated as an acceptable cost rate. The reserve levels attained by the end of 1969 in all cases except Vermont and Washington were below the two to three times "reserve multiple" regarded as prudent practice.

Responsibility for the chronic underfinancing that characterizes many states can probably be attributed to three factors: the effects of experience-rating in undermining employer-taxpayer responsibility, outmoded concepts of reserve financing, and the existence of separate state funds without any pooling of risk.

The original rationale for experience-rating as a tax incentive to induce employment-stabilizing behavior has all but vanished

TABLE 8

Tax Rates 1964–1969 and "Reserve Multiple" 1969 of States That Borrowed
or Applied for Loans from the Federal Loan Fund by the End of 1975

	Average Tax Rates[a]							"Reserve Multiple" End of 1969[b]
	1963	1964	1965	1966	1967	1968	1969	
Arkansas	1.04	1.04	1.07	1.06	.81	.77	.75	1.53
Connecticut	1.12	1.09	1.08	1.03	.86	.94	.86	1.56
Delaware	1.35	1.22	.96	.56	.48	.43	.42	1.28
Hawaii	1.21	1.51	1.32	1.20	1.13	1.12	1.10	1.96
Maine	1.41	1.29	1.09	.91	.73	.78	.77	1.27
Massachusetts	1.61	1.68	1.59	1.49	1.18	1.16	1.02	1.79
Michigan	1.66	1.44	1.22	1.12	.80	.63	.65	.89
Minnesota	.78	.72	.73	.88	.81	.74	.70	1.17
Montana	.97	.95	.95	.89	.89	.88	.86	1.20
Nevada	1.77	1.71	1.27	1.24	1.26	1.22	1.13	1.37
New Jersey	1.29	1.21	1.18	1.12	1.05	1.07	1.04	1.21
Oregon	1.86	1.54	1.23	1.20	1.16	.87	.84	1.46
Pennsylvania	1.79	1.89	1.78	1.61	1.40	.78	.73	1.30
Rhode Island	1.87	1.82	1.77	1.45	1.38	1.23	1.21	1.82
Vermont	1.13	1.33	1.54	1.89	1.55	1.20	1.00	2.02
Washington	1.48	1.44	1.42	1.24	1.18	1.01	.81	2.54

[a] Total tax paid as a percentage of total wages.

[b] Reserve ratio (percent of total wages) as a multiple of highest 12-month benefit cost rate since Jan. 1, 1958.

because of Keynesian economics and the principles established in the Full Employment Act of 1946. Responsibility for the vigor of the economy rests with taxing, spending, and monetary authorities. Experience-rating persists, nevertheless, and not just as a monument to the quaint ideas of the past. It now has new justifications and apologists. It is widely believed in the business-taxpayer community that experience-rating is the only way this kind of tax can be kept low and a low tax continues to be the main concern of large segments of the business community. Thirteen states have even pushed the minimum experience-rate to zero, and another 17 states have minimum rates at one-tenth of 1 percent or less.

The desire to perpetuate low rates has also encouraged certain questionable practices in fund management, one of which is allowing optional contributions to secure a lower rate on a given schedule. Another is using a previous year's benefit-cost rate, some multiple of it, or an average of recent years rather than a past high-cost period as the solvency standard. Still another is delaying fund recoupment too long to handle recessions that quickly follow one on another. Finally, a number of states still fail to use "total payrolls" as the base for calculating the "trigger" for higher tax rates, depending instead on flat dollar amounts or taxable payrolls, each of which becomes ineffective in time.

In the early 1960s, an important innovation in fund management was the use of an array of rates to produce a predetermined yield. The desired yield, when expressed as a proportion of the taxable wage base, becomes the central rate; other rates of the schedule fall above and below in such a manner that the distribution of rates produces the desired yield. This approach concentrates attention on essentials—the revenue-raising capacity of each schedule. Despite its advantages, this method has not been widely adopted by the states.

Imprudent fund management is a matter of neglect in some states, but in others it is an overt policy. These states follow an out-and-out policy of brinksmanship in which the objective is to keep reserves low as one way of resisting demands for higher benefits.

Finally, and this is perhaps the most obvious cause of underfinancing, there is the structure of state-by-state underwriting, in which each state assumes all the risk within its borders and shares none outside. Total risk is necessarily greater with such a system. State economies differ, and a recession in one state is not necessarily mirrored in every other one. One of the lessons of the 1970s recession is that in order to achieve solvency, it will be necessary hereafter to have either larger or more effective reserves. The cheaper course is more effective reserves, which could be obtained through some system of pooling of high-cost experience.

Conclusions

The jobless-pay program established in the thirties has been monitored chiefly by its labor beneficiaries and its employer taxpayers. Although there has been a modest liberalization even with the moving wage levels, the program still falls short, particularly from the perspectives of manpower and poverty policy and the insufficiency of its financing. It would appear desirable to infuse more public-interest participation in policy-making in order to supplement the constituent roles.

Labor called attention early to the dangers of hinging the financing structures to purposes other than underwriting benefits. While there are other objectives that may be of interest, such as stimulating stable employment practices, maximizing countercyclical effects, or placing the cost burden consistent with the most productive economic incentives, and while any of these and other objectives can be legitimately claimed, the primary aim should be to assure adequate and continuing payments. The present fiscal crisis of the system is mute testimony that this objective has not been achieved.

Confusion in objectives would, of course, be a defect in a more centralized system, but had the federal government taken more of a role in shaping the program, the subversion of goals could not have occurred in the shadows of half a hundred state legislatures where there usually is not even a written record of what transpires.

If one lesson emerges from this history, it is the danger of establishing a decentralized system with no explicit hierarchy of purposes.

CHAPTER 5

Fair Labor Standards

RUDOLPH A. OSWALD
Department of Research, AFL-CIO

Fair labor standards—"a floor under wages," a "ceiling over hours," and "a break for children"—was enshrined in federal legislation in 1938 as the last major building block of the New Deal. However, minimum wage and maximum hour legislation is as old as 1900 and as new as 1976, when new amendments were considered in Congress and the Supreme Court handed down a major decision on the Fair Labor Standards Act, barring its application to most employees of state and local governments.

This basic wage and hour legislation continues to be a major public policy issue—with the arguments advanced by proponents and opponents in the early 1900s still bandied about today as if nothing had happened in 40 years of favorable experience under federal legislation and a generally favorable experience under the various state wage and hour laws.

The idea of minimum standards of labor had been developed originally in behalf of children and women, the most exploited in the extremes of the industrial revolution and the new factory system. However, a second major theme crystallized in this early period, emphasizing the notion of a minimum "living wage," which today would be called "a step above poverty."

At the turn of the century, many studies by various social reform organizations, government commissions, and others described in detail the exploitation of children and women in the nation's factories, mines, and farms. The earliest efforts were to prohibit the employment of very young children, particularly those below the ages of 12 or 14. These children not only worked long hours— sometimes 12 to 14 a day, or all night—but they also were paid lower wages than adults, thus pulling down the adult wage.

In 1904, the National Child Labor Committee was formed to protect "children by suitable legislation against premature or otherwise injurious employment." Famous leaders of this group included Florence Kelley, Jane Addams, and Felix Adler. Their efforts were supported by religious leaders such as Rev. John Ryan of St. Paul Theological Seminary, Walter Rauschenbusch, and others, as well as by educators such as John R. Commons of the University of Wisconsin and many others.

Simultaneously attempts were made to improve the conditions of working women. The legislative drive was to restrict hours of work to 8 or 10 hours a day, to prohibit nighttime work for women, and to set a minimum wage. In the forefront of this drive were the National Consumers' League, under the direction of Florence Kelley, and the Women's Trade Union League, under Rose Schneiderman.

The labor movement of that day supported protective legislation for women and children as well as the eight-hour law for public employees, but for male workers in private industry they believed that union pressure was the best solution. AFL President Samuel Gompers was of the opinion that the undercutting of standards by women and children was a major obstacle to organizing workers into effective unions.

The notion of a minimum "living wage" was also broadly discussed at the turn of the century. A basic impetus came from the 1891 encyclical of Pope Leo XIII, Rerum Novarum, generally called "On the Condition of the Working Classes," in which he spoke of an obligation of employers to provide at least a minimum living wage. In his doctoral dissertation in 1906, Father Ryan justified the principle of the "living wage" on religious and moral as well as economic grounds.[1] He called for the state to assure a minimum living wage by appropriate direct and indirect legislation. The direct method was a minimum wage law, while the indirect methods included an eight-hour day, no child labor under age 16, as well as the establishment of an old-age pension system and low-cost housing for purchase by workers.

The living-wage theme was also developed in the late 1890s in England by Beatrice and Sidney Webb. It became an underlying foundation of minimum wage legislation in England as well as Australia and New Zealand, although the approach in these

---

[1] John A. Ryan, *A Living Wage: Its Ethical and Economic Aspects* (New York: Macmillan Co., 1906–12) .

countries was on an industry basis rather than a general floor under all wages. In the United States, the principle of a living wage was adopted as a fundamental World War I policy by the War Labor Conference Board.

At the turn of the century, studies were made of what it would cost a U.S. working woman to support herself properly. Father Ryan reported in a speech in 1912 that such cost estimates varied from $7 to $10 a week, while three-fifths of the women workers earned less than $6.25 a week. He concluded, saying: "Try to figure what it means, that so many women . . . are getting so much less than enough to maintain them decently."[2]

Proponents of the minimum wage legislation argued that the traditional "laissez-faire" economics of letting the market set the wage did not provide women and children, those at the bottom of the economic structure, protection from being exploited. They warned that unless such safeguards were provided by the state, unscrupulous employers would tend to drive down wages for the weakest in society to a starvation level. Opponents argued that interference with the free market system would be catastrophic. In legal terms they alleged that minimum wage laws violated the rights of an employee to contract for his or her services with the employer. These basic arguments, with minor variations, still underlie many of the current discussions of labor standards.

These arguments gradually were rejected, however, first in regard to child labor, then in terms of women's hours, and finally minimum wage laws. In the late 1800s various states prohibited child labor, and by 1909 all but six states had adopted some limitation on the age of employment in factories. By 1913, 19 states had succeeded in passing an eight-hour law for working children under age 16.

During this period, the health of women workers in factories created great concern. In 1903, Oregon adopted a 10-hour law for women in industry, and five years later the U.S. Supreme Court upheld the law for women in *Muller* v. *Oregon*. This sparked the enactment of similar maximum-hour laws in numerous other states.

The first minimum wage law for women and children was adopted in Massachusetts in 1912. During the next decade, some 17 states enacted minimum wage laws. Such laws seemed to be legally

---

[2] Rev. John A. Ryan, speech to the National Child Labor Committee, Jan. 26, 1912, reported in *Child Labor Bulletin*, vol. 1 (June 1912), p. 170.

acceptable after the Supreme Court, by a split decision, let stand an affirmative verdict of the Oregon Supreme Court upholding the Oregon minimum wage law. But in 1923, by a 5 to 4 decision, the U.S. Supreme Court ruled the District of Columbia minimum wage law unconstitutional. In that case, *Adkins* v. *Children's Hospital,* the Court held that such legislation contravened the Fifth Amendment, violating the implied freedom of contract. The Court reasoned that the moral right of an individual to a living wage was outweighed by the moral right of an employer to refrain from paying more than a "just wage," and it was assumed that whatever an employer paid was a "just wage."

But this was not the universal opinion. Chief Justice William Howard Taft dissented in the *Adkins* case, stating: "Legislatures in limiting freedom of contract between employee and employer by a minimum wage proceed on the assumption that employees, in the class receiving the least pay, are not upon a full level of equality with their employer and in their necessitous circumstances are prone to accept pretty much anything that is offered. They are peculiarly subject to the overreacting of the harsh and greedy employer. . . . It is not the function of this court to hold congressional acts invalid simply because they are passed to carry out economic views which the court believes to be unwise or unsound."

Laws regulating the labor of children were upheld by the courts as long as they were confined to individual state acts, but when Congress attempted to discourage child labor in factories, first through the regulation of interstate commerce (1916) and later through the exercise of the taxing power (1919), the Supreme Court invalidated both statutes, in 1918 and 1922, respectively.[3] To remedy this situation, Congress adopted a constitutional amendment in 1924, but by 1932 only six states had ratified it.

As a first step toward legislating a type of minimum wage, Congress passed the Davis-Bacon Act in 1931, establishing a minimum prevailing wage standard applicable to federal construction contracts. Although the Davis-Bacon Act was not a general floor under wages, it was a protection to building trades workers employed on federal building projects. While government contracts continued to be awarded to the lowest bidder, the new legislation assured the

---

[3] *Hammer* v. *Dagenhart,* 247 U.S. 251 (1918), and *Bailey* v. *Drexel Furniture Co.,* 259 U.S. 20 (1922).

worker that the lowest bid was not at his expense. No longer would the lowest bidder be the one who paid his workers the least. In each county where federal construction contracts were undertaken, the minimum rate for each type of craft was established, based on rates prevailing in that locality.

The New Deal Era

When President Roosevelt took office in 1933, his Secretary of Labor, Frances Perkins, had a minimum wage proposal ready for immediate action. However, Roosevelt considered its approach too narrow and incorporated minimum wage and maximum hour standards into a more comprehensive bill, called the National Industrial Recovery Act (NIRA), enacted during his first 100 days in office. The NIRA called upon employer and labor representatives in each industry to formulate codes of fair competition specifying maximum hours of labor, minimum rates of pay, and the abolition of child labor under age 16. The NIRA also dealt with fair pricing of commodities, safety and health standards, collective bargaining rights, and a variety of other subjects. In 1935, the Supreme Court held the NIRA unconstitutional.[4] In that case the Court decided that the activities of a poultry slaughter house in New York City exerted only an indirect and remote effect on interstate commerce and did not "affect" commerce as defined under the law.

While the National Industrial Recovery Act provided for minimum wage legislation, the first broad wage and hour bill was introduced in 1934 by Senator Hugo S. Black (D. Ala.) and Representative William P. Connery (D. Mass.) (H.R. 8492, 73d Cong., 2d Sess., 1934). However, this bill did not go anywhere until the Supreme Court reversed its position in regard to minimum wage legislation.

Although the NIRA was struck down on constitutional grounds, it did demonstrate that compliance with labor standards could be secured on a national scale. To try to rescue some of the minimum wage protections of NIRA, the Congress passed the Walsh-Healey Act in 1936, establishing a minimum prevailing wage standard for federal procurement of goods. Minimums were set by the Secretary of Labor on an industry or product-line basis after hearings allow-

---

[4] *Schechter Corp. v. U.S.*, 298 U.S. 495 (1935).

ing industry and union participants to set forth their recommendations. This procedure was somewhat similar to the industry committee procedure under NIRA.

In 1936 the Supreme Court's *Tipaldo* decision invalidated a new (1933) New York State minimum wage law as a "violation of liberty of contract."[5] The 5 to 4 ruling held the New York law a violation of the due process clause of the 14th Amendment. A year later, in *West Coast Hotel Co.* v. *Parrish,* the Court reversed its earlier positions and upheld the minimum wage law of the State of Washington.[6] This time the 5 to 4 vote reversed the *Adkins* decision of 1923 and with it the 1935 ruling in *Tipaldo.* Justice Owen J. Roberts had switched his position from the earlier case, joining Justices Benjamin Cardozo, Louis Brandeis, Harlan F. Stone, and Charles E. Hughes.[7] Fourteen days later, the Court upheld the National Labor Relations Act, accepting with it an expanded definition of interstate commerce that allowed Congress to regulate industrial and labor relations.[8] In the *Parrish* decision, Chief Justice Hughes put to rest the "implied" doctrine of "freedom of contract." Referring to the interpretation of the 14th Amendment that had blocked fair labor standards legislation for many years, he asked: "What is this freedom? The Constitution does not speak of freedom of contract. It speaks of liberty and prohibits the deprivation of liberty without due process of law." Hughes cited many previous decisions to show that contracts between employer and employee could be restricted in the public interest.[9] This decision restored the chance for federal legislation. As a matter of fact, few states could afford to enact wage and hour legislation on their own for fear of losing business to states where labor standards were not regulated and labor costs were lower.

Less than two months after the Supreme Court decision, President Roosevelt sent a message to Congress requesting legislation to establish federal fair labor standards, stating: "All but the hopelessly reactionary will agree that to conserve our primary resources of manpower, government must have some control over maximum

---

[5] *Morehead* v. *Tipaldo,* 298 U.S. 597 (1936).
[6] 300 U.S. 391 (1937).
[7] John W. Chambers, "The Big Switch: Justice Roberts and the Minimum Wage Cases," *Labor History,* vol. 10 (Winter 1969), p. 60.
[8] *NLRB* v. *Jones & Laughlin Steel Co.,* 301 U.S. 1 (1937).
[9] 300 U.S. at 393.

hours, minimum wages, the evil of child labor, and the exploitation of unorganized labor."

Senator Black and Representative Connery revived their bills to establish a fair labor standards law. The legislation was strongly backed by Secretary of Labor Perkins and the National Consumers' League. Secretary Perkins urged that wage minimums be set on an industry basis rather than a general minimum wage applicable to all industry. The industry approach was similar to that under the NIRA.

The Black and Connery bills were amended many times before mid-June 1938 when both houses adopted the final conference report. The proposed law set forth standards to promote "the maintenance of the minimum standard of living necessary for health, efficiency, and general well-being of workers." Yet Congress attempted to be moderate and flexible, allowing industry time to adjust to the new minimum wage without undue hardship or substantial curtailment of employment.

Sharp differences were voiced in Congress, proponents arguing that the legislation was essential to eradicate poverty among the working poor, to eliminate the sweatshop, and to expand job opportunities for the large numbers of unemployed. To these humanitarian and social considerations, various economic arguments were added. Minimum wage standards would maintain purchasing power, and such purchasing power itself would contribute to sustaining higher levels of employment. A floor under wages would prevent a further downward spiral in wages. The proponents argued that the employer who pays decent wages and observes other adequate labor standards should be legally protected against the competition of unscrupulous sweatshop employers. They believed this was possible only through federal legislation, since industries were in competition in a national market. The imposition of premium pay for hours worked above a certain maximum would lead to a spreading of available work and to the hiring of the unemployed.

Contrarily, opponents of the legislation felt that there should be no governmental interference with the "market system." They argued that any minimum wage would be arbitrary and artificial, and hence counterproductive. They saw rising costs which, in turn, would drive down real wages as well as employment. Moreover, they did not believe that the federal government should, nor that it legally could, establish minimum labor standards. Generally, the bill was opposed by the growing conservative opposition in Congress, frequently made up of southern Democrats and Republicans.[10]

The proponents of a "living wage," of a decent hour standard, and of child labor protection won out in the Congress in 1938. However, the basic arguments have been repeated through the following decades.

In 1937, a number of industry representatives appeared in support of the bill, arguing that prosperity required the raising of substandard wages to increase purchasing power and shorter hours to absorb the unemployed. Labor, however, had been urging a 30-hour law through much of the Depression, but had not supported a general minimum wage for men. After introduction of the new minimum wage bill in 1937, the AFL executive council endorsed the bill subject to additions to be offered by President William Green. Unions had been concerned that a minimum wage would become the maximum wage and that it would interfere with a collectively bargained wage. The AFL was opposed to setting rates by industry committees, and called instead for a flat 40-cent minimum. John L. Lewis, testifying for the CIO, supported the bill, but also called for various amendments. Sidney Hillman of the Amalgamated Clothing Workers was the only labor leader who approved the bill substantially as introduced.

Joint hearings were held by the Senate and House Labor Committees to speed the legislative process. On July 31, 1937, the Senate passed the bill in amended form, by a vote of 56 to 28. The House Labor Committee reported out an amended bill on August 6, but the Rules Committee refused to let the bill go to the floor of the House and Congress adjourned without acting on it.

President Roosevelt called a special session of Congress for November 15, 1937, and declared in his message: "I believe the country as a whole recognizes the need for immediate congressional action if we are to maintain wage increases and the purchasing power of the nation against recessive factors in the general situation." Following his call for immediate passage of the Fair Labor Standards bill, it was brought to the House floor by a discharge petition. After five days of debate in December, the bill was ordered

---

[10] For further discussion of this aspect, see James T. Patterson, *Congressional Conservatism and the New Deal* (Lexington: University of Kentucky Press, 1967).

recommitted by a vote of 216 to 198, a near-fatal defeat for minimum wage legislation.

In January 1938, the House Labor Committee again reviewed the bill and reported out an amended version, but the Rules Committee for the third time refused to let the bill be brought to the floor. However, a discharge petition quickly gathered enough signatures after two southern Democratic primaries in May elected staunch supporters of minimum wage legislation.[11] After Administration adherents beat down some 50 amendments, losing only a few exempting certain agricultural and fishery workers and adding on the "Shirley Temple" amendment exempting child actors from child labor provisions, the House passed the bill, 314 to 97. The final form of the Fair Labor Standards Act was a compromise between the House and Senate versions, as written by the conference committee.[12] It contained enough exemptions on coverage and on hours to pacify many hesitant senators and congressmen. It compromised between a flat rate applicable to all industries and an industry rate-setting procedure.

The initial minimum rate was set at a flat 25 cents an hour effective October 24, 1938, increasing to 30 cents a year later and to 40 cents on or before October 24, 1945, as determined by industry committees. The Act also set up the following workweek schedules: Effective October 24, 1938, a maximum workweek of 44 hours was established, decreasing to 42 hours a year later and to 40 hours on October 24, 1940. Work above the maximum would be penalized at the rate of at least one and one-half times the employee's regular rate of pay.

The 1938 Act also prohibited the employment of "oppressive child labor" in the production or distribution of goods and services. "Oppressive child labor" was defined first as employment of minors under 16 years of age in manufacturing and mining, and second, as employment of minors under 18 years of age in hazardous occupations. Exemptions could be made for minors between 14 and 16 under certain conditions.

---

[11] Lister Hill of Alabama and Claude Pepper of Florida were the two primary winners. Among those signing the discharge provision was a young Texas congressman, Lyndon B. Johnson.

[12] For additional detail, see Elizabeth Brandeis, "Protective Legislation," in Labor and the New Deal, eds. Milton Derber and Edwin Young (Madison: University of Wisconsin Press, 1961).

The law also provided authority for triparite industry committees representing labor, management, and the public to speed up the
pace of minimum wage increases to 40 cents an hour in various
industries. In fact, all of the industry committees had established
the 40-cent-an-hour rate by 1943, two years before the legally
required date.

The Fair Labor Standards Act (FLSA) adopted on June 25,
1938, became the last of the great cornerstones of social-economic
legislation of the New Deal. While it was updated a number of
times during the ensuing decades, its elements have remained substantially unchanged. With poverty and unemployment still rampant in the Great Depression, the law was a beginning in limiting
the exploitation of workers through low wages and long hours.
While 25 cents an hour, or $550 a year, for a 44-hour workweek
was not a munificent sum, it was a substantial improvement for
millions of workers.

Expecting a challenge to the Act's constitutionality, the Congress
provided fairly narrow coverage. About 12.6 million workers were
estimated to be covered in April 1939, or about 23 percent of the
civilian labor force. These workers were primarily engaged in
manufacturing, transportation, mining, and wholesale trade. Of
the 12.6 million workers covered by the new law, the Labor Department estimated some 200,000 had their wages increased because
of the 25-cent minimum, and 1,384,000 workers either had their
workweeks reduced to 44 hours or received overtime compensation
for the longer hours.[13]

The new law did not cause an increase in unemployment or a
run of bankruptcies, as the opponents of the bill had forecast.
The Wage-Hour Administrator reported on Labor Day 1939 that
"all indices show employment, payrolls, and profits for this year
far ahead of last year. Obviously the new wage and hour regulations
have not harmed business."[14]

Publicity of conditions found in early inspections also led to
greater general acceptance of the need for the law. A description
by the Wage and Hour Administration of existing conditions reads
as follows:

[13] William S. Tyson, "The Fair Labor Standards Act of 1938: A Survey and
Evaluation of the First Eleven Years," *Labor Law Journal*, vol. 1 (January 1950),
p. 280.
    [14] Tyson, p. 281.

It was found that girls working in a Massachusetts shoe factory for $4 and $5 a week were forced to falsify their payroll records in order to keep their jobs. A woman in Georgia walked many miles to a factory, worked eight hours and returned home at night with 50 cents as her day's pay. Women were found working in an Eastern clothing factory for two cents an hour—eighty-eight cents for a forty-four-hour week—because their employer said that it took from nine months to a year for an employee to learn to operate a sewing machine. A small community which had welcomed a "gypsy" plant as an opportunity for employment of its people found that its relief agencies were forced to supplement the workers' earnings of eight cents an hour or less in order to enable them to exist.[15]

A Wage and Hour Administration was set up to handle interpretation and enforcement of the Act. To achieve compliance with the Act, that governmental bureau undertook an education program on the law's requirements, investigations of employer payroll records, and interviews of employees. Employers whose violations were serious or willful were brought into courts by injunction proceedings or by prosecutions to enforce the criminal penalties of the Act.

After the wage and hour law had been in effect for six months, the Wage-Hour Administrator reported one complaint for each 11,000 workers covered, which he called "pretty good evidence of general compliance." This overall compliance with the law became one of its hallmarks throughout the following decades.

As expected, the Fair Labor Standards Act was challenged in the courts, and in 1941 the Supreme Court's *Darby* decision unanimously upheld its constitutionality.[16] The opinion, written by Justice Stone, said: "Since our decision in *West Coast Hotel Co.* v. *Parrish,* it is no longer open to question that the fixing of a minimum wage is within the legislative power and the bare fact of its exercise is not a denial of due process under the Fifth more than under the Fourteenth Amendment. Nor is it any longer open to question that it is within the legislative power to fix maximum hours."

---

[15] Tyson, p. 281.
[16] *United States* v. *F.W. Darby Lumber Co.,* 312 U.S. 100 (1941).

"Similarly the statute is not objectionable because [it is] applied alike to both men and women," the decision stated.

The Postwar Era

The *Darby* decision put to rest the basic constitutional challenge to the Fair Labor Standards Act, but it was far from the end of the minimum wage story. As economic conditions shifted, so did the law—with major updating and expansion approved in 1949, 1955, 1961, 1966, and 1974. In 1963, equal pay provisions were added to the basic standards already incorporated into the Act, and in 1965 prevailing minimum wage standards were enacted to protect workers employed on federal service contracts. Even as late as 1976, the constitutionality of the Act's application to employees of state and local government was still an issue.

During World War II, wages generally improved, pushing even low-wage industries and areas far above the 40-cent figure. After the war, both the AFL and the CIO called for a higher statutory rate without bothering with the industry committee procedure to recommend increases on an industry-by-industry basis, as was used for effectuating the 40-cent rate. In 1945, labor asked for a 75-cent rate, and by 1948 for $1 per hour.

In 1949, after hearings spread out over four years, Congress approved an increase in the minimum wage from 40 to 75 cents an hour, effective January 25, 1950. The overtime provisions were revised slightly, and additional protection was provided for young people. Coverage was slightly narrowed by changing the reference to production of goods for interstate commerce.

The 75-cent minimum wage brought increases to an estimated 1 million workers.[17] Although the increase from 40 to 75 cents amounted to 87 percent, the impact was slight because wages had generally increased substantially during World War II. Again employment increased in the year following the higher minimum wage. However, this was an abnormal period as it encompassed the beginning of the Korean War.

The 1949 amendments removed from the Act the provision for wage-setting by industry committees and wage orders for mainland industries, which had been used to accelerate the timing of the

---

[17] Tyson, p. 284.

40-cent rate, but the tripartite industry committee procedures, begun in 1940, were retained for Puerto Rico and the Virgin Islands.

In 1955, the minimum wage was increased from 75 cents to $1, effective March 1, 1956. This legislation was a compromise between the 90-cent-an-hour rate proposed by the Republican Administration, and the $1.25-an-hour rate urged by labor. The U.S. Chamber of Commerce opposed any increase. But Senator Paul Douglas (D. Ill.), chairman of the Labor subcommittee, cut through the various conflicting elements and carried the legislation through the Senate; speedy House action followed. Although Secretary of Labor James Mitchell had originally urged that coverage be extended to large retail and service firms, President Eisenhower later opposed any extension of coverage, and the final bills simply increased the minimum wage. As early as 1953, Secretary of Labor Martin Durkin had recommended a $1 minimum wage, but had failed to receive any support from President Eisenhower. The amendment also called for detailed studies by the Secretary of Labor on the effects of the minimum wage legislation.

In its studies of the effects of the increase from 75 cents to $1, the Labor Department estimated that the increase added $560 million to U.S. wages, only 0.7 percent of the yearly total of wages paid to all workers covered by the Act.[18] These direct effects of the increase were not augmented by any major secondary effects. According to these studies, wage increases up to the minimum in covered industries had little tendency to spread to workers above the new minimum or to noncovered industries. Studies of the effects of the $1 minimum wage in seven low-wage communities or cities and in ten low-wage industries demonstrated that increases in average hourly earnings in industries subject to the Fair Labor Standards Act were not accompanied by similar increases in industries not covered by the Act, and even within covered industries wage increases were generally limited to those paid below the minimum or within a few cents of the minimum.[19]

After attempts in 1959 and in 1960 to both raise the minimum

---

[18] U.S. Department of Labor, *Report Submitted to Congress in Accordance with the Requirements of Section 4(d) of the Fair Labor Standards Act,* January 1962, p. 3.

[19] U.S. Department of Labor, Wage and Hour and Public Contracts Divisions, *Studies of the Economic Effects of the $1 Minimum Wage, Effects in Selected Low Wage Industries and Localities,* January 1959.

wage and extend coverage, attempts strongly opposed by the Eisenhower Administration, President John F. Kennedy made minimum wage legislation an early order of business in his new Administration. The bill had tough sledding, with the Administration bill losing to a weakened substitute on the House floor by a 216 to 203 vote. The Senate adopted the basic Kennedy Administration bill that had been introduced by Senator Patrick McNamara (D. Mich.). After weakening amendments had been rejected, the Senate passed the FLSA amendments by a vote of 65 to 28.

The minimum wage was raised to $1.15 an hour effective September 3, 1961, and to $1.25 two years later. In addition, the coverage of the Act was broadened to include some 3.6 million additional workers in large enterprises, sales of which affected commerce. New coverage included large retail and service enterprises and local transit with $1 million or more in annual sales, and construction enterprises with $350,000 in annual sales. For the newly covered, the minimum hourly wage went from $1 on September 3, 1961, to $1.15 in 1964, and to $1.25 in 1965. Most of the newly covered also received overtime protection after 44 hours a week beginning September 3, 1963, and the standard was reduced to 42 hours a year later and to 40 hours the following year.

In extending coverage, Congress attached an "enterprise concept" to the original statute. Under the 1938 law, the Act's protection was confined to employees whose individual activities were in interstate and foreign commerce or in the production of goods for such commerce. However, a large number of employees were specifically excluded from the Act's protection by numerous exemptions mainly contained in Section 13 of the Act. Under the new "enterprise concept," the test of coverage under the Act shifted from one that measured the activities of individual employees to one that evaluated whether the enterprise had employees engaged in commerce or production for commerce, "including employees handling, selling, or otherwise working on goods that have been moved in or produced for such commerce." Congress applied this new coverage standard to comparatively large enterprises doing business of $1 million or more a year. An annual sales volume test for coverage was also applied to each single establishment of covered enterprises in the retail and service industry. The establishment test was set at $250,000 of sales per year.

In the year following enactment, Secretary of Labor Arthur J. Goldberg found little effect from the increase since the legal minimum affected only a minor fraction of the labor force. As a result, the changes had a relatively "small impact on the total costs, total employment or total income and consumption."[20]

Four years later, after all the provisions of the amendments were effective, Secretary of Labor W. Willard Wirtz reported to Congress "that the available evidence" shows:

1. that the 1961 amendments to the act have resulted in significant raising of wage levels; that this had not produced unemployment; that it has had no unstabilizing effect on wages or prices, and

2. that a substantial further increase in the coverage and minimum wage levels of the act will contribute to the elimination of poverty without producing either unemployment or inflation.

The Equal Pay Act of 1963 amended the Fair Labor Standards Act to prohibit discrimination on the basis of sex in the payment of wages to employees covered under the Act. Basically, the law required that males and females be paid the same, provided skill, effort, and responsibility were equal and provided the job was performed under similar working conditions. The Congress noted in its declaration of policy that a wage differential based on sex: " (1) depresses wages and living standards for employees necessary for their health and efficiency; (2) prevents the maximum utilization of the available labor resources; . . . (3) constitutes an unfair method of competition."[21]

The Equal Pay Act reenforced the goals of the Fair Labor Standards Act to eliminate poverty and expand employment opportunities. The addition of the prohibition of sex discrimination highlighted another basic concept underlying the law—namely, that there was to be a basic job rate, not to be deviated from because of sex. The following year the Civil Rights Act of 1964 extended the prohibitions against job discrimination to include such other nonjob-related factors as race, religion, or national origin. Sex was again restated in that law's broad protection of equal

---

[20] USDL, *Report*, 1962, p. 6.
[21] Sec. 2 (a) , Public Law 88–38.

employment opportunities. However, these aspects of the Civil Rights Act were to be administered by a new agency, the Equal Employment Opportunity Commission.

Another prevailing minimum wage law was enacted in 1965. This one, the McNamara-O'Hara Act, covered federal service contracts. Basically, it was similar to the Davis-Bacon Act and the Walsh-Healey Act. Rates including fringe benefits prevailing in a locality were set as minimum guarantees for various classes of service workers.

After 25 years of administering FLSA, the Wage and Hour Administration undertook a detailed analysis of compliance with the Act to develop an overall measure of how well the Act was being observed. According to the 1965 *Compliance Survey*, approximately 6 percent (or 1.8 million workers) of the 27 million workers protected by the Act were underpaid, and they were employed in some 200,000 establishments representing 18 percent of all covered establishments. That study also showed continued child labor violations, with 72,400 minors estimated to be illegally employed.[22] This study documented the success of the Wage and Hour Administration in educating employers concerning the Act and enforcing the Act against recalcitrant employers.

In 1966, amendments to the Fair Labor Standards Act brought the hourly rate to $1.40 an hour on February 1, 1967, and to $1.60 one year later. The Act's protection was further extended by substantially broadening the enterprise coverage accomplished through lowering the dollar volume annual sales test from $1,000,000 to $250,000. Specific exemptions were also deleted or changed to cover laundries, restaurants, hotels, hospitals, and nursing homes. Also covered were employees of certain governmental units, local transit, hospitals, and schools, as well as federal wage board employees and federal employees paid from nonappropriated funds. Farm workers employed on large farms were protected for the first time. More extended adjustment periods were allowed for employers of newly covered workers, with wages of all workers reaching a minimum of $1.60 an hour by February 1971, except for the farm workers whose minimum wages stopped at $1.30 an hour.

The Johnson Administration had announced a "War on

---

[22] U.S. Department of Labor, Wage and Hour and Public Contracts Divisions, *Compliance Survey, 1965* (Washington: May 1966).

Poverty," and the 1966 amendments were part of that "War." A detailed analysis of the characteristics of poverty families showed that over half of the families were headed by a man or woman who worked. Moreover, half of these employed family heads, representing almost 30 percent of all poor families, held a full-time job for the entire year. These latter families accounted for 40 percent of all the children growing up in poverty families.

In order to meet the goals of the "War on Poverty," the minimum wage was set at $1.60 an hour or $3,200 a year for a year-round, full-time worker, just above the poverty line for a family of four. In signing the legislation, President Johnson said:

> The new minimum wage—$64 a week—will not support a very big family. But it will bring workers and their families a little bit above the poverty line—$3,000 a year. . . . It will help them carry on. It will help them to not worry about three meals a day. It will enable them to help themselves develop skills so that they can someday earn more. . . . It will help under-income areas—Appalachia and some areas in my own South. It will help minority groups who are helpless in the face of prejudice that exists.

The 1966 amendments also extended the Act's protections to many workers in retail and service industries that had traditionally been low-wage sectors of the economy. The new provisions added some 9 million additional workers to coverage, bringing the total to nearly 80 percent of all nonsupervisory employees protected by the Act.

One of President Johnson's proposals that was not accepted by the Congress was that the overtime penalty premiums be increased from time-and-one-half to doubletime. This new overtime premium was to be effective initially after 48 hours a week, and eventually after 45 hours, and was designed to restore the original deterrent effects of the overtime premiums that had been eroded by the large growth of fringe benefits since 1938.

At the completion of the first phase of the 1966 amendments, Secretary Wirtz reported to Congress on January 31, 1968, as follows: "When the 1966 amendments went into effect on February 1, 1967, about 4.5 million workers had to be given wage increases averaging 12 cents an hour. Despite repeated predictions to the contrary, the facts clearly indicate that desirable social gains were achieved without economic disruptions. . . . At the same time as wages were increased employment continued to rise."

In the years when the various phases of the 1966 amendments were being implemented, several different Secretaries of Labor filed reports on the effects of the legislation. In each case the reports emphasized that those industries most affected by the changes in the statute had little difficulty in adjusting to the changes and the condition of workers improved. For example, in 1970 the report submitted to Congress by Secretary of Labor George P. Shultz concluded:

> There was continued economic growth during the period covering the third phase of the minimum wage and maximum hours standards established by the Fair Labor Standards Amendments of 1966. Total employment in nonagricultural payrolls (seasonally adjusted) rose in 28 out of the 32 consecutive months between January 1967 and September 1969. In the most recent 12-month period, employment climbed 3.2 percent, from 68.2 million in September 1968 to 70.4 million in September 1969. Employment rose in all major nonagricultural industry divisions in the 12-month period between September 1968 and September 1969. In the retail, services and State and local government sectors—where the minimum wage had its greatest impact in 1969, since only newly covered workers were slated for Federal minimum wage increases—employment rose substantially.[23]

In 1971, the report to the Congress from Secretary of Labor James D. Hodgson stated: ". . . it is significant that employment in retail trade and services—the industries where the newly covered group is largely concentrated and hence most likely to manifest some impact from the wage increase—fared better than industries unaffected by the statutory escalation in the minimum wages."[24]

The 1970s

Active consideration of updating the minimum wage began

[23] U.S. Department of Labor, *Report Submitted to Congress in Accordance with the Requirements of Section 4(d) of the Fair Labor Standards Act,* January 1970, pp. 1–2.

[24] U.S. Department of Labor, *Report Submitted to Congress in Accordance with the Requirements of Section 4(d) of the Fair Labor Standards Act,* January 1971, p. 5.

in 1971. In that year the Nixon Administration proposed an increase, in stages, to $2 an hour but with a subminimum wage for youth.

The Administration recommendation of a lower rate for teenagers came only a short time after the Department of Labor had completed a comprehensive study of the relationship between youth unemployment and minimum wages. The Secretary of Labor stated in his 1971 report to Congress: "This study provides information useful in evaluating the teenage unemployment problem. A significant finding was that it was difficult to prove any direct relationship between minimum wages and employment effects on young workers."[25] Despite this conclusion and the fact that the Youth Unemployment Study[26] came up with negative results in its effort to relate youth unemployment to minimum wages, the Administration pushed hard for a subminimum wage for youth.

During 1971 and 1972, both the House and Senate passed alternatives to the Administration bill to amend the Fair Labor Standards Act. The question of a "youth subminimum" was primarily responsible for blocking all efforts at effecting a compromise. Although each chamber had passed a bill, the House refused even to appoint a conference committee to meet with the Senate to reconcile the two bills. The House bill would have raised the minimum to $2 an hour in 1974 and would have authorized subminimum wages for workers 21 years or younger. The Senate version would have raised the minimum to $2.20 in 1973 and extended coverage to 6,000,000 additional workers, but it contained no subminimum youth rates.

In the spring of 1973 the Administration again made recommendations on amending the Fair Labor Standards Act. The 1973 recommendations included a four-step increase in the minimum wage to $2.30 an hour as well as the elimination or phasing down or out of some of the exemptions. But once again, a subminimum wage for youth was a major provision and a major focus of debate.

The bill passed by Congress in August 1973 and vetoed by

[25] USDL, *Report*, 1971, p. 3.
[26] U.S. Department of Labor, Bureau of Labor Statistics, *Youth Unemployment and Minimum Wage*, Bull. No. 1657 (Washington: 1970).

President Nixon in September would have raised the minimum wage to $2.20 an hour by July 1974 and extended minimum wage and overtime protection to most public employees as well as to household workers. The House, on a 259 to 164 vote, failed to obtain the two-thirds votes necessary to override President Nixon's veto.

A renewed effort in 1974 to update the Fair Labor Standards Act, by Senator Harrison A. Williams (D. N.J.) in the Senate and Representative John Dent (D. Pa.) in the House, was finally successful.

During the debate on the 1974 amendments, many of the same arguments that had been heard each time the Act had been considered were repeated. Representative Claude Pepper (D. Fla.), a member of the House or Senate nearly continuously since 1938, when the minimum wage bill was the issue in his campaign for the Senate, characterized the opposition to the bill as "the same kind of opposition . . . the same specious reasons given against it." He asserted: "It has been a blessing to millions of our fellow countrymen who needed help; . . . it has made America stronger and better."[27]

However, Senator Barry Goldwater (R. Ariz.) argued the contrary, stating: "Instead of creating new jobs, instead of bringing in more income, the minimum wage actually, throughout history, has decreased jobs and has not had a salutary effect on wages. The minimum wage only starts a chain of increases which sometimes—many times—cannot be afforded in the business. We sometimes forget that it is the intent of the American economic structure to provide profits. Without profit, there can be no growth; without growth, there can be no jobs."[28]

The disemployment effects were vigorously denied by Representative Harold Donohue (D. Mass.) who maintained that "every advance in the minimum wage since World War II has resulted in additional employment opportunities for older workers, men and women, for minority groups and for teenagers."[29]

---

[27] U.S. Senate, Committee on Labor and Public Welfare, Subcommittee on Labor, *Legislative History of the Fair Labor Standards Amendments of 1974* (Washington: U.S. Government Printing Office, 1976), p. 1292. Hereinafter cited as *Legislative History.*

[28] *Legislative History,* p. 919.

[29] *Legislative History,* p. 1287.

Senator Harrison Williams (D. N.J.) answered the charge that a minimum wage starts a chain of increases by pointing to the various Labor Department studies on effects of minimum wage increases. He pointed out that these studies "have documented the fact that when the minimum is raised, the wage spread is narrowed and there is no general upward movement of wages."[30]

Representative Dent had tried to put to rest the "myth" of inflation in his introduction of the bill to the House floor. He pointed to the testimony of the Chamber of Commerce whose witness responded to a question: "We do not contend, unlike some of the witnesses that appeared before you apparently, that the minimum wage is inflationary. Quite the opposite. Inflation is not caused by minimum wages." Mr. Dent then went on to say: "In actual fact, inflation adversely affects the lowest income worker—including minimum wage earners—more harshly than any other. He is its sorriest victim."[31]

Congressman Mario Biaggi (D. N.Y.) decried the President's veto, stating: "The President's claim that the bill would be inflationary and would create unemployment is a rash judgment founded on nonexistent facts."[32]

Some congressmen, such as John Rarick (D. La.) were still concerned with government interference in the market system. He denounced the bill as "intermeddling" in the free enterprise system.[33] John Erlenborn (R. Ill.) was concerned with the interference "in the contract relationships between local units of government and their employees."[34] Both of these arguments seemed passé after 1938, but they still cropped up in the 1974 debate.

Others, such as Robert Dole (R. Kan.), were still concentrating on the impact of the bill on rural areas. He argued that the legislation would adversely affect rural development and would fall hardest on the farmers.[35] Similarly, Congressman Robert Bauman (R. Md.) insisted that the seafood processing industry would be adversely affected.[36] Both of these arguments had been made

[30] *Legislative History*, p. 1646.
[31] *Legislative History*, p. 236.
[32] *Legislative History*, p. 1259.
[33] *Legislative History*, p. 2287.
[34] *Legislative History*, p. 249.
[35] *Legislative History*, p. 1035.
[36] *Legislative History*, p. 2286.

for over 30 years, although there had been no evidence of adverse effects. As a matter of fact, the Secretary of Labor had made intensive studies of nonmetropolitan areas and of the seafood processing industry in response to previous allegations and had found that these sectors adjusted easily to previous minimum wage increases.

One of the major issues debated in the early 1970s was the proposal for the subminimum wage for youth. Senator James Buckley (R. N.Y.), who proposed a youth differential at 85 percent of prevailing minimum wage rates, said:

> Someone who understands how wages are determined will realize that when low-productivity teenagers are hired at their free-market wage, they are not simply replacing higher paid adult workers. Teenagers usually compete for different types of jobs than adults do. First, their low-skill level makes them unqualified for the jobs most adults hold. In addition, teenagers are often seeking part-time or summer employment rather than full-time jobs. All of this means that, if teenagers are permitted to receive low wages, new jobs will be created for them. In other words, the father will not be fired to hire the son.[37]

This concept was answered most succinctly by Congressman Robert Drinan (D. Mass.):

> Aside from the absence of evidence to support the idea that low wages create jobs, studies have found that minimum wage rates have no adverse effect on employment opportunities for teenagers. The administration strongly desires a subminimum for broad categories of young workers. Yet the Congress has considered the concept and rejected it in favor of a limited subminimum for full-time students working in certain occupations. Further, the law already exempts learners and apprentices from the minimum. The Congress has determined that a general youth subminimum would violate the basic objective of the law. That is, the raising of wages of the poorest paid who are in no position to bargain for themselves.[38]

Constitutionality also was a question in regard to the 1974

---

[37] *Legislative History*, p. 905.
[38] *Legislative History*, p. 1232.

amendments, with some senators arguing that the coverage of domestics was beyond the scope of interstate commerce,[39] while others questioned the constitutionality of extending the Act to all nonsupervisory state and local government employees.[40] These arguments were answered by "legal briefs entered into the record which pointed to previous Court decisions on congressional authority as the basis for coverage of domestics."[41] Similarly, coverage of state and local government employees was based heavily upon the 1968 Supreme Court decision *(Maryland* v. *Wirtz)* that upheld the 1966 coverage of employees of state and local hospitals and schools.

Elimination of poverty was certainly a key theme in the discussion. The House Committee report indicated that the "simplest, most direct and least expensive way to eliminate poverty is to modernize the Fair Labor Standards Act."[42] The passage of a higher minimum was directly related to welfare conditions by Senator Williams who said: "Establishment of a minimum wage rate at a level which will at least assure the worker an income at or above the poverty level is essential to the reduction of welfare rolls and overall reform of the welfare system in the United States."[43] Congressman Dent pointed out that "no fewer than 20 states and the District of Columbia provide higher amounts in the welfare payments plus food stamps to a family of four, than the minimum wage rate provides to that family's breadwinner."[44] Congressman Carl Perkins (D. Ky.) observed: "[I]t appears we have been more willing to hand out welfare payments than to guarantee a decent wage to people willing to work and lucky enough to have a job."[45]

The House Committee report restated the purpose of the Act in these terms:

> Its basic purpose has been and continues to be the raising of wages of that small proportion of employees at the bottom of the wage scale who are in no position to bargain for themselves. It is not a substitute for col-

[39] *Legislative History,* p. 949.
[40] *Legislative History,* p. 1795.
[41] *Legislative History,* p. 962.
[42] *Legislative History,* p. 2128.
[43] *Legislative History,* p. 1646.
[44] *Legislative History,* p. 236.
[45] *Legislative History,* p. 1226.

lective bargaining or the operation of the free labor market. It protects the fair employer from unfair competition from chiseling employers. The minimum wage set under the Fair Labor Standards Act is not an average wage. It is the "lowest" wage which may be paid employees in activities covered by the Act. It is paid to the unskilled, untrained, inexperienced worker who frequently is young or black or a woman.[46]

The amendments increased the minimum wage for most covered workers to $2 an hour on May 1, 1974, to $2.10 in January 1975, and to $2.30 in January 1976. The bill signed by President Nixon in April was virtually identical with the one that had been vetoed some months earlier.

The Act's coverage was again extended; this time it included just about all nonsupervisory employees in the public sector—federal, state, and local government. In addition, significant proportions of domestic workers were added under the Act's protective umbrella. Again extended adjustment periods were allowed for newly covered and recently covered enterprises to meet the new requirements. Farm workers were also to be brought up to the general uniform standard of $2.30 an hour by 1978.

Congressman Dent introduced a new minimum wage bill (H.R. 10130) in 1975 to increase the minimum wage, in steps, to $3 an hour and to provide for automatic increases after the $3 rate became effective. That bill also would have increased the overtime premium from time-and-one-half to doubletime. The automatic adjustment of the minimum wage was not novel; it had congressional support in the late 1940s. Representative Samuel K. McConnell, Jr., expressed an interest in linking the minimum wage to the Consumer Price Index in 1947, as did Senator Allen J. Ellender (D. La.) and Senator Robert A. Taft, Sr. (R. Ohio) in 1949. The latter senator proposed that minimum wage adjustments be set at 60 percent of average hourly earnings in manufacturing. Picking up on this theme, there were congressional discussions in 1976 of tying changes in the minimum wage to changes in average hourly earnings of nonsupervisory employees in private nonfarm employment. However, the 94th Congress ad-

---

[46] *Legislative History*, p. 153.

journed in 1976 without seriously considering any minimum wage legislation.

The extensions of coverage brought new constitutional challenges to the Fair Labor Standards Act. The U.S. Supreme Court had upheld the constitutionality of the enterprise concept introduced in the 1961 amendments, and coverage of state and local government employees was initially accepted by the Court as it related to public school and hospital employees in a 1968 decision.[47] The latter decision was reversed in 1976 in *League of Cities* v. *Usery*,[48] a case that challenged the 1974 extension of FLSA coverage to all nonsupervisory governmental employment. Particularly controversial was the coverage of police officers and firefighters.

In the earlier case, the Court, by a 6 to 2 decision, held that Congress had the power to extend the FLSA to state and local government school and hospital employees. Justice John M. Harlan, writing for the majority, found that "while the commerce power has limits, valid general regulations of commerce do not cease to be regulations of commerce because a state is involved. If a state is engaging in economic activities that are validly regulated by the Federal Government when engaged in by private persons, the State too may be forced to conform its activities to federal regulation."[49]

However, eight years later, by a 5 to 4 split decision, the Court found that coverage of state and local government employees was an infringement by the federal government of state sovereignty as set forth in the Tenth Amendment to the Constitution. The case was originally argued on April 16, 1975, but the Court failed to reach a decision in that session. The case was reargued on March 2, 1976, with the decision rendered on June 24. William H. Rehnquist delivered the opinion of the Court, joined by three other justices: Chief Justice Warren Burger, Potter Stewart, and Lewis F. Powell. Harry A. Blackmun filed a concurring opinion. A sharp dissent was written by William J. Brennan, joined by Byron White and Thurgood Marshall. John P. Stevens wrote another short caustic dissent.

[47] *Maryland* v. *Wirtz,* 392 U.S. 183 (1968).
[48] *League of Cities* v. *Usery,* Nos. 74–878 and 74–879 (1976).
[49] *Maryland* v. *Wirtz,* at 18; Wage and Hour cases 449.

The majority found that "one undoubted attribute of state sovereignty is the States' power to determine the wages which shall be paid to those whom they employ in order to carry out their governmental functions, what hours those persons will work, and what compensation will be provided where these employees may be called upon to work overtime."[50]

This opinion seemed to contradict the decision of the Court a year earlier in *Fry* v. *United States.* In that case the Court found no invasion of state sovereignty by the wage control program that had placed a ceiling on wage increases made by state governments as well as by private employers.

In his dissent in the *League of Cities* case, Justice Brennan wrote:

> I cannot recall another instance in the Court's history when the reasoning of so many decisions covering so long a span of time has been discarded roughshod. That this is done without any justification not already often advanced and consistently rejected, clearly renders today's decision on *ipse dixit* reflecting nothing but displeasure with a congressional judgment.[51]

Justice Stevens ridiculed the decision, stating:

> The Federal Government may, I believe, require the State to act impartially when it hires or fires the janitor, to withhold taxes from his pay check, to observe safety regulations when he is performing his job, to forbid him from burning too much soft coal in the capitol furnace, from dumping untreated refuse in an adjacent waterway, from overloading a state owned garbage truck or from driving either the truck or the governor's limousine over 55 miles an hour. Even though these and many other activities of the capitol janitor are activities of the state qua state, I have no doubt that they are subject to federal regulations.[52]

Overall, employers have substantially abided by the requirements of the Act throughout the years. However, wage-hour inspections, largely in response to employee complaints, disclosed

---

[50] *League of Cities*, at 12.
[51] *League of Cities*, 74–879, at 16.
[52] *League of Cities*, 74–879, at 26.

that over a half million workers were underpaid a total of $120 million in fiscal year 1976. These violations are a clear indication that vigorous enforcement is a continuing necessity to ensure compliance with the minimum wage, overtime, equal pay, and child labor requirements of the Act.

Child labor violations were described in detail in 1970. In that year, 13,000 violations were discovered by investigators, including nearly 1,500 children under the age of 14 illegally employed, including some children as young as 6 years old. Examples cited included a cooperative produce association that used children ages 6 to 12 to grade vegetables, some motels that used 12-year-old girls as night maids and linen workers, and some hamburger chains that employed children below the age of 16 for up to 65 hours a week, during school time. Children ranging from 7 to 15 years old were hired to cultivate shade-grown tobacco under a cheesecloth canopy, where this crop is usually grown.[53]

An Overview

At the turn of the century, many opponents of minimum wage legislation predicted that government regulation of a floor under wages would bring disastrous unemployment and bankruptcies. Throughout the years, economists using existing data or economic models reached various conclusions concerning the effects of the minimum wage. This chapter has not attempted an analysis of the large number of conflicting economic points of view, but instead has concentrated on the broad sweep of the legislation and court interpretations through this century and the results reported in the voluminous studies by various Secretaries of Labor, both Democratic and Republican. The experience has indeed shown that it is possible to raise the wages of the lowest paid workers by governmental action without adverse effects. It has happened throughout the last 40 years in the United States.

The standard 40-hour workweek, unchanged since the initial legislation, is again being reviewed in light of the high unemployment of 1975 and 1976. Maybe an adjustment in this standard is also due. The penalty for overtime, established at time-and-

[53] U.S. Department of Labor, Wage and Hour Division, *Working Children, A Report on Child Labor*, W.H. Publication 1323 (Washington: 1971).

one-half in 1938, is also being reconsidered. Because of the growth of fringe benefits, the penalty payment, based on wage rates and not on total earnings, has lost its deterrent effect.

As for child labor legislation, the recent trend has been to nibble at child labor restrictions. Public support of child labor laws has weakened amid broad concern for high teenage unemployment rates and rising levels of juvenile delinquency. However, the basic necessity to protect children from exploitation by unscrupulous employers remains as valid today as it was at the turn of the century. Moreover, many believe that any weakening of the child labor standards will have disastrous consequences for adult employment, while further alienating the youth.

The basic function that government assumed in 1938—the establishment of minimum standards of employment—remains a vital governmental role in the 1970s. The floor under wages needs to be kept current, the ceiling on hours needs to be reviewed, and the child labor standards need to be reaffirmed.

The New Deal sought to eliminate poverty. No single program was comprehensive enough to meet the various facets of poverty. For the elderly poor, social security went part of the way; for the unemployed, unemployment compensation went part of the way; for the disabled and dependent children, welfare went part of the way; and for the working poor, minimum wage went part of the way. The detailed poverty studies of the 1960s and 1970s indicated that approximately half of all families in poverty were headed by someone who held a job. Thus, their poverty was related to low wages, short hours, and intermittent unemployment, or sometimes large families. Without minimum wage legislation, their conditions would undoubtedly be much worse. The Fair Labor Standards Act has gone far toward its goal of providing a "minimum standard of living necessary for health, efficiency, and general well-being of workers."

CHAPTER 6

Manpower Policies and Worker Status Since the 1930s

GARTH L. MANGUM
University of Utah

There are, of course, similarities and differences between the manpower policies of the 1930s and those of more recent years, and the same will be sayable 20 years from now. The future is always more like than unlike the past, but it is also markedly different. Comparative manpower policies over time are best understood if visualized within the broad historical sweep of industrialization. That is the approach of this paper: What were the historical social and economic forces that led to the manpower policies of the 1930s? What were the responses to those policies? What were the social and economic forces emerging to produce the explosion of manpower-related policies and programs of the 1960s? What are the particular responses, and how did they work out? What are the social and economic forces extant and foreseeable today that will underlie the policies of the years ahead? But first, what is this stuff we call "manpower policy" anyway?

What Is Manpower Policy?

Policy is defined by a standard dictionary as "a definite course of action, selected from alternatives, and in light of given conditions, to guide and determine present and future decisions." Upon reading that definition, one is inclined to respond to public policy, "We've never had any." The political world simply does not work that way. Be that as it may, there are always governmental decisions in any important area of activity related to the public welfare that can be dignified by the term "policy."

Manpower (a notably sexist term for which no one has yet found a satisfactory substitute—"personpower"?) has come by usage and logic to refer to the efforts of human beings in employed activities. It is a subset of human resources which, though even more vague, seems to encompass human beings in all of their productive activities, whether or not in paid employment. Thus, manpower policy refers to all of those policies directly concerned with the participation of human beings in paid employment at any or all occupational levels. Its concerns are employability, employment, and productivity as they occur in labor markets. It recognizes that people are the most essential factor in any form of production and that employment is the primary source of family income in an industrial society. It acknowledges that employment policy is related to but is not coextensive with manpower policy. Since the demand for labor is a derived demand, jobs are created only by the spending of money for the purchase of goods and services. Generation of purchasing power and motivating its use are the keys to employment at the aggregate level.

However, manpower policy involves itself only in the labor market. It has few tools to affect that vital product-market generation of derived demand. In general, manpower policy is recognized as dealing with all labor-supply concerns—foreseeing need, motivating people to seek employment, preparing them to perform jobs, and helping them to find jobs. On the demand side, it is particularistic—how to assure that there are specific employment opportunities for particular groups and that the structure of employment opportunities is compatible with the labor-supply structure.

Essentially, manpower policy has two overriding concerns: (1) the development of human resources and their allocation within labor markets to those activities upon which society has placed the highest priority, and (2) satisfactory working careers (involving income, status, and job satisfaction) for all individuals who can be prepared and motivated to prefer paid employment as their primary source of income.

The Sweep of Industrialization

Labor markets, supply of labor, demand for labor, paid employment—these are the terms that gained meaning only within the context of industrialization. Specialization of labor, production techniques involving an interface between people and machines, interdependence and exchange of goods and services, and income in cash from paid employment were its essence. Its advent in the United States can be dated from 1870, the decennial Census when, for the first time, the number of people working in agriculture began to be exceeded by the number engaged in other productive activities. Natural resources, particularly the fertility of the soil, had keyed the preindustrial society. Capital resources (hence capitalism) were the critical concern of industrialization. Nevertheless, a new relationship emerged for the human resource which, because it (the individual) was the end as well as the means in society, required policies to assure its welfare.

Industrialization everywhere has had similar consequences for worker status: (1) increased material abundance; (2) greater insecurity from (a) a declining economic role and a more vulnerable status for the young and the old, (b) the disappearance of a moral and legal claim on a share in society's means of subsistance, (c) the fluctuations of the business cycle, and (d) assigning to others—employers—the right to allocate available employment opportunities and to determine their nature; (3) a concern among employers that workers adapt themselves to the requirements of the machine.

There have also been everywhere, as responses, the emergence of (1) some form of organization through which workers participate in making the rules which govern the workplace; (2) employer practices directed toward developing a symbiosis between man and machine for maximum productivity; (3) public policies for the protection of workers against economic insecurity and the physical hazards of employment; and (4) a system of mass education, the purpose of which, among other things, is to prepare the labor force for industrial participation.

The nature of these developments differs by the cultural setting within which industrialization emerges, but they all are there in the industrial society, whether it be democratic or totalitarian, socialistic or private enterprise.

American Industrialization and the 1930s

The 1930s are best understood as the period when the political power of America's industrial workers first became sufficient to enable them to do something about the consequences of industrialization. It was not that the consequences had not been felt during the previous 60 years, but not until then had sufficient time passed for the number of industrial workers to increase as a proportion of the body politic as well as of the labor force to have an impact in a pluralistic society governable only by coalition among social and economic interests. Also, events occurred that were sufficiently dramatic to diminish adulation for the industrialist-hero of American progress and to develop sympathy for the plight of the worker. The need was already recognized at the intellectual level, and now conditions were ripe. Unemployment, which never for a dozen years dropped below 15 percent and peaked at 25 percent of the labor force, provided the immediate setting for long-range reform.

The permanent reforms were the National Labor Relations Act, the Social Security Act, the Fair Labor Standards Act, the banking and securities reforms, and, though it came a decade later, the Employment Act of 1946. The latter legislation required a spread of Keynesian thought and the wartime demonstration that a country could spend itself into prosperity.

The work-relief programs that more generally characterize the New Deal in the public mind were emergency, short-run, and disorganized as compared to the more unique and carefully developed permanent reforms. They had been used before, though never on such massive scale, and they emerged without planning from the necessity to do something immediately, which the long-term reforms could not do. The most significant factors in the context of this recital were (1) their magnitude, and (2) the precedents for the 1960s and 1970s. It should be enough to point out that if similar tools were in use today proportionate to the labor force and the GNP, the combination of public-service and youth employment programs would enroll 5.8 million persons at a budgetary cost of $39 billion.

The Second World War and Its Aftermath

Manpower policy in the 1950s and 1960s can be analyzed in the contexts of both the long-term advance of industrialization and the more immediate forces of the times. The second world war was the bridge between the two, accelerating long-run trends to the critical levels necessary for political action. Beginning in the late thirties, with the necessity to supply material support to allies already at war and later, at the end of 1941, for all-out war, the dozen years of labor-market slack ended suddenly in the strongest demand for labor the nation had ever experienced. The 10 or 11 million people who, on the average, made up the armed forces of 1941–1945 were not only the heart of the labor force— prime-age males 18–35, predominantly—but also its bulk since they were drawn from a prewar labor force of 45 million (1940: 34 million males). At the same time, the nation had not only to feed, arm, and transport this fighting force, but also to do the same for its allies while continuing to support the civilian population. The production challenge was unprecedented, requiring draconic measures and producing irreversible changes in the U.S. manpower system. These interacting war-motivated developments were the social and economic forces to which the manpower policies of three decades later are still responding. The most important were:

1. A speed-up of rural-to-urban migration. Output per manhour in agriculture, which had been following a long-term rising trend of 1 percent per year, leaped to an annual average increase of 6 percent and has not yet dropped below 5 percent as a continuing trend.

2. A faster pace of technological change, overall. A sharp shift in output per manhour from an average annual rise of 2 percent per year before the war to around 3 percent per year during and after it is the simplest representation.

3. Rising labor-force participation of women. The 19 percent of adult women in the labor force before the war became 27 percent by 1947 and 44 percent by 1975. Meanwhile, the age-pattern of that participation changed from "enter the labor force in the teens and leave at marriage" to "enter, leave at the birth of first child, and return when the last child enters school," to "have fewer children and put them in day-care situations so as to pursue a continuous working career."

4. The increased sophistication of military technology. Civilian spinoffs and continuing cold-war developments made new demands on the structure and preparation of the labor force.

5. The post-war baby boom. The high birth rates of the 1947–1957 period, falling off in the next decade to a new low plateau after 1967, predetermined youth employment problems from 1963 to sometime in the 1970s.

6. The World War II G.I. Bill. Whether by cause or effect, educated people became available, engineers designed technology assuming an educated labor force, employers expected it, and labor-market competition demanded it.

Item 4 (above) had the first notable impact on postwar man-power policy. The others were time-bombs ticking away inexorably toward the 1960s. For the 1950s, the perceived need was for scientific, engineering, and technical manpower, not so much for the sake of economic development as for national defense. Since our international competitors were obviously not as smart as we, it must have been spies who enabled them to crack our nuclear monopoly. But executing spies did not prevent them from beating us into space, where no one could have stolen the secret since we were not there yet. We had to increase our flow of high-talent manpower or our technological superiority would wither away—hence, the National Defense Education Act and related developments.

Meanwhile, everything was related to everything else. The old rural-urban migration had seen European peasants migrating to America's new industrial cities. Their first requirement was housing and, since the immigrants were poor, this meant cheap housing, which, of course, was in the oldest or central parts of cities from which previous residents had progressed outward. The next pressing need was for unskilled and semiskilled jobs which, by happy coincidence, were contiguous with the cheap housing. With those needs met, their children could be educated to sound and look American and join the trek to suburbia, leaving a vacuum for the next wave.

But the post-World War II wave was a domestic migration from the rural South and Southwest and Puerto Rico. The war-time wave, which had not been heavily shared by minorities, had ensconced its participants on seniority rosters in plentiful semi-skilled jobs. But in the postwar era, that happy contiguity of housing and job for the immigrant was shattered. The new tech-nology now required continuous process industry and technically skilled workers. The open space and favorable property tax rates for the former and the location of the latter subsized by housing programs, was now suburban. Yet the economies of housing and racial discrimination in its distribution trapped the new migrants in the central city where there were mainly two kinds of jobs: (1) the white-collar office jobs held by commuting suburbanites because the central city residents lacked the required education, skills, and cosmetic attributes, and (2) low-skilled, lowly paid jobs servicing those commuters and the central city.

School systems everywhere were simply too overwhelmed by sheer numbers of baby-boom and migration products to worry about quality or relevance to emerging needs. With traditionally female jobs more plentiful than those for males, the central-city family structure was burdened by economically impotent fathers and working mothers.

Pent-up shortages from war-time and the demands of the cold war reduced interest in the Full Employment bill of 1945 and resulted in the largely rhetorical Employment Act of 1946. Following the close of the Korean conflict, unemployment trended persistently upward through a series of short, mild recessions and recoveries. With each recession, unemployment rose higher and, with each recovery, left behind a higher residual. Every elementary economics text had the proper prescription: A most modest stimulus to purchasing power would have prevented the accumulation of unemployment and the persistent deficits in the federal budget. But notions of budget balance and fear of balance-of-payments consequences tied fiscal and monetary policies to past orthodoxies.

Meantime, off in another corner, some black youth in North Carolina could not understand why they could not sit down and drink their cokes like the white kids did, and a black woman could not understand why she should sit in the back seats of a bus, behind a curtain, when she paid the same fare as the white folks. And in the 1960 presidential campaign, a rich man's son from Boston first saw poverty face-to-face in West Virginia. All the forces—long-, medium-, and short-run—were in place for the manpower policy developments of the 1960s.

Manpower Policy Responses During the 1960s

Three essential differences distinguish the manpower-related policies of the 1960s from those of the 1930s: (1) Those of the 1960s were based on less careful analysis and forethought. (2) Those of the 1960s were far smaller in magnitude, relative to the size of the economy and labor force. (3) Training and other preparation for employment played a major role in the 1960s, but none in the 1930s. These three points will be easier to demonstrate after a brief review of the policy responses that occurred during the 1960s.

Despite having narrowly won an election on the slogan, "Get America moving again," the Kennedy Administration was remarkably ill-prepared to get into motion. There were many hypotheses but no consensus on what was wrong and what needed to be done. General economists in and around the Council of Economic Advisers were convinced that all that was needed was a healthy fiscal stimulus to raise the rate of economic growth. Labor economists in and around the Labor Department had discovered "structural unemployment"—concentration by age, sex, race, education, and location. Swirling around were kibitzers convinced that automation was the source of all ills, with the most extreme suggesting that the nation give up full employment and prepare for the coming world of full unemployment.

Since the Administration was not prepared to move, the initiative lay by default with Congress. Senators and congressmen tended to see the world from the vantage points of their own constituencies and to be influenced by the popular press rather than the professional journals. Structural unemployment best represented the level of detail at which they were prepared to operate: Who is unemployed from what past job in my district? Not, how many are unemployed nationwide related to what aggregate purchasing power?

The depressed-areas bill of Paul Douglas had been thoroughly aired by twice passage in the Senate and once in the House, followed by veto by President Eisenhower. It needed only reintroduction as the Area Redevelopment Act for passage. Never mind that aiding limited spots of persistent depression in a generally bouyant economy is something quite different from trying to attract industry to such locations when the entire economy is operating below its capacity.

The unemployed the legislators knew best in 1961 were white male family heads of long labor-force attachment. Who now stood at the work stations where they were formerly employed? Often, a machine. Apparently, those whose substantial skills had suffered technological obsolescence now needed retraining. After all, witnesses as prestigious as the chairman of the Federal Reserve Board and the former chairman of the Council of Economic Advisers had testified before congressional committees that there was no lack of jobs. Anyone who could read the newspaper help-wanted ads could see that. The problem was one of square pegs in round holes. The people did not fit the jobs.

Designed in 1961 and passed in March 1962, the Manpower Development and Training Act was not funded until the autumn, and the first enrollments were during the winter of 1962–1963. But by the spring of 1963, unemployment of married men had fallen from the 4.5 percent of 1961 to 3.2 percent. With the first products of the postwar baby boom now turning 16 years of age, youth unemployment jumped to 17 percent. With the experienced male adult workers being recalled, the characteristics of those enrolling in the new MDTA program soon demonstrated that what was needed was not a retraining program, but a training program for those who had never had substantial skills or stable work experience. But this was not going to be like training high school seniors and graduates in vocational schools. Remedial adult basic education, orientation to the world of work, guidance in occupational choice for those of limited work exposure, personal counseling, and other supportive services would be needed and could be best provided within the training institution. Since the techniques never had been developed, there was no base in experience, nor any institutions capable of supplying the needed services. Years of trial-and-error development were necessary before the MDTA institutional training program became viable. Even then, it became viable only for those locations where jobs existed and housing, transportation, race and sex discrimination, and other social pathologies were not overwhelming. Where they were, training too often provided a "hunting license" to search for jobs that did not exist or were out of reach.

Meanwhile, trial-and-error experimentation continued with a 1963 emphasis on youth and a 1964 addition of poverty and race. The Vocational Education Act of 1963 represented the first serious reconsideration of federal vocational education legislation since its inauguration in 1917. The influence of industrialization's progress was obvious. The Morrill Act of 1862, recognizing the need for engineering skills in agriculture and in the infant industry, established the agricultural and mechanical land-grant colleges. By the time of the first world war, industrialization was entering adolescence, and the need for a limited number of skilled tradesmen was recognized. The Smith-Hughes Act of 1917 offered matching grants to the states for vocational training in the specific occupational categories designated by the Congress. Education and training still were not prerequisites for employment for most people. The Vocational Education Act of 1963, appropriate to maturing industrialism, reversed that philosophy. Not the skill needs of the labor market, but the employment needs of people was the new focus. Rather than occupational categories, the 1963 Act prescribed population groups to be served.

The New Deal had not involved education or training. Among the long-run reforms, formal preparation for jobs was not yet that important. Why train for jobs that do not exist? The total short-run concentration was on temporary job-creation. Whether or not there were enough jobs to go around, it was clear that youths were not getting them. And had not the Civilian Conservation Corps and the National Youth Administration been the least criticized of the work-relief programs of the 1930s? Senator Hubert H. Humphrey had introduced and guided through the Senate in 1957 a bill to reestablish these programs, but it had died in the House. A Youth Employment Act of 1963, with the same two provisions, had the same experience. All that could be done for youth in 1963, beyond the longer range reforms of vocational education, was to increase the youth component of MDTA training. But the stage was partially set for 1964.

There were other pieces of staging. The civil rights movement had progressed beyond lunch-counter sit-ins, bus boycotts, and freedom rides to demands for equal access to jobs. Continuing interest in Appalachia and the gradual discovery of the central city generated a flow of popular literature on poverty. Staff analysts within government began to search income data to explore the incidence and extent of poverty. These pressing problems and a proposed massive tax cut, representing the Administration's conversion to Keynesian economics and a conviction that unguided recovery was inadequate, represented the three major proposed thrusts of the Kennedy Administration as assassination cut it short.

However, a southern President with civil-rights sympathies and "arm-twisting" abilities was better situated than his predecessor to win the Civil Rights Act of 1964 with its Title VII prohibition on racial and ethnic discrimination in employment. That the trickery of enemies who thought to make Title VII unenforceable by tossing the three-letter word "sex" into its machinery backfired is a historical quirk. A President who visualized his Texas background as poverty could also say, upon being briefed as to impending proposals, "That's my kind of program" and publicly declare "war on poverty" without asking "What shall we use as weapons?" The presidential honeymoon and sympathy for the fallen champion could also sell an unprecedented job-creating tax cut—but more on that later.

Under pressure to devise strategy for the already declared antipoverty war and to do so at a cost no greater than $1 billion the first year (part of the deal to get the tax cut), the interagency task force designing the new Economic Opportunity Act was limited largely to bits and pieces of programs, legislation, and experience scattered about the landscape. The New Deal precedents were large among the contributions.

The Neighborhood Youth Corps was the reincarnation of the National Youth Administration. The Job Corps conservation centers were direct descendents of the Civilian Conservation Corps. The Job Corps urban centers were new. The Defense Department was then under pressure to close obsolete defense facilities and proposed using them as residential vocational schools. The Labor Department suggested a full-scale reinauguration of the Works Progress Administration (WPA) work-relief program financed by a cigarette tax. Its proposal was rejected as too expensive and was folded into the Title V Work Experience and Training program to allow welfare recipients and other poor to earn the equivalent of public-assistance benefits. Its vindication came year by year as EOA was amended to add Operation Mainstream (a miniscule rural WPA for older workers) and the New Careers program (to provide jobs as subprofessional aides), and as the Emergency Employment Act of 1971 (first vetoed in 1970 as a "WPA") and subsequent "public service employment" provisions made special job-creation targeted by socioeconomic group and locality an apparently permanent part of the manpower tool kit.

A catchall paragraph can wind up an already overlong description of developments during the 1960s and prepare for a few comparative observations before moving on to signposts concerning the future of manpower policy and worker status. The most innovative aspect of the Economic Opportunity Act was the Community Action Program (other nonmanpower provisions of EOA are ignored as unimportant in this context). It had its precedents, of course, but was unique in its assumptions that all existing governmental machinery was disinterested in and incapable of serving the poor. A whole new set of institutions— Community Action Agencies involving "maximum feasible participation of the poor"—was created and provided with federal funding to coordinate local activities on behalf of the poor. Central-city unrest soon focused almost complete attention there to the exclusion of rural and suburban poverty. Private employers were recruited by subsidies to hire disadvantaged workers in place of the more advantaged who might be available. Rising AFDC costs and enrollments became a political issue, and rhetoric took a punitive turn: "Make taxpayers out of taxeaters and get them off welfare rolls onto payrolls." The difficulty of adapting nationally designed programs to the needs of local individuals and labor markets generated an interest in decentralizing manpower decision-making to the labor-market level and in breaking down the fixed categorical limits on the types of services to be offered.

Such was the manpower-policy development through 1968. Only the Vocational Education Act of 1963 and its 1968 amendments evidenced the careful study and preparation which went into the National Labor Relations Act and the Social Security Act. All other legislation and administratively created programs of the 1960s were more comparable to the emergency New Deal work-relief programs. They were trial-and-error efforts forced by crisis and designed by intuition.

The legislation of the 1930s went to the heart of worker status. It guaranteed the right of workers to be represented by collective bargaining agents of their own choosing and required employers to bargain with those agents. It insured the worker in a major way against the insecurities of the business cycle and dependent status during old age. It created emergency jobs for 6.6 percent of the labor force and persisted in doing so for a total of nine years. It chose for those jobs a series of activities— construction, art, writing projects—which made a permanent contribution to the infrastructure of communities and the quality of life. All of these programs, long and short term, were designed for the mainstream industrial labor force and their children. There were other provisions for rural recovery (which inadvertently had the effect of driving marginal farmers off the land). No one seems to have worried much about non-European minorities and others at the margins of society.

Manpower programs of the 1960s never achieved enrollments of the equivalent of 1 percent of the labor force nor 1 percent of the federal budget. There were no basic reforms in worker security and worker status and only one significant intervention in the way labor markets work—the equal-employment-opportunity legislation and machinery. There was trial-and-error experimentation and significant, though small-scale, success at bringing the "outs" in to share whatever was available at the lower margins of the labor market. The almost total emphasis was on the problems of minorities and other groups facing competitive disadvantages in central-city labor markets. There was no consensus on the basic cause of the problems: Was it behavioral characteristics that caused individuals to be disadvantaged, or was it the institutional structure of society and the labor market? However, there was relatively more emphasis on changing people (primarily through skill-training) than on changing institutions.

Manpower Policy and Worker Status, 1968–1975

All of the three significant manpower-policy developments during the 1968–1975 period were extensions of proposals or programs of earlier years. Two were actually legislated in December 1967 but implemented and emphasized later. Only one had important implications for worker status.

Prior to 1965, there had been a notable correlation between unemployment and public assistance. AFDC rolls rose as unemployment increased, and as unemployment declined, the welfare load would diminish. But when unemployment decreased sharply after the 1964 tax cuts and the escalation of the Vietnam war in 1965, AFDC did not decline; instead, it accelerated.

By the end of 1967, Congress was aroused. Something had to be done to make "taxpayers out of those taxeaters." Still not having recognized the new phenomenon of the female-headed family, Congress thought it would be a simple task to solve the problem by purging the welfare rolls of all but mothers of preschool children. They should all be placed in jobs or trained for jobs, or jobs should be created for them in a Work Incentive Program. The normal initial-letter approach to an acronym, WIP, was modified as sounding too coercive, but, as originally conceived, WIP would have been more descriptive than WIN, the acronym chosen. Because funding was not sufficient to finance the day-care and job-creation load that would have been required, WIN became primarily a training and placement program for welfare mothers. It actually came very near to being swallowed up in a more promising approach to the solution of the problem—a combination of a guaranteed income for all families with children and a negative income tax work-incentive. Those for whom employment was not practical would have a basic income guarantee, while all families with potentially employable members would have an economic incentive to work. But after carrying the new concept closer to passage than most observers had expected, both the Administration and the Congress drew back from the enormity of the change.

At the same time the WIN program was introduced, Congress also amended the Economic Opportunity Act to decentralize much of the decision-making in its manpower programs to the community level. It followed up this trend in 1968 by also enlarging the state role in MDTA decisions. The concern was that nationally uniform programs were not sufficiently adaptable to local situations. "Decentralize and decategorize" was the new slogan. Fold all of the several categorical programs into one, with authority to provide any or all of the services formerly under the various agencies. Then give decision-makers at the local labor-market level authority to decide within limits whom to serve, what services to provide, and whom to use as deliverers of the services. Congress gave the Department of Labor and the Office of Economic Opportunity clear instructions to do just that. Both agreed philosophically with the directive, but they never complied with it because they could not agree upon which local agencies should be assigned the decision-making functions. It was exactly four years later, in December 1973, that decentralization and de-categorization became a fact with the passage of the Comprehensive Employment and Training Act (CETA). By that time Congress had answered the difficult question: Decentralize to the governors, mayors, and county officials who face voter retribution if they do not perform satisfactorily.

The impact of the first of these three significant manpower-policy developments from 1968 to 1975 was on a group that was either outside of or only marginally in the labor force. The second was an administrative change that may or may not noticeably affect worker status. The third was that often-advocated reinauguration of work-relief programs, but in a form very different from the 1930s model.

The public-job-creation proposals of the 1960s had focused, as had most other manpower policies of the period, on those unable to compete successfully in normal labor markets. The philosophy was "government as employer of last resort," but first to use fiscal and monetary policy aggressively to create high levels of employment and then to abolish discrimination and use training programs and relocation allowances to enable workers to compete more successfully for the available jobs. For those still left out, useful jobs providing needed public services would be created, and sheltered workshops for the severely handicapped would be added. Finally, there would be income-maintenance programs for those not employable under any conditions. That proved to be an unsalable recipe.

Public-service employment came into being because of reluctance to use the job-creating tools of fiscal and monetary policy. Having little control over general economic policy, Congress could mandate a contracyclical, direct job-creation program by offering local governments and public agencies additional funds to expand their work forces. Title II of CETA was conceived as a permanent program of public job-creation in those areas suffering above-average unemployment. But the Emergency Employment Act of 1971 and Title VI added to CETA in 1975 were everybody's second-best solution to the job-creation problem. They echoed the thirties, but only dimly. Unemployment, though high (peaking at 8.9 percent), did not approach 1933's 25 percent. The construction industry was now a high-technology and well-organized sector, no longer an outlet for masses of unskilled labor. Large components of the unemployed were women and youth, few of whom were accustomed to common labor. Adding members here and there to already large governmental staffs was more appropriate in the current occupational structure, but it was not massive job-creation.

Perhaps most significant in the 1968–1975 period was the perception of one Administration that lower middle- and middle-class workers felt that their status was threatened by policies favoring the disadvantaged, and the perception of another that it did not matter what anyone below the middle thought. The first sought to win away traditional Democrats into a "new Republican majority" by attacking "the Great Society." Thus, the first Nixon Administration, with its doubtful mandate, actually expanded manpower expenditures, whereas the short-lived second one, with its overwhelming but tenuous mandate, set out to dismantle the structure. The Ford Administration seemed impelled to destroy the support that anyone dependent upon cyclically vulnerable employment might be conditioned to give it.

Manpower Policy, Worker Status, and Labor Markets

It must be said for most of the manpower programs from 1960 to 1975 that, in general, they worked. That is, from the best information available, most of the people who went through such programs came out sufficiently better off in employment stability and income to justify the expenditure. But usually the average gain was from well down in the poverty ranks to its upper levels. The improvements were significant, but less than the rhetorical promises.

It must also be said that only the civil rights and equal-employment-opportunity policies had a significant impact on the way labor markets work and on the status of the body of working men and women. Everything else was designed to make those on the margins of the labor market less marginal or to provide income alternatives for those unable to "make it" in the job market.

In retrospect, it is quite clear that little could be expected of a manpower policy under which programs were designed without full recognition of the realities of functioning labor markets. Not that labor markets are sacred and beyond intervention. People can be aided to participate in labor markets only if those aids are consistent with the workings of labor markets. To intervene in labor markets to make their results more consistent with policy objectives requires a sensitive understanding of labor-market functions and what is possible without undesirable effects.

A few examples should make the point: Accept as three of the "first principles" of labor economics the truisms that (1) the demand for labor is a derived demand, (2) jobs are created only by the spending of money for creation of goods and services, and (3) the primary function of a labor market is to allocate labor supplies among alternative uses according to social priorities. A nation concludes that it must take anti-inflation actions which, by cutting purchasing power, destroys four million jobs in the private sector of the economy, and then it uses as its main lines of defense $18 billion of unemployment insurance and some 300,000 temporary public-sector jobs purchased at a cost of some $2.5 billion. Are the policy decisions consistent with the labor-market premises?

Manpower-training activities for women were concentrated in clerical and health occupations, but for men the training occupations were automotive repair, machine operation, welding, building service, food service, and upholstery—mostly occupations where formal skill-training is not the normal entry route. That many of the disadvantaged were at a subentry level was a justification, but lack of skill was the major barrier to job entry for few. Inadequate attention was given to the concept of ports of entry through which program graduates could find attractive employment; thus, most ended up employed in marginal firms.

Despite a great deal of empirical research over the years, practical theory capable of describing and predicting labor-market behavior and suggesting ways it could be improved is remarkably limited. Take as another example the major conceptual hypotheses concerning labor-market functioning that have been the basis for major policy prescriptions over the past 15 years: The staffs of the Council of Economic Advisers and the Joint Economic Committee viewed the supply side of the labor market as a simple queue, with the entire labor force ranked in order of individual productivity. Employers usually started at the front and went down the line until they had met the demands of their customers. Reducing unemployment was a simple process of increasing aggregate demand until the desired point in the queue was reached. My own contribution was the substitution of a shape-up for the queue, with workers ranked by whatever criteria employers chose to use—objective ones related to skill and productivity perhaps, but also subjective ones related to age, race, sex, education, etc. Increasing aggregate demand could increase the demand for labor, but might motivate employers to compete more vigorously for the most desired workers rather than simply to pick up the next best. High aggregate demand was a necessary but not a sufficient condition. Training programs, remedial education, antidiscrimination laws, relocation allowances, subsidized private employment, etc., could at the same time reduce employer reluctance and change relative rankings by making the disadvantaged more competitive. Government as the employer of last resort for those at the back of the line after all else was done, with income maintenance for those who could not even get into the line-up, was the logical completion of that formulation.

Piore and Doeringer added further sophistication in their dual labor market theory. To them, both of the previous formulations were faulty in that (1) they did not account for the fact that jobs had desirability rankings also and some might be rejected by workers, and (2) they failed to recognize that there was a primary and a secondary labor market with an almost impervious wall between. That is, in the labor market there are good jobs and bad jobs, the former typically secure, steady, well paid, and accompanied by a variety of fringe benefits; the latter, the opposite. There are employers who restrict themselves to one or the other of these markets, and there are workers who, by choice or lack of opportunity, are restricted to them. For those restricted to the secondary labor market, there is no advantage in being steady and productive since jobs available have no future and other jobs, no better and no worse, are readily at hand. The policy implication of that concept is that programs concentrating on the supply side, to change people, are useless. Only efforts on the demand side, to open access to primary jobs, can change economic opportunity.

Few refute the usefulness of the dual labor market concept, but the imperviousness of the wall is challenged. Most youth, it is argued, go through something like a secondary labor market on the way to the primary one. Workers can be assisted to vault the wall into the primary market.

Others have carried the dual labor market concept further into a theory of labor-market segmentation. A variety of protected enclaves of attractive employment is posited, each shielded from the competition of outsiders. Some find the source of the segmentation in a conspiracy of "capitalists" to keep the workers in subjection, apparently unaware that the secondary labor market encompasses generally the competitive sector of the economy. Others attribute it to the natural desire of the "ins" to protect themselves from competition from the "outs."

It may be more useful to conceive of the labor market as a stacked pinochle deck, one half a stack of jobs ranked by their desirability and the other half a stack of labor-force participants ranked by socioeconomic status. The shuffle, by and large, matches the best jobs with the most advantaged workers, but occasionally a job-seeker from the bottom of the deck does manage to make it to the top.

All of these conceptualizations are useful to the extent they aid simplified understanding of complex reality, predict results, and prescribe solutions. The critical issue is that there are only so many good jobs, even in the best of times and in the country with the most widespread opportunity. Policy alternatives can range over expansion of opportunity and sharing of that which exists. The enhancement of worker status was pursued in the 1930s by strengthening the hand of workers vis-à-vis their own employers and protecting them against times when no employment opportunities existed. The Employment Act of 1946 represented an emphasis on the total supply of jobs, but it has never been fully implemented for fear of inflationary consequences. The emphasis of the 1960s was on equal access to whatever opportunity existed, whether enforced by antidiscrimination rules or promoted by adding to the competitive abilities of those not enjoying their share of opportunity.

That is where manpower policy stands stymied in the mid-1970s. The traditional solution of enlarging a pie by economic growth so that each slice gets bigger without redistributing the relative shares seems blocked by fears of inflation, environmental concerns, resource constraints, and a possible long-term decline in the rate of productivity growth. Yet growth offers no real solution as long as each expansion of opportunity further raises expectations. No matter what the total supply of opportunity may be, jobs still vary in relative attractiveness. There may be more jobs, but there are still good ones and bad ones. The sharing approach is blocked by the perpetual reluctance of the "haves" to share with the "have nots" and by the desire of the former "have nots" to protect their gains against new insurgents.

Yet there are no other than the three alternatives: (1) convert the whole social philosophy from a competitive struggle to a cooperative sharing; (2) move the whole structure upward through economic growth, maintaining the "stacked deck" structure of good and bad jobs, in the hope that those on the bottom will compare their progress with their own past status rather than with the relative distance between themselves and those who are ahead; or (3) continue to plug away at the dual piecemeal task of opening access to segmented markets and preparing the "outs" to slip in one by one. The first is such a sharp departure from tradition to be unrealistic, and who would know how to do it if it were possible? The second appears to have lost much of its charm, but it is a prerequisite to the third: Maintaining a rapid rate of economic growth and job-creation while compromising as little as possible with environmental quality and finding other means than unemployment for restraining inflation, tinkering with the job structure while chipping away at obstacles to equal access, and preparing individuals to compete for what is available is a messy formula but the only one available. It offers little departure from the policies of the 1930s and 1960s, but where is the realistic alternative?

The Socioeconomic Base of Future Policies

The long sweep of industrialization and the more immediate

consequences of depression and war were identified as the major determinants of worker status and manpower policies in the 1930s and the 1960s. What will be the major social and economic forces that will determine worker status and to which manpower policy will respond in the years ahead? Undoubtedly there will be many surprises, but some of those forces are already apparent.

The rural-to-urban migration so critical to the postwar scene could not continue at its old pace. In fact, a mild reverse trend seems to be beginning—not enough to drain the cities but enough to generate significant economic development and jobs in rural settings. It is always dangerous to declare an end to technological change, but it does seem unlikely that anything as dramatic as the electronics, computer, television, nuclear power, wonder drugs, etc., of 1945–1975 will be equalled in 1975–2000. Maintaining the current average pace of productivity increases is likely to be a tough challenge in the years ahead. Demographers have been caught by surprise before, but it does not seem likely that the nation will rediscover how to make babies at the 1947–1957 rate. Only the labor-force participation of women, generated by the second world war, appears likely to continue unabated.

Demographically, a slower rate of labor-force growth and an aging labor force already seem foreordained. Implied also is a rising ratio of the retired to the economically active population, unless trends toward earlier retirement reverse. Perhaps an increase in the second-career trend will be the resolution. Immigration is already an important component of labor-force growth after a 50-year gap, and it may become the most important source of new manpower.

Productivity gains will depend increasingly on what happens in the service and government sectors. Opportunities for greater efficiency are present but unlikely to be as pervasive as those in manufacturing, communications, transportation, etc., have been in the past. It seems doubtful that the near 3-percent pace of productivity increase to which we have become accustomed in the postwar period can continue. The labor force and productivity outlet together forecast slower economic growth, a reduced rate of improvement in standards of living, and persistent inflationary pressures as various claimants attempt to maintain their customary rises in living standards.

With all these developments, youth unemployment should be a decreasing problem, though the black/white differential will probably persist and the transition from school to work will always include some pain. Racial discrimination in employment, which took 300 years to become engrained, is not about to disappear, though continued slow progress is likely.

The deterioration of the nuclear family, after virtual disappearance of the extended family, will continue. Female-headed families, now one out of eight white families and one of each three black families, will remain the core of the public-assistance problem. It is not a labor-market problem and cannot be solved there, though the creation of employment opportunities can help.

Nothing on the horizon suggests that the industry and occupation structure will depart markedly from the trends of the past quarter-century. Energy concerns will favor revival of the coal industry, expansion of nuclear power, and the beginnings of coal gasification and oil-shale development, all of which will have important localized impacts. The auto industry will be permanently impacted by smaller cars requiring less labor per unit, but overall the dislocations will not be major. Educational attainment will rise more slowly but will continue upward. The oversupply of college graduates will be responded to by rising educational requirements for jobs rather than by unemployment among the educated. The gap in educational attainment between men and women and black and white will disappear, but the income differential will not, though it will shrink. Geographical trends in jobs will be diverse—to the central city, suburban centers, and rural areas—but without favoring the most disadvantaged workers. Poverty populations should become less concentrated. The South, Southwest, and Mountain West should be the major population growth centers, with less tendency toward megalopolis on the coasts and around the Great Lakes.

Militant unionism will continue to sweep across the public sector into the private white-collar and professional ranks, with the blue-collars relatively quiet. Internationally, continued population pressures and food shortages cannot help but have an impact upon the United States and its labor markets.

Other critical forces can undoubtedly be identified and forecast by more knowledgeable minds. The point of this review is that, after the experiences of the period 1930–1975, manpower policies for the years ahead should be carefully planned in full recognition of (1) demographic, social, and economic trends, and (2) labor-market realities.

Whither Manpower Policy or Worker Status?

The manpower policies of the 1930s and 1960s were responses to both the long sweep of industrialization and its immediate consequences. Those of the 1930s, which were designed for permanence, were more fundamental, better thought through, and more significant for worker status. Those of the 1960s were primarily responses to changing demographic, social, and economic trends accelerated by the second world war and its immediate aftermath. They were generally successful, but only marginal in their impact. Their major shortcoming was failure to take labor-market reality into account in their formulation.

Now a new set of demographic, social, and economic forces has emerged, and policies of the next 25 years must be responsive to them. Everyone who will enter the labor force in the early 1990s is now born. Technological surprises do not overwhelm an economy in a few short years, though we now know that international relations may. There will be surprises, but a great many of both the supply and the demand developments can be foreseen a quarter-century ahead.

Manpower policy now seems stalled dead center. It has not progressed far beyond the 1930s, and few of the innovations of the 1960s were fundamental. Only the equal-employment-opportunity emphasis deserves that title. Now is not a time for new legislation. We would not know which way to move if we were compelled to do so. It is a time for basic and thorough reexamination. Any lasting improvement in worker status that is produced by manpower policy must rest on realistic understanding of labor markets and the practicality of various interventions into their workings. What is now needed is the same kind of fundamental thinking that went into the Social Security Act and the National Labor Relations Act, but extended 25 years out from 1975.

CHAPTER 7

The Transformation of Fair Employment Practices Policies

JAMES E. JONES, JR.
University of Wisconsin–Madison

I. Introduction

The writing of an essay on the transformation of federal fair-employment-practices policies since the 1930s is to undertake a review of the major portion of the story of the growth and development of the entire field. While one could assert, with some degree of validity, that federal fair employment efforts go back at least to the Emancipation Proclamation of 1863[1] and the establishment of the Freedmen's Bureau in 1865,[2] the modern fair-employment story is of much later vintage.

A generous dating of the beginning of federal policy in point would start with the Civil Service Act of 1883,[3] when Congress first adopted the principle of merit for federal employment. However, it was primarily in the interest of government efficiency that this law was enacted, and its effect upon minority employment was minimal at best.[4]

---

[1] After all, slavery is the ultimate in employment discrimination. One might argue, however, that the proclamation of the President was not a fair-employment measure, but a matter of wartime strategy. See Irving Dillard, "The Emancipation Proclamation in the Perspective of Time," 23 *Law in Transition* 95 (1963), at 95–100; see also Derrick Bell, *Race, Racism and American Law* (Boston: Little, Brown and Co., 1973), ch. 1.

[2] 13 Stat. 507 (1865). In an attempt to aid the former slaves, emancipated by the war and the law, Congress established the Freedman's Bureau in March 1865. The Bureau was directed by General O. O. Howard, appointed by the President, and, pursuant to its congressional mandate, provided "destitute and suffering refugees and freedmen and their wives and children" with, among other things, food, clothing, fuel, land, and work. The Bureau was created initially for the duration of the war and one year thereafter, but was continued by Congress over President Johnson's veto in July 1866. (14 Stat. 173)

[3] The Pendleton Act of 1883, 22 Stat. 403 (codified in scattered sections of 5 U.S.C.).

[4] See Frances Cousens, *Public Civil Rights Agencies and Fair Employment* (New York: Praeger Publishers, 1969), p. 5.

Section 42 U.S.C. 1981, one of the Reconstruction Acts of 1866, was potentially a fundamental fair-employment protection, but the early federal laws of 1866 through 1875 were effectively repealed by Supreme Court interpretation[5] and Section 1981 has only recently been resuscitated.[6]

The New Deal period should be mentioned in passing for the actions taken by the legislative and executive branches in originating the federal policy of equal opportunity in employment and training created through federal funds. These policies extended not only to direct federal employment and employment by federal contractors, but also to employment and training opportunities provided by grants-in-aid programs.[7]

While there was an abundance of policy pronouncements in statutes[8] and in administrative regulations where no statutory provisions existed,[9] these efforts were of little effect because there were no criteria whereby "discrimination" might be determined and rarely any administrative machinery or effective sanctions for enforcement.[10]

During the later 1930s and early 1940s, the advent of World War II brought about an upturn in the economy as the nation was forced into the dual role of producing for defense and rapidly raising and training a greatly expanded armed force. Even with the stress such "guns and butter" production placed upon manpower resources, the percentage of blacks in manufacturing was at a 30-year low. Only one in 20 defense workers was black, although blacks comprised 10 percent of the population, and

---

[5] See, e.g., *Civil Rights Cases,* 109 U.S. 3 (1883). See also Civil Rights Act, 42 U.S.C. 1981 (1870); Civil Rights Act, 42 U.S.C. 1982 (1866); Civil Rights Act, 42 U.S.C. 1984 (1875).

[6] See *Jones* v. *Alfred Mayer,* 392 U.S. 409 (1968), discussed *infra;* also, Note, "Jones v. Mayer: The Thirteenth Amendment and the Federal Anti-Discrimination Laws," 69 *Colum. L. Rev.* 1019 (1969).

[7] See Civil Rights Commission, *Employment, 1961 Commission on Civil Rights Report* (Washington: U.S. Government Printing Office, 1961), Book 3, ch. 2. See also Unemployment Relief Act of 1933, 48 Stat. 22 [no longer in effect]; First Supplemental Civil Functions Appropriations Act, 54 Stat. 1048 (1941).

[8] *Employment, supra* note 7, at 168, fns. 21–23.

[9] *Id.,* at 168, fn. 24.

[10] *Id.,* at 9. See also Marc Kruman, "Quotas for Blacks: The Public Works Administration and the Black Construction Worker," 16 *Labor History* 37 (Winter 1975), for a discussion of the Public Works Administration (PWA) program, a well-intentioned yet largely ineffective attempt to eliminate discrimination in the construction industry.

there was no more than 3 percent Negro participation in the skilled work force in the construction industry.[11]

[11] Herbert Northrop, *Organized Labor and the Negro* (New York: Harper and Bros., 1944), p. 19; also Louis Kesselman, *The Social Politics of FEPC* (Chapel Hill: University of North Carolina, 1948), p. 6.

TABLE 1*
EMPLOYMENT—14 YEARS OLD AND OVER—1940—BY RACE

Employment Status	All Classes	White	Negro
		%	
In Labor Force	52.2	51.6	58.2
Employed (except public emergency work)	47.7	44.3	48.4
At work	43.6	43.2	47.6
With a job but not at work	1.1	1.1	.8
On public emergency work	2.5	2.4	3.4
Seeking work	5.0	4.9	6.4
Experienced workers	4.3	4.1	5.7
New workers	.8	.8	.7
Not in Labor Force	47.8	48.4	41.8
Engaged in own housework	28.6	29.3	21.9
In school	8.9	9.0	8.1
Unable to work	5.2	5.1	6.5
In institutions	1.2	1.1	1.8
Others and not reported	3.9	3.9	3.6

* *Statistical Abstract of the United States*, 1944–45, p. 126.

TABLE II*
PERCENTAGE OF EMPLOYED PERSONS, 14 YEARS OLD AND OVER, IN MAJOR OCCUPATIONAL GROUPS, 1940

	Total Empl. Excluding Emerg. Wk.	Prof. Wkrs.	Semi-Prof.	Farmers & Fm. Mgrs.	Props., Mgrs. & Off. Wkrs.	Clerical, Sales., etc.	Craftsmen, Foremen, etc.
Total	45,166,083	6.4	1.0	11.5	8.4	16.8	11.3
White	40,495,089	6.9	1.1	11.1	9.2	18.5	12.3
Non-white	4,670,994	2.5	0.2	15.1	1.4	2.0	3.0

	Operatives etc.	Domestic Service	Service Workers	Farm Lab. Wage Wkrs.	Farm Lab. Unpaid (Family)	Laborers (excl. Farm)
Total	18.4	4.7	7.7	4.3	2.6	6.8
White	19.3	2.7	7.2	3.5	2.1	6.0
Non-white	10.5	21.9	11.8	11.1	6.6	14.0

** *American Year Book*, 1944.

When the defense program got under way, "Negroes were only on the sidelines of American Industrial Life."[12] Early efforts to determine the feasibility of voluntary absorption of blacks into defense industries revealed widespread resistance to their utilization, except in such minor capacities as porters and cleaners, by both management and labor.[13]

National, state, and local governments were also opposed to antidiscrimination programs, and discrimination was common in government agencies themselves. Segregation was the rule and was constitutionally acceptable. Thus, as the nation prepared for the war to make the world safe for democracy, its employment practices, as well as other aspects of life in America, revealed a most embarrassing contradiction.

> The wide use of democratic symbols by the government in an effort to unify the population and to wage psychological warfare upon the Axis nations helped to sharpen the contrast between ideals and realities. Negroes became increasingly agitated over their lot; some observers even despaired of their loyalty in the event of war. While succeeding events proved their loyalty was unimpeachable, deepening bitterness on the part of blacks was ample cause for concern.[14]

Efforts to accommodate the interests of blacks and other workers in organized labor is as painful a story as any other historical account of race in America.[15] It is perhaps naive to expect organized labor to reflect an attitude substantially different from that of the society from which it comes, but for two centuries black unionists have sustained the hope that such would be the case. And blacks have consistently made efforts to gain support of the labor unions.[16]

---

[12] Robert Weaver, *Negro Labor* (Port Washington, N.Y.: Kennikat Press, 1946), p. 15.

[13] Kesselman, *supra* note 11, at 3–9.

[14] *Id.*, at 13.

[15] See Philip Foner, *Organized Labor and the Black Worker, 1619–1973* (New York: Praeger Publishers, 1974).

[16] See Marc Karson and Ronald Radosh, "The American Federation of Labor and the Negro Worker, 1894–1949," in *The Negro and the American Labor Movement*, ed. Julius Jacobson (Garden City, N.Y.: Doubleday and Co., 1968). See also Philip Taft, *The A.F. of L., from the Death of Gompers to the Merger* (New York: Harper and Bros., 1959); Charles Wesley, *Negro Labor in the United States* (New York: Russell and Russell, 1927).

This is not a biography of A. Philip Randolph. However, as organizer and leader of the Brotherhood of Sleeping Car Porters, Randolph was a constant irritant to the leadership of the American Federation of Labor (AFL) as he fought continuously against discrimination. His initial attitude toward the AFL reflected black workers great distrust of the Federation, and he originally felt that a new federation had to be built on some basis other than trade autonomy and the exclusion of unskilled workers. At one time he asserted that the AFL was the most wicked machine for the propagation of race prejudice in the United States.[17] While this was Randolph's view in 1919, ten years later he had decided to seek admission of the Sleeping Car Porters to the AFL, not as an abandonment of his fight against discriminatory practices but with the view that the organization should take its place within the AFL where it could combat racial discrimination more effectively.

In 1933 the Sleeping Car Porters had a membership of 35,000. Even so, the Brotherhood was accepted not as an international organization, but on the basis of charters to separate local unions directly affiliated with the AFL.[18] While carrying on the fight against discrimination, against exclusion of blacks from union membership, and against auxiliary (segregated) locals within the House of Labor, Randolph also assumed the leadership among blacks to compel the government to address racial discrimination in hiring and other conditions of employment.

The Congress of Industrial Organizations (CIO), almost of necessity, took a different approach to the racial-discrimination matter. Founded upon the fundamental principle of organizing all workers and often engaged in competition with the AFL, the CIO viewed the exclusion of black workers from membership as a handicap too serious to overcome.

It has been noted that the CIO commitment to racial equality, while unquestionable, was pursued more through CIO influence in the general political process than through direct action. CIO strength supported such progressive measures as were adopted— such as the war-time FEPC—but did not, and probably could

---

[17] See Karson and Radosh, *supra* note 16, at 161–62.
[18] *Id.*, at 162.

not, initiate or decisively shape any of them.[19] It has been suggested that most advances secured by black industrial workers during the CIO's lifetime were due to dominant economic forces, such as prolonged labor shortages, rather than to the power of the CIO unions. "CIO affiliates gladly capitalized on these conditions to secure concessions for Negro workers from employers; AFL affiliates were in many cases far more resistant to these forces, and did not generally welcome the threat that they posed to traditional racial patterns and practices. Nevertheless, CIO practices altered those of AFL Unions often to a considerable extent."[20] It has also been noted that by the time of the AFL-CIO merger (1955) the CIO had largely abandoned any vigorous commitment to improve the position of blacks through direct union action and that it did not seriously fight to obtain the incorporation of the CIO union's standard of conduct in this regard in the merged organization.[21]

Some commentators claim that the CIO unions sparked the transformation of American labor from an autocratic, ineffectual minority into the largest labor movement in the Western World. In addition to transforming industrial relations in the mass-production industries, it organized thousands of blacks and broke down historic barriers between blacks and trade unions. The new generation of leaders developed in the CIO included for the first time numbers of blacks, some of whom reached high posts. However, even Sidney Hillman was unable to persuade President Roosevelt to adopt a fair employment practices commission. It was only the threat of the first modern march on Washington, led by A. Philip Randolph, that eventually forced the President's hand.[22]

A. Philip Randolph and the March on Washington Movement

Although there had been previous protests lodged and meetings called to oppose job discrimination in defense industries,[23]

---

[19] See Sumner Rosen, "The C.I.O. Era 1935–55," in Jacobson, *supra* note 16, at 188, 208.

[20] *Id.*, at 190.

[21] *Id.*, at 190.

[22] *Id.*, at 207–208.

[23] Julius Jacobson, "Union Conservatism: A Barrier to Racial Equality," in Jacobson, *supra* note 16, at 12.

the first direct action was taken by Randolph, president of the predominantly black Brotherhood of Sleeping Car Porters, when he convened a conference of top black leaders in February 1941. Out of this effort emerged the March on Washington movement, embodying his theory of nonviolent direct action. This initiative proved to be the catalyst for the eventual establishment of the "first government-wide administrative machinery designed to implement a national policy of non-discriminatory employment and training."[24]

Randolph threatened a March on Washington for July 1, 1941, of 10,000 people—eventually raising the ante to 100,000[25]—unless the government took some meaningful action. President Roosevelt, after unsuccessful attempts to dissuade Randolph,[26] and recognizing the possible international reaction to such a demonstration, issued Executive Order 8802 establishing a Fair Employment Practices Committee in the Office of Production Management.[27]

Executive Order 8802—The Executive's Mobilization of the Federal Power of Purse

The full story of presidential fair-employment-practices committees has yet to be told and would far exceed the dimensions of this paper.[28] However, brief mention is warranted of the five-man Fair Employment Practices Committee (FEPC) established under the original Executive Order. The order declared it to be the policy of the government "to encourage full participation in the national defense program by all citizens of the United States, regardless of race, creed, color, or national origin, in the firm belief that the democratic way of life within the Nation can be defended successfully only with the help and support of all groups within its borders."[29]

---

[24] *Employment, supra* note 7, at 10.
[25] Duane Lockard, *Toward Equal Opportunity* (New York: Macmillan Co., 1968), p. 17.
[26] Kesselman, *supra* note 11, at 13, 14.
[27] Executive Order No. 8802, 3 C.F.R., 1938–43 Comp., 957.
[28] For discussions of fair employment practice committees from 1941 to 1963, see Paul Norgren and Samuel Hill, *Toward Fair Employment* (New York: Columbia University Press, 1964), pp. 148–79. See also Michael Sovern, *Legal Restraints on Racial Discrimination in Employment* (New York: Twentieth Century Fund, 1966), chs. 2, 5.
[29] Executive Order No. 8802, Preamble, 3 C.F.R., 1938–43 Comp., 957.

The order was broad in scope, applying to all defense contracts and vocational-training programs administered by federal agencies and, arguably, to employment by the federal government, though there is some dispute as to the clarity of this coverage. It imposed upon both employers and labor organizations the duty to provide for full and equitable participation of all workers in the defense industry without discrimination.

The FEPC was authorized to receive and investigate complaints, to take "appropriate steps" to redress valid grievances, and to recommend to federal agencies and the President whatever measures it deemed necessary and proper to carry out the purposes of the order. However, the FEPC had no funds to operate regional offices and a staff of only eight people. As its potential effectiveness in investigating and processing complaints was limited, it concentrated its activities on drafting policy and conducting public hearings throughout the country. Lacking any direct enforcement powers, it had to rely primarily on publicity, moral suasion, and negotiations to effect any recommendations it made, or upon referral of matters to the President.[30]

Most noteworthy about the first FEPC order was the fact that it was issued at all. Its legality rested on two presidential prerogatives, the power of the administrative head of the executive branch to determine conditions under which the government would do business, and the power of the commander-in-chief to assure adequate supplies for military forces.[31]

After interagency disputes precipitated the resignation of some of the members of the earlier FEPC, President Roosevelt issued Executive Order 9346 establishing a new FEPC as an autonomous agency in the Executive Office of the President. It had a full-time chairman and six part-time members selected from the ranks of labor, industry, and the public. The authority with respect to labor organizations was extended to include discrimination in union membership, and its powers previously restricted to the redress of individual grievances, were enlarged to allow it to take appropriate measures to eliminate discrimination. Additionally, and perhaps more importantly, it was provided with an increased

---

[30] See *Employment, supra* note 7, at 9–12.
[31] See Kesselman, *supra* note 11, at 15, fn. 31.

budget that enabled it to employ a staff of 120 people and to open 15 field offices. During the three-year period of its existence, it processed some 8,000 complaints and conducted 30 public hearings. However, the Committee still lacked enforcement powers.

Perhaps the only lasting significance of these early endeavors is the assertion of the power of the presidency to address discrimination. Although the issue has not yet been addressed directly by the Supreme Court, argument can be made that the constitutional admonition that the President "take care that the laws and the Constitution[32] are faithfully executed" provides him with sufficient responsibility and authority to act, independent of congressional actions.

Less notable, but of some import, are the early attempts to use the tripartite arrangement—representatives of management, labor, and the public—in the administration of what was at best an unpopular program. One might argue that the first FEPC was tripartite plus one, since the major minority group as well as labor, management, and the public, were represented in its membership. However, while involving representatives of the affected groups in the administration of a program is an acceptable principle of the human-relations-in-industry school, its effectiveness in programs aimed at employment discrimination has yet to be demonstrated. Efforts were made to secure congressional support for the program and to endow the committee with enforcement powers. Although success was to elude the advocates for 20 years, the earlier programs demonstrated the necessity for congressional action if effective and lasting antidiscrimination programs were to be achieved.

The Roosevelt wartime FEPC eventually succumbed to congressional attack. The Russell rider, which was passed in 1944, provided that no appropriations could be allotted to any agency established by executive order and in existence for more than one year if Congress had not specifically appropriated the money for such agency or specifically authorized the expenditure of funds

---

[32] The commands of the Fifth and Thirteenth Amendments to the Constitution are not to be violated by federal executive action.

for it.[33] The FEPC was granted appropriations; but in 1945 it was given just enough money to liquidate its affairs, and it went out of existence with the issuance of its final report in 1947.[34]

The following year, in an effort to clarify the Russell rider, Congress enacted the Independent Office Appropriation Act of 1946, which made it clear that interdepartmental committees were not subject to the Russell rider prohibition.[35] This interagency exception to the Russell rider proved to be the salvation of future presidential activity in the equal-employment area. To get around the strictures of the previous Act, it was only necessary to appoint representatives of two or more federal agencies to the committees, along with such other members as would be necessary and appropriate. In this format the presidential committee structure survived until 1965.

A final comment on the early FEPC's significant contributions: President Roosevelt having set in train the exercise of executive authority to deal with the employment-discrimination problem, each subsequent president has utilized that authority in some fashion, either by executive order of his own or by continuing those programs inherited from a predecessor. Between the Roosevelt orders and the initiative of John Kennedy 20 years later,[36] no novel concepts emerged from presidential programs that would be deserving of comment in a brief overview.

II. The Courts and the Duty of Fair Representation in Phase I, Steele v. Louisville Railroad Co. and Its Progeny (1944–1955)

In 1944, in *Steele* v. *Louisville Railroad Co.,* the Supreme Court ruled that the black firemen might be entitled to both

---

[33] See Independent Officers Appropriation Act (Russell amendment), Tit. II, Sec. 213, 58 Stat. 387 (1944), as amended 31 U.S.C. §696 (1958).

[34] See *Employment, supra* note 7, ch. 2.

[35] Tit. II, §214, 59 Stat. 134 (1945), as amended 31 U.S.C. §691 (1958): "Appropriations of the executive departments and independent establishments of the Government shall be available for the expense of committees, boards or other interagency groups engaged in authorized activities of common interest to such departments and establishments and composed in whole or in part of representatives thereof who receive no additional compensation by virtue of such membership: Provided that employees of such departments and establishments rendering service for such committees, boards or other groups, other than as representatives, shall receive no additional compensation by virtue of such service."

[36] Discussed *infra.*

injunctive relief and damages for the union's breach of duty of fair representation and declared:

> So long as a labor union assumes to act as a statutory representative of a craft, it cannot rightly refuse to perform the duty, which is inseparable from the power of representation conferred upon it, to represent the entire membership of the craft. While the statute does not deny to such a bargaining labor organization the right to determine eligibility to its membership, it does require the union, in collective bargaining and in making contracts with the carrier, to represent non-union or minority union members of the craft without hostile discrimination, fairly, impartially, and in good faith.[37]

The brave potential of the duty-of-fair-representation doctrine was demonstrated by a decision by the Supreme Court of Kansas in *Betts* v. *Easley*.[38] The Kansas Supreme Court interpreted the doctrine to reach all aspects of labor-management relations as well as the internal affairs of the union organization, except those internal matters unrelated to the collective bargaining process— that is, social integration. This broad application of the doctrine was not followed by other courts, and in spite of a decision on point issued the same day as *Steele*,[39] it was not conceded until 1955 that unions under the National Labor Relations Act had the same obligations as the brotherhoods under the Railway Labor Act.[40]

The doctrinal base for the statutory interpretation of the existence of the duty of fair representation that emerged from *Steele* was that to rule otherwise would raise grave constitutional questions. It is interesting to speculate what might have been the impact of the doctrine of the duty of fair representation that emerged from *Steele* v. *Louisville*[41] if that case had come after the deci-

---

[37] *Steele* v. *Louisville & Nashville Railroad Co. et al.*, 323 U.S. 192 (1944), at 204.

[38] *Betts* v. *Easley*, 169 Pac.2d 831 (1946).

[39] *Wallace Corp.* v. *NLRB*, 323 U.S. 248 (1944).

[40] See *Syres* v. *Oil Workers International Union Local No. 23*, 223 F.2d 739 (5th Cir. 1955), rev'd 350 U.S. 892 (1955). See also Neil Herring, "The Fair Representation Doctrine: An Effective Weapon Against Union Discrimination," 24 *Maryland L. Rev.* 113 (1964), at 114–15.

[41] 323 U.S. 192 (1944).

sions of the Supreme Court in the late 1940s and early 1950s, culminating in *Brown* v. *Board of Education*.[42] The potential effectiveness of the doctrine of the duty of fair representation has yet to be realized in spite of its more than 30 years of existence within the judicial arsenal.[43] The doctrine as a judicial construct has survived the passage of Title VII of the Civil Rights Act of 1964 and continues as viable federal labor policy with even more potential as an unfair labor practice under the National Labor Relations Act.[44]

III. The Responsive States—The Emergence of Little FEPCs (1945–1948)

In our march of time from the 1930s to the present, we should note that between 1945 and 1949, eight fair employment practice measures were enacted into state law.[45] These early laws were passed in states in which there were heavy concentrations of blacks, and there is an obvious relationship between these factors.[46]

---

[42] Mr. Justice Murphy, who concurred in the *Steele* decision, thought the issue should have been squarely faced on constitutional grounds. However, he was not that persuasive, for it was not until *Shelley* v. *Kraemer*, 334 U.S. 1 (1947), and *Hurd* v. *Hodge*, 334 U.S. 24 (1947), that the Supreme Court adopted the view that the Fourteenth Amendment's equal-protection clause prohibited the enforcement of restricted covenants by state courts. In *Hurd* v. *Hodge*, the Court found judicial enforcement of restrictive covenants by the District of Columbia courts to violate public policies expressed in statute. The Court, however, did not reach the Fifth Amendment issue. It is significant, I believe, that not until *Brown* v. *Board of Education of Topeka*, 349 U.S. 294 (1954), holding separate inherently unequal and violative of the Fourteenth Amendment, do we have the Fifth Amendment question squarely faced. In the companion case of *Bolling* v. *Sharpe*, 347 U.S. 497 (1954), the Court, though it did not quite equate the equal-protection clause of the Fourteenth Amendment and the due-process clause of the Fifth Amendment, nonetheless held that racial segregation in public schools in the District of Columbia was a denial of due-process of law guaranteed by the Fifth Amendment.

Later, in 1961, in *Burton* v. *Wilmington Parking Authority*, 365 U.S. 715 (1961), the Supreme Court started to unravel those fact situations in which the government agency is so intertwined with private discrimination as to make such private discrimination state action. Had these three concepts been more firmly fixed in 1944, or had *Steele* v. *Louisville* been perhaps a 1962 case, the duty of fair representation concept might have made a more effective contribution in securing the status of minority workers.

[43] See, e.g., Herring, *supra* note 40.

[44] See discussion of "The Duty of Fair Representation, Phase 2," *infra*.

[45] Lockard, *supra* note 25, at 22–24.

[46] *Id.*, at 24–27.

IV. Marches, Sit-ins, and Other Protests—The Turbulent Fifties

As of May 7, 1954, "separate but equal was the law of the land"; however, "separate but unequal was, and still is, a practice and a reality."

The American Negro of the Fifties lived in a state of constant humiliation. His dignity as an individual was not admitted in the North or the South, and his

TABLE II

THE TIMING OF PASSAGE OF ANTIDISCRIMINATION
LAWS HAVING ADMINISTRATIVE ENFORCEMENT*

Year	Fair Employment Practices	Public Accommodations	Private Housing
1945	New York, New Jersey		
1946	Massachusetts		
1947	Connecticut		
1948			
1949	New Mexico, Oregon, Rhode Island, Washington	Connecticut, New Jersey	
1950			
1951			
1952		New York, Rhode Island	
1953		Massachusetts, Oregon	
1954			
1955	Michigan, Minnesota, Pennsylvania		
1956			
1957	Wisconsin, Colorado	Washington, Colorado	
1958			
1959	California, Ohio		Massachusetts, Connecticut, Colorado, Oregon
1960	Delaware		
1961	Illinois, Kansas, Missouri	Ohio, Pennsylvania	New Jersey, Minnesota, New York, Pennsylvania
1962			
1963	Alaska, Indiana, Hawaii	Alaska, Indiana, Kansas, Michigan	Alaska, California, Michigan
1964		Delaware, Maryland	
1965	Arizona, Maryland, Nevada, Utah, New Hampshire, Nebraska	Arizona, Minnesota, Missouri, New Hampshire	Indiana, Rhode Island, New Hampshire, Ohio, Wisconsin
1966	Kentucky	Kentucky	

* The FEP, public accommodation, and housing laws without enforcement powers are not included; therefore the dates indicate the time when enforcement powers were acquired, not necessarily the original date of passage.

worth was so demeaned that even other non-white peo-
ples of the world had little respect for him. School desegregation, disfranchisement, segregation of public facilities and overt police brutality aside, the true condition
of the Negro is best reflected by his relative position
as a wage earner and professional man in American Society. . . .

Professional Pollyannas, particularly among white liberals, point with pride to the fact that the American
Negro has more income today than he has ever had before. That is not the issue; everybody has more income
today than he ever had before, and consumer goods cost
more today than they ever have before. The crucial issue
is that the income of the American Negro family showed
no progress in relation to the income of the white family
during the decade of the Fifties. As a matter of fact, the
relative average income of the Negro family declined
during the last two years of the Fifties.[47]

The late Louis Lomax, a black writer in the early 1960s, thus
captured the condition of the American Negro as of the date of
the *Brown* v. *Board of Education* decision. Although there is no
dearth of writing covering the period 1954–1960, the mere mention of a few critical incidents from the period should evoke
memories of the "social climate of the times":

On the surface the school integration cases involved the
right of children of taxpayers to attend public schools.
But the real issue was deeper than that; it involved the
entire status of the black man as an individual in American society. The lynching of Emmett Till—the mur-
derers were exonerated then confessed in Look magazine—
and the harassed Negro students ducking in and out of
previously all white schools were but current symptoms
of a malady that had afflicted the nation. . . .[48]

The explosion—and no one would have taken it for
that—came on December 1, 1955, the day Mrs. Rosa Parks
boarded the Cleveland Avenue Bus in Montgomery, Alabama. And the Negro revolt is properly dated from the

---

[47] Louis Lomax, *The Negro Revolt* (New York: Harper and Row, 1962),
p. 67.
    [48] *Id.*, at 76.

moment Mrs. Parks said "No" to the bus driver's demand that she get up and let a white man have her seat.[49]

Thus, the bus boycott in Montgomery, Alabama, was launched, and a young Baptist minister, Dr. Martin Luther King, was elected president of the Montgomery Improvement Association and went on to fame and martyrdom.

On February 1, 1960, four freshmen from the all-Negro Agricultural and Technical College at Greensboro, North Carolina, walked into the local Woolworth dime store and sat down at the all white lunch counter. When told to move, they refused; when the manager closed down the counter, the students opened their textbooks and began to study their lessons; when the local radio station interrupted its program to flash the news, scores of other students from A and T poured into town and joined the demonstration.

The 2nd major battle of the Negro revolt was underway. . . .[50]

On February 1, 1961, forty-year-old James Farmer became national director of the Congress of Racial Equality. On March 13, CORE announced that it would conduct freedom rides through the South to test racial discrimination in interstate travel terminals. On April 28, CORE wrote President Kennedy and advised him that the rides would soon be underway and asked for federal protection. On May 4, after three days of training and indoctrination, the freedom riders began their journey for Washington, D. C.[51]

The noted black historian, John Hope Franklin, writing in 1965 captures the hope and the climate at the beginning of the sixties.

The drive to destroy the two worlds of race has reached a new, dramatic, and somewhat explosive state in recent years. The forces arrayed in behalf of maintaining these two worlds have been subjected to ceaseless and powerful attacks by the increasing numbers committed to the elimination of racism in American life. Through tech-

---

[49] *Id.*, at 81.
[50] *Id.*, at 121.
[51] *Id.*, at 133.

niques of demonstrating, picketing, sitting-in, and boy-cotting they have not only harassed their foes but mar-shalled their forces. Realizing that another ingredient was needed, they have pressed for new and better laws and the active support of government. At the local and state levels they began to secure legislation in the 1940's to guarantee the civil rights of all, eliminate discrimina-tion in employment, and achieve decent public and pri-vate housing for all.

While it is not possible to measure the influence of public opinion and the drive for equality, it can hardly be denied that over the past five or six years public opin-ion has shown a marked shift toward vigorous support of the civil rights movement. . . .

The models of city ordinances and state laws and the increased political influence of civil rights advocates stim-ulated new action on the federal level. Civil rights acts were passed in 1957, 1960, and 1964—after almost com-plete federal inactivity in this sphere for more than three quarters of a century. Strong leadership on the part of the executive and favorable judicial interpretation of old as well as new laws have made it clear that the war against the two worlds of race now enjoys the sanction of the law and its interpreters. In many respects this consti-tutes the most significant development in the struggle against racism in the present century.[52]

V. The Golden Sixties and the Advent of Affirmative Action—Executive Order 10925 and the Kennedy/Johnson Era

When John F. Kennedy assumed the presidency, the prospects for orderly process in civil rights were far from bright. Years of inaction during the preceding adminis-tration were yielding a predictable harvest of discontent. The civil rights movement was both accelerating and as-suming new and more demanding forms. The strategy of almost exclusive reliance on court action, brilliantly led by the legal staff of the National Association for the Advancement of Colored People, was giving way to tech-niques of mass protest and non-violent direct action. . . .

---

[52] John Hope Franklin, "The Two Worlds of Race," 94 *Daedalus* 899 (Fall 1965), at 917–18.

Crisis was no longer the occasional and accidental by-product of court directed change, but the continuing and conscious result of planned confrontation between opponents and defenders of the existing racial order. . . .[53]

Kennedy's earliest and most promising executive action was the issuance in April 1961 of Executive Order 10925 on equal opportunity in federal and federally connected employment. (It was supplemented in 1963 by Executive Order 11114 regulating employment in federally assisted construction.) The Order greatly strengthened standards of compliance and methods of enforcement applying to contractors and federal agencies. It also established, under the chairmanship of then Vice-President Lyndon B. Johnson, a committee of public and private members with broad powers of regulation and review of the agencys' programs. Civil rights spokesmen greeted the order as impressive evidence that in Mr. Johnson's words, "we mean business." Administrators of federal programs affected by the directive also saw the action as an indication of strong presidential concern, conferring high priority on the employment effort.[54]

The most significant aspects of Executive Order 10925 were (1) the requirements that contractors "take affirmative action to insure that applicants are employed, and that employees are treated during employment without regard to their race, creed, color or national origin"; and (2) the fact that sanctions, which might be imposed for violation of these contractual obligations, along with procedures providing for elementary due process in imposing such sanctions, were specifically enumerated in the order.[55]

By far the most important contribution of the Kennedy Executive Order was the creative utilization of affirmative action, a remedial concept usually imposed after determination of guilt, as a requirement for doing business with the government. The "legislative history" of this order suggests that it was an out-

---

[53] Harold C. Fleming, "The Federal Executive and Civil Rights: 1961–1965," 94 *Daedalus* 921 (Fall 1965), at 921.

[54] *Id.*, at 932.

[55] Executive Order No. 10925, Sec. 312–314, 3 C.F.R., 1959–63 Comp., 448 (1961).

growth of the experiences of an earlier committee chaired by Richard Nixon when he was Vice-President.[56]

The threat of enforcement implicit in the inclusion of provisions for the imposition of sanctions as well as procedures to protect the rights of contractors gathered dust for the first five years of the new Executive Order. A voluntary approach symbolized by the Plans for Progress program was in the ascendency during that period.[57]

The Kennedy order utilized the tripartite committee structure of earlier executive approaches, and persons from national labor unions served on the President's Committee on Equal Employment Opportunity (PCEEO) as they had on committees under predecessor orders. The Kennedy order directed its committee to use its best efforts to cause any labor union representative of workers who are or may be engaged in work on government contracts to cooperate with the purposes of the order. The committee was also authorized to hold hearings, to submit reports to the President, and to recommend remedial action in connection with union practices as well as to refer such matters to agencies—state, local or federal—that might have enforcement authority.

The Executive Order directed contractors to obtain statements in writing from the labor union officials with whom they did business to the effect that the union's practices did not discriminate and that the unions would affirmatively cooperate with the implementation of the policies and provisions of the Executive Order.

In connection with the Plans for Progress, under which major contractors took the pledge to promote the policies of the Executive Order, leaders of national unions were also asked to sign statements committing their organizations to nondiscrimination. By the winter of 1962, 67 national labor organizations, all affil-

---

[56] The President's Committee on Government Contracts was appointed by President Eisenhower in September 1952 and continued in operation for more than seven years. See *Pattern for Progress, Final Report to President Eisenhower from the Committee on Government Contracts* (1960). See also Norgren and Hill, *supra* note 28; *Employment, supra* note 7.

[57] See Richard Nathan, "Jobs and Civil Rights, the Role of the Federal Government in Promoting Equal Opportunity in Employment and Training" (Washington: U.S. Government Printing Office, 1969); Fleming, *supra* note 53. See also James E. Jones, Jr., "Federal Contract Compliance in Phase II—The Dawning of the Age of Enforcement of Equal Opportunity Obligations," 4 *Georgia L. Rev.* 756 (1970).

iated with the AFL-CIO, formally adopted the program. However, 17 national AFL-CIO affiliates and a number of unaffiliated organizations either refused or failed to sign the pledge.[58]

One of the obvious difficulties with the program, resting as it did on the contracting authority, was the extent to which jurisdiction was lacking over those with whom no contract existed. Such is the structural weakness in the Executive Order approach. However, as later developed, resort to the courts to prohibit union interference with the contractual relationship between the government and the employer proved to be a viable sanction.[59]

In evaluating the program under Executive Order 10925, in 1966 Michael Sovern called it "a phenomenon familiar to biology as well as politics—the powerful offspring of feeble progenitors." He went on to evaluate the gains, probably attributable to the Committee, as both substantial and trivial. Assessing progress statistically, for example, he noted an increase in the employment of blacks in the total work forces of 103 Plans for Progress companies from 5.1 percent to 5.7 percent. At the same time he pointed out that a study of 4,600 establishments filing the appropriate forms indicated an increase in the representation of blacks among their white-collar workers from 1.2 percent to 1.3 percent, or a rise of one tenth of one percentage point. However, expressed in gross figures, those gains are substantial. The less-than-1-percent gain among the Plans for Progress signers occurred because blacks were hired to fill 40,998 of the companies' 341,734 vacancies, or 12 percent of all the vacancies. The white-collar rise represented a net gain of 1,830 white-collar jobs, or an increase of 17.4 percent of Negro white-collar employment at at time when total white-collar employment among the companies increased by only 1.9 percent.[60]

Harold C. Fleming,[61] however, in his evaluation of the pro-

[58] See Norgren and Hill, *supra* note 28, at 175–76.

[59] See *Local 189, United Papermakers and Paperworkers and Crown Zellerbach Corp* v. *U.S.*, 416 F.2d 980 (5th Cir. 1969), *cert. den.* 397 U.S. 919 (1970). See also *U.S.* v. *Sheet Metal Workers Local 36*, 280 F.Supp 719 (E.D.Mo. 1968), *rev'd* 416 F.2d 123 (8th Cir. 1969); *U.S.* v. *Building and Construction Trades Council*, 271 F.Supp. 454 (E.D.Mo. 1966); *U.S.* v. *Building and Construction Trades Council*, 271 F.Supp. 497 (E.D.Mo. 1966); *Local 53, Heat and Frost I. & A.W.* v. *Volger*, 407 F.2d 1047 (5th Cir. 1969).

[60] Sovern, *supra* note 28, at 160.

[61] Fleming, *supra* note 53, at 921–47.

gram, concluded that despite the energetic performance of the earlier years, the implementation of the Executive Order 10925 had fallen below expectations. He attributed the shortfall in part to the lack of jurisdiction over labor unions, the advent of automation and resulting decline in less skilled jobs, inadequate education and training and therefore limited supply of qualified blacks for jobs, and so forth. He pointed out, however, that two things that were vitally necessary for effective use of the contracting power were "steady insistence on the employers' obligation through the channels of contract management, including the use of sanctions when necessary, and strong and continuing backing for this approach from high officials in the administration. Voluntary action going beyond the requirements of the Order could be a desirable adjunct, as long as it was kept wholly distinct from, and secondary to, the contractual obligation."[62] Unfortunately, these administrative conditions were not fully maintained and the high sense of priority and presidential interest initially communicated to contracting agencies soon diminished. Moreover, the committee was beset with internal dissension over the balance to be struck between persuasion, education, and promotion of voluntary action, on the one hand, and systematic compliance-enforcement efforts on the other.[63]

The years 1962 and 1963 again saw the nation racked with racial turmoil. The demonstrations against the enrollment of James Meredith in the "ole Miss" law school in Oxford, Mississippi, and the rioting on the campus there, the weeks of demonstrations in Birmingham, Alabama, where marching blacks were harassed by savage police dogs, fire hoses, and mass arrests, the murder of the NAACP's Medgar Evers in Jackson, Mississippi, and the bombing of the black church and the death of children in Sunday school in Birmingham shocked the nation and triggered a chain reaction of protests. In one 10-week period, the Justice Department counted a nationwide total of 758 racial demonstrations.[64]

The culmination of these activities was a massive march on Washington in the Summer of 1963. It would be difficult to

---

[62] *Id.*, at 933.
[63] *Id.*, at 933–34.
[64] *Id.*, at 941–42.

attribute the subsequent enactment by the Congress of the historic Civil Rights Act of 1964 solely to that march on Washington. However, it is also difficult to avoid the symbolic association between the passage of the Civil Rights Act of 1964 and the march and the initiation of the first FEP program in response to a threatened march in 1941. It would also be remiss to fail to mention that in the forefront of the massive march was one A. Philip Randolph, 74-years-young, as well as innumerable representatives of the American labor movement. Although what eventually emerged from Congress was less than the hoped-for national fair-employment-practice legislation (and there are some who might have preferred no bill to the compromise that emerged), the Civil Rights Act of 1964 was a comprehensive measure, one section of which, Title VII, was devoted to equal employment opportunity.

Clearly, the labor movement is entitled to claim some political credits for the passage of the Act in 1964. It is also deserving of credit, or blame, for some of the ambiguities in the law, if not some of its major weaknesses. It would hardly be fair to saddle George Meany with responsibility for the Mansfield-Dirksen compromise, but specific aspects of the law, which will be discussed below with regard to limitations on so-called preferences, are attributable to organized labor's influence. So, too, are efforts to use Title VII to kill the Executive Order program on affirmative action.

Michael Sovern[65] provides a contemporaneous analysis of the new Title VII of the Civil Rights Act of 1964 as well as of other programs current at the time. I doubt that the EEOC will ever escape the phrase-making Sovern who dubbed Congress's creature "a poor enfeebled thing with power to conciliate but not to compell."[66] On the positive side, "Congress at last" enacted a measure at the federal level purporting to provide comprehensive protection against employment discrimination. Unexpectedly, and in the minds of most people an act of mischief by Congressman Smith of Virginia, the prohibitions of the law were extended to discrimination on the basis of sex.

There are a number of factors worth noting about the Civil

---

[65] *Supra* note 28.
[66] Sovern, *supra* note 28, at 205.

Rights Act of 1964 as it existed for the first eight years. First, the administrative structure did not follow the National Labor Relations Act model, a more comprehensive and uniform approach to labor problems. Moreover, it did not follow the usual competing model of the Fair Labor Standards Act. The Commission was neither fish nor fowl nor good red herring. It had only the power to investigate and conciliate and then to refer. The Justice Department was provided with a separate jurisdictional base to litigate pattern-and-practice cases. Upon the failure of the process of conciliation, the private plaintiff was entitled to seek his or her own lawyer and go to court. Thus, ultimate judicial enforcement of individual claims was on the slender financial shoulders of the plaintiffs. A curious lapse of drafting did permit the Commission to go into court to seek enforcement of orders that might have been obtained through private litigation, and in its early days the Commission made creative use of *amicus* appearances.

As we have grown accustomed to anticipating when a new regulatory apparatus is established, those entities that are to be subject to its regulation immediately seek position and influence in the administration of the program. The fledgling EEOC was no exception, and close scrutiny of earlier appointments could probably track many of them to employers, unions, civil rights organizations, and other constituencies.

What is amazing about the Commission's role in the early enforcement of the Act is that so reckless an entity had any effect at all. However, while the emerging equal-employment law was influenced primarily by the energies of private attorneys representing the plaintiffs, and secondarily by the Justice Department's strategic litigation under its pattern-and-practice authority, the "poor enfeebled thing" is entitled to a share of the credit. How much credit? Perhaps less than its share of blame for the many criticized shortcomings of the program during its first eight years.

The Duty of Fair Representation in Phase 2—The NLRB and the Failure in the Duty as an Unfair Labor Practice

Michael Sovern, writing in 1963,[67] noted that the resistance

---

[67] Michael Sovern, "Race Discrimination and the National Labor Relations Act: The Brave New World of Miranda," *New York University, Sixteenth Annual Conference on Labor* (New York: Matthew Bender and Co., 1963), p. 3.

of blacks to the pattern of discrimination by unions rarely evoked the unequivocal holdings of *Steele* and the decisions that followed it. He observed that resort to the courts to redress a union's failure to represent had occurred on an average of less than once a year since *Steele* was decided in 1944, an omission attributable at least in part to the difficulty in obtaining counsel familiar with the intricacies of federal labor legislation. This may be an indirect or unintended comment on the exclusion of blacks from labor law practice, intentionally or accidentally, during most of the period following enactment of federal labor law.

The obvious advantage of going to the National Labor Relations Board was, and is, that the NLRB acts in the public interest, and the cost of pursuing remedies before it, or before the courts, are borne by the government. However, prior to the "Brave New World" of *Miranda*,[68] the NLRB's remedies were minimal and largely ineffectual. For years, the most available to minority supplicants was the revocation of the certification of the union, a remedy rarely, if ever, invoked.[69] On a number of occasions, the NLRB had indicated its willingness to revoke a certification, but it did not exercise the power until 1964. In an important bridge decision, *Pioneer Bus Co.*,[70] the Board stated, in dicta, that the execution of a racially discriminatory contract warranted the revocation of the certification of the union. That particular case involved the removal of the contract bar to election, although the offending union had a collective bargaining agreement that had not expired. The Board said:

> The Board will not permit its contract bar rules to be utilized to shield contracts such as those here involved from the challenge from otherwise appropriate election petitions. We therefore hold that, where the bargaining representative of employees in an appropriate unit executes separate contracts, or even a single contract, discriminating between Negro and white employees on ra-

[68] *Id.* This refers to *Miranda Fuel Co.*, 125 NLRB 454 (1959), *rev'd* 284 F.2d 861 (2d Cir. 1960), *cert. granted* 366 U.S. 763 (1960); *on remand*, 140 NLRB 181 (1962), *enf. den.*, 326 F.2d 172 (2d Cir. 1963).

[69] See *Larus & Bros. Co.*, 62 NLRB 1075 (1945); *Hughes Tool Co.*, 104 NLRB 318 (1953), and cases cited therein.

[70] 140 NLRB 54, 51 LRRM 1546 (1962).

cial lines, the Board will not deem such contracts as a
bar to an election.[71]

In the *Miranda Fuel Co.*,[72] case, the NLRB, in a split decision, decided that Section 7 of the NLRA gave employees the
right to be free from unfair or irrelevant or invidious treatment
by their bargaining agent in matters affecting their employment.
Among the rights protected by Section 7 is the right to be represented fairly. Therefore, when a union represents an employee
unfairly or fails to represent him at all, it coerces or restrains
him in the exercise of his Section 7 rights and thereby violates
Section 8 (b) (1). Moreover, when an employer accedes to a
union's request made in violation of the duty, he, too, has interfered with the employee's Section 7 rights and accordingly is
in violation of Section 8 (b) (1). Additionally, the Board held
that a statutory bargaining representative and an employer also
violate Sections 8 (b) (2) and 8 (a) (3) when, for arbitrary or irrelevant reasons, the union attempts to cause or does cause an
employer to derogate the employment status of an employee. The
Miranda Fuel case did not involve race. However, on the heels
of the controversial decision, the Board was presented with a race
case in *Hughes Tool Co.* and issued its decision in 1964.[73] The
Hughes Tool case involved separate locals for blacks and whites
operating under a joint certification, a practice the Board had
previously approved and which practice aided and abetted segregation and was maintained throughout the South by various
labor organizations. In brief, a black officer of Local No. 2 applied for a job opening covered by an apprenticeship provision
restricted to members of Local No. 1. Upon the company's declaration that the grievant was ineligible for the posted opening,
the union refused to process the grievance. The plaintiff and the
black local filed unfair labor practice charges alleging a violation
of 8 (b) (1) (9). It was concluded that by failing to investigate
and handle the request, the union did violate 8 (b) (1) and restrained the plaintiff in the exercise of his Section 7 rights; it

---

[71] *Id.*, at 55.

[72] 140 NLRB 181 (1962).

[73] *Hughes Tool Co.* (Independent Metal Workers Local No. 1), 147 NLRB
1573 (1964); see also *Local Union No. 12, United Rubber Workers and the
Business League of Gadsden*, 150 NLRB 312 (1964), enf'd 368 F.2d 12 (5th Cir.
1966), cert. den. 389 U.S. 837 (1967).

violated 8 (b) (2) by causing the employer unlawfully to discriminate against the employee in violation of 8 (b) (3) ; and it violated 8 (b) (3) by refusing to bargain on his behalf. Moreover, the Board also concluded that the discrimination required the revocation of the certification of the separate black and white local unions.

Declaring breach of the duty of fair representation to be an unfair labor practice was, conceptually, the most novel development in labor law in the mid-1960s. However, the fears expressed at the time that the NLRB would usurp the functions of the newly created Equal Employment Opportunity Commission have not been realized. Despite the interjection of the race issue and its application to sex discrimination,[74] there has been no general exodus to the National Labor Relations Board of civil rights complaints from the court enforcement procedures provided under Title VII.[75]

Although the NLRB has not yet accepted the proposition, and it has not been directly addressed by the Supreme Court, the Court of Appeals of the District of Columbia has ruled, as a matter of law, that an employer policy on racial discrimination can also be an unfair labor practice.[76]

While the process of accommodating the more recent interpretations of the National Labor Relations Act and the newly enacted Title VII of the Civil Rights Act of 1964 is likely to occupy the courts for the next several decades unless, of course, Congress steps in and harmonizes the two by legislation, it seems fair to assert at this time that the duty-of-fair-representation doctrine as developed and the sanctions available to the Board hold great potential for perfecting the rights of minority workers. However, the multiplicity of tribunals involved in the same or similar set of facts under the NLRB promises a great deal of over-

---

[74] See *Jubilee Manufacturing Co.*, 202 NLRB 272 (1973), which applied the concept to sex discrimination.

[75] See *Vaca v. Sipes*, 386 U.S. 171 (1967), where the Supreme Court recognized the Board's characterization of failure in the duty of fair representation as an unfair labor practice, but declined to interpret the assumption of jurisdiction by the Board as giving the Board exclusive jurisdiction under the preemption doctrine.

[76] See *United Packinghouse Workers* v. *NLRB*, 416 F.2d 1126 (1969), *cert. den.*, *Farmers Co-op Compress* v. *United Packinghouse Workers*, 396 U.S. 903 (1969) ; see also *Emporium Capwell Co.* v. *Western Addition Community Organization*, 420 U.S. 50 (1975).

lap and confusion that may detract substantially from the potential benefits of NLRB involvement. Not even the most ardent apologists for the National Labor Relations Board would accuse it of having been a pro-civil-rights activist. Therefore there is little in history to suggest that the Board will become aggressive and creative in the use of its potential in civil rights matters. It seems more likely that it will be a reluctant follower of other developed legal doctrines and will be persuaded to exercise only a small fraction of its enforcement potential.

VI. The Johnson Era and the Dawning of the Age of Enforcement—Executive Orders 11246 and 11375

"Of underrated significance in a program, the legitimacy of which had long been a subject of congressional debate, was the express congressional recognition of the Executive Order 10925 and successor orders in the language of the Civil Rights Act of 1964."[77] This congressional blessing of the President's efforts, along with subsequent appropriation action of Congress in specifically providing funds for the executive's program, provided legal authority for a bolder approach to the utilization of presidential power. President Johnson issued a series of orders, including Executive Order 11246,[78] which, in addition to incorporating the substantive aspects of the Kennedy orders, changed the organizational structure of the President's program substantially. With arguable congressional approval, it was no longer essential to maintain the intra-agency committee approach out of deference to the applicability of the Russell rider.[79]

Full authority was delegated to the Secretary of Labor to administer the provisions of the Executive Order relating to nondiscrimination in employment by government contractors and subcontractors. The substantive aspects of the Executive Order remained the same as in the preceding order. However, what had been quasi-legislative, executive, and adjudicatory functions lodged in the President's committee were now powers and duties devolved upon the Secretary of Labor and upon the contracting

---

[77] Jones, *supra* note 57, at 759. See 42 U.S.C. 2000 (c) , 8 (d) , 2000 (e) (15) (1964) .

[78] Executive Order No. 11246, 3 C.F.R., 1964–65 Comp., 339.

[79] Veteran's Preference Act of 1944, 58 Stat. 387 (1944) , amending 31 U.S.C. 696 (1954) .

agencies. The Secretary established the Office of Federal Contract Compliance as the operating arm of the new power and subdelegated all his authority except that for promulgating general rules. It is interesting to speculate whether this change in format affected the extent of influence upon the program by management, labor, or the public. However, to the extent that the tripartite device was eliminated, that avenue for formal input into the decisional process of the executive's antidiscrimination program also was eliminated. Of course, to the extent that the interest groups affect staffing and have informal access to policy-makers, one would expect business as usual. But without formal membership there is less identification with the program and less motive for the interest groups to insure that it is a success. Moreover, being uninvolved in the "running of the show," one can attack and oppose the program more readily without a sense of conflict.

Whether the nature of the activities was directly related to the form of the administrative mechanism cannot be determined. However, from 1961 to 1966, when the tripartite approach was in place, the activities of the President's committee were essentially of the "jawbone" variety. Despite heavy hints of enforcement in the order itself, as well as tough talk and hard negotiations, the existing muscle was, in fact, not utilized.

Beginning in late 1966 and continuing through 1968, the Office of Federal Contract Compliance emerged as the resident ogre of equal employment opportunity. The responsibilities of the fledgling organization were staggering. With only 14 professional employees, it was expected to develop an enforcement program both in the industrial sector and in the construction industry, to develop mechanisms for monitoring the compliance activity of the federal agencies that were directly responsible for securing compliance with the Executive Order, and to develop policies for the guidance of everybody and procedures whereby its mandates could be carried out. It is perhaps a startling success story that any of these responsibilities were carried out—all the more startling because it took place in the last two years of a Democratic administration that was facing a strong Republican challenge at the national level and, therefore, had to be especially sensitive to trade union influence as well as concerned about the political views of its most numerous minority group. Despite these impediments, what emerged from that period was the establishment of an enforcement posture. The Labor Department actually formulated procedures for holding hearings for the purpose of determining violation of the contractual requirements and for the imposition of sanctions; pursuant thereto, eight notices of proposed debarment were issued.[80]

Of those original enforcement hearings, only *In re: Allen Bradley* and *In re: Bethlehem Steel* proceeded to the point of decision; the *Bethlehem Steel* case took five years. They did, however, establish that the government could and would utilize the process, and they provided a basis for subsequent action by the contracting agencies with prime responsibility.[81]

Perhaps as significant to the program as the establishment of the possibility of enforcement that emerged from these early efforts was the impact upon the federal agencies, which were charged with the prime responsibility of securing compliance, of the Office of Federal Contract Compliance's seizing jurisdiction of a case and taking it through hearings. By implication at least, when the Labor Department determined to impose sanctions on its own authority, it was because the agency with the prime responsibility either could not or would not carry out the law. While the effectiveness of the assumption of jurisdiction by such a small staff can be called in question, the potentiality of the device, along with appropriate public relations, is obvious.

In addition to these administrative contributions of the first OFCC, there were substantive contributions as well:

1. The Office of Federal Contract Compliance's involvement with Crown Zellerbach consummated in litigation from which emerged two principles fundamental to the equal employment program: (a) that an injunction is available to restrain a union from striking against an employer's compliance with his government contract even though such compliance requires a unilateral modification of the collective bargaining agreement, and (b) that even a seniority system predating Title VII is subject to modifi-

---

[80] See Jones, *supra* note 57, at 760–64.

[81] See, e.g., *In re Edgely Air Products*, U.S. Department of Health, Education, and Welfare, Docket No. CC-1 (March 23, 1971).

cation pursuant to equal employment dictates despite the legitimacy of such seniority provisions under a preexisting collective bargaining agreement.[82]

2. From continued OFCC efforts to provide a viable program in the construction industry emerged the first substantive statement of goals and timetables. In the St. Louis Arch experience, involving very minimal efforts to integrate the construction industry, it was demonstrated that the federal agencies could cooperate and act if there was the will. When the labor organizations boycotted the St. Louis Arch because of the presence of minorities on the job, the government secured an injunction through the National Labor Relations Board that brought an end to the walkout.[83] More importantly, the use of numerical goals and timetables as a requirement for participation in government construction jobs gained currency in Cleveland in 1967[84] and proliferated until the Comptroller General of the United States declared them illegal.[85]

As these administrative and conceptual contributions to more effective enforcement emerged from the fledgling OFCC, there was undisguised opposition and hostility on the part of the labor movement. While it was no surprise that the building trades would oppose effective job-sharing and job-integration, in the *Crown Zellerbach* and *Bethlehem Steel* cases the issues involved the "sacred" seniority interests of the industrial unions. The emergence of these issues contributed to the widening rift between liberal and labor circles and the organizations of blacks. The divisiveness continues to the present time.

---

[82] *U.S.* v. *Local 189, United Papermakers and Paperworkers,* 282 F.Supp. 39 (E.D.La. 1968), *aff'd* 416 F.2d 980 (5th Cir. 1969); see also *Quarles* v. *Phillip Morris Co.,* 279 F.Supp. 505 (E.D.Va. 1968). See, e.g., *U.S.* v. *Sheet Metal Workers Local 36, supra* note 59.

[83] *IBEW Local 1,* 164 NLRB 313 (1967). Litigation relating to the St. Louis Arch experience, however, continued in federal court; see *U.S.* v. *Sheet Metal Workers Local 36, U.S.* v. *Building and Construction Trades Council,* and *U.S.* v. *Building and Construction Trades Council, supra* note 59.

[84] See, e.g., *Ethridge* v. *Rhodes,* 268 F.Supp. 83 (S.D.Ohio 1967); *Weiner* v. *Cuyahoga Community College District,* 238 N.E.2d 839 (C.P. 1968), *aff'd* 19 Ohio St.2d 35, 249 N.E.2d 907 (Ohio Sup. Ct. 1969), *cert. den.* 396 U.S. 1004 (1970). See also James E. Jones, Jr., "The Bugaboo of Employment Quotas," 1970 *Wis. L. Rev.* 341, at 348–61, for a discussion of the emergence of goals and timetables.

[85] See Jones, *supra* note 84, at 358–64, for a sequel to the goals and timetables story.

Initiation of Enforcement Hearings Under
Executive Order 11246

The first modern action, and generally believed to be the first effort at enforcement of the Executive Order under authority of the President in its 30-year existence, involved an action by the Office of Federal Contract Compliance of the Department of Labor against the Allen Bradley Corp. of Milwaukee.[86]

There are two notable aspects of the *Bradley Corp.* case. The first is that the government actually scheduled and conducted a hearing for the purpose of approving sanctions for violations of the contractual requirements prohibiting racial discrimination and requiring affirmative action under Executive Order 11246.[87] Perhaps even more significant than this first enforcement action is that the allegations against the company included not only acts of discrimination, but failure in its obligations to engage in affirmative action, a very ill-defined concept even in the minds of the federal government. The decision of the Secretary of Labor in the *Allen Bradley* matter ultimately issued on August 8, 1969.[88] By that time the case was before the Secretary of Labor for a second time, and for the first time before the new secretary, George Shultz. Significantly, it was held that the company had failed to take affirmative action to broaden its recruitment base to increase the flow of minority applicants in violation of its Executive Order undertaking. There was mediation effort on the part of the panel appointed by the Secretary of Labor to hear the case, and the mediation recommendations were incorporated into the secretary's decision.

During the period 1966–1968, the Office of Federal Contract Compliance instituted a number of debarment proceedings, but except for this brave enforcement posture assumed by the Department of Labor and the many difficulties it encountered in attempting to carry out its bluff, nothing startling or novel emerged from those endeavors.[89]

---

[86] See Notice of Hearing, *In re Allen Bradley Corp.*, 33 Fed. Reg. 10479 (July 23, 1968).

[87] See 30 Fed. Reg. 12319 (1965) and 41 C.F.R. Sec. 60-1.

[88] See 1 CCH Employ. Proc. Guide, ¶1634 (1973).

[89] See *In re Bethlehem Steel Corp.*, 33 Fed. Reg. 11438 (1968), which began in 1968 and took five years to resolve in an administrative proceeding that was intended to be relatively informal.

The most noteworthy act of the Office of Federal Contract Compliance in its early enforcement phase involved a case in which debarment proceedings were not initiated. In the *Crown Zellerbach Corp.* matter, information negotiations with the Office of Federal Contract Compliance directly and indirectly resulted in two separate law suits.[90]

Worthy of comment here is the indirect action that resulted in a successful assault by the government upon discriminatory seniority systems despite their lawful status under the National Labor Relations Act. Moreover, the government successfully obtained an injunction against a threatened strike called to frustrate the implementation of the Executive Order requirements, despite the Norris-LaGuardia Act's limitations upon the jurisdiction of the federal court to intervene in and grant injunctions in labor disputes.[91]

The Changing of the Guard from Wirtz to Shultz, from Johnson to Nixon, 1968–1969

As a new administration took over, and after the usual period of virtual suspended animation that accompanies any change of administration, the government under the new management eventually got around to assessing the equal employment program. A review of the Executive Order program that the new Secretary of Labor, George P. Shultz, inherited would have found the following major problems:

1. An understaffed Office of Federal Contract Compliance with limited capacity to carry out its primary responsibilities of monitoring the compliance performance of contracting agencies and lacking in capacity to take over those compliance activities through assumption of jurisdiction of cases for enforcement purposes. The OFCC had pending, in one form or another, eight enforcement actions that threatened to consume all of its staff capacity to the exclusion of important developmental work and other activities

---

[90] See *Crown Zellerbach Corp.* v. *Wirtz*, 281 F.Supp. 337 (D.D.C. 1968), in which the company and the union successfully obtained a preliminary injunction against the Secretary of Labor enjoining him from undertaking any enforcement action prior to an administrative hearing. See also *U.S.* v. *Local 189, United Papermakers and Paperworkers, supra* note 82.

[91] Norris-LaGuardia Act, 29 U.S.C. §§101–115 (1932). See, e.g., *U.S.* v. *Local 189, United Papermakers and Paperworkers, supra* note 82, at 43–44 and 996–97.

more normal to an agency whose prime responsibility was policy development and program oversight.

2. A construction program in total disarray because of a formal opinion of the Comptroller General that the use of summary tables was contrary to procurement law and illegal.

3. Legislative intervention pursuant to criticisms of the Defense Department for contracting with major textile companies despite determinations of the Department of Labor that such companies were not in compliance with the Executive Order.[92]

4. The addition of sex to the protected class by President Johnson's Executive Order 11375 in 1965, to be effective in 1966, without any comparable program having been developed to accommodate the new complaint universe of women.

5. No affirmative action concept to be applied even to those classes protected in the original order.

6. A conflict with the Department's natural constituency over the issue of seniority, brought about by the initiatives in the *Crown Zellerbach* and the *Bethlehem Steel* (Sparrows Point) cases of the previous administration.

In response to some of these problems, the Department of Labor went through the first of a series of reorganizational "musical chairs," but despite these efforts, the OFCC was unable successfully to manage the program it was created to run.[93]

VII. Affirmative Action Emerges from the Shadows

The Philadelphia Plan and the Flap over Goals or Quotas

Although the emergence of the revised Philadelphia Plan[94] was an attempt by the new administration to mount an equal employment initiative by revitalizing the construction industry

---

[92] See Equal Employment Opportunities Hearings Before the Subcommittee on Administrative Practices and Procedures, Senate Committee on the Judiciary, 91st Cong., 1st Sess. (March 27, 28, 1969). See also Hearings Before Congressman Ryan's Ad Hoc Committee (December 3, 4, 5, 1968); Hearings on S. 2453 Before the Subcommittee on Labor, Senate Committee on Labor and Public Welfare, 91st Cong., 1st Sess. (August 11, 1969) (statement by Secretary of Labor Shultz).

[93] *The Federal Civil Rights Enforcement Effort—1970* (Washington: U.S. Government Printing Office, Sept. 1970), pp. 105–262. See also *The Federal Civil Rights Enforcement Effort—1974* (Washington: U.S. Government Printing Office, 1975), Vol. V, ch. 3.

[94] 2 CCH Employ. Proc. Guide, ¶16, 175; 16, 176 (1969).

program, the most significant by-product was that it provided a fundamental underpinning that made it possible to articulate standards for affirmative-action programs applicable to nonconstruction employers. Governmental imposition of quotas or goals, as a condition for construction contracts, was not novel.[95] However, in reconstructing the Philadelphia Plan, departmental activists were not proceeding with this history in hand, and experience provided no reliable court decisions around which to fashion such an initiative.

The fundamental problem within the competence of the Comptroller General involved the inclusion of manning tables in the contract specifications prior to bidding. Their omission had been the defect identified by the Comptroller General in the Department's previous attempt to use manning tables in affirmative-action programs. As a legal or an administrative chore, it was easy to repair that defect by simply including them in the specifications. However, there was still some fear that their inclusion in bid specifications might be declared an imposition of illegal quotas, contrary to the Constitution as well as to the antipreference provision of the Civil Rights Act of 1964.[96]

The Department decided to go ahead with the initiatives and to utilize the rule-making process to establish: (1) the nature of the problem in the Philadelphia area, and (2) the statistical basis upon which "reasonable" goals and timetables could be prescribed for those employers subject to the plan. The hearings sought to establish the exclusion of nonwhites from the construction unions in the subject area; a continuing need for skilled construction workers brought about by both attrition and the creation of new jobs, which need was not normally being filled by union apprenticeship programs; and the availability in the Philadelphia area of minority employees with sufficient skills to

---

[95] See Kruman, *supra* note 10.
[96] Civil Rights Act of 1964, 42 U.S.C. §2000e-2 (j) (1964). The Comptroller General first raised the issue of the compatibility of goals and timetables with Title VII in an opinion issued on November 18, 1968 (48 Comp. Gen. [B-163026] Nov. 18, 1968). In similar and subsequent opinions, the Comptroller General held that where federal contracts are awarded on the basis of competitive bidding, minimum requirements relating to acceptable affirmative action programs must be made known to the bidders; see 48 Comp. Gen. ([B-163026] Feb. 25, 1969), 48 Comp. Gen. ([B-163026 (4)] April 11, 1969), 48 Comp. Gen. ([B-163026 (6)] May 6, 1969), 48 Comp. Gen. ([B163026 (6)] May 12, 1969).

participate in the construction industry. The goals, which were to be achieved over a four-year period, were modest. They represented no more than half of the projected job openings. If the maximum goals had been achieved on all contracts, the percentage of minority employees in the skilled trades would still have been less than the percentage of black workers already participating in the entire construction industry in the area. Moreover, the requirements that the employer make only a good-faith effort to achieve the goals and that he not engage in "reverse discrimination" in the process were designed to relieve the plan of the curse of an "illegal inflexible quota."[97]

After the Secretary of Labor set up the goal-range system of the revised Philadelphia Plan, the Comptroller General again found the plan illegal on the ground that it was in violation of Title VII, and he refused to approve expenditures on projects covered by it.[98] The Attorney General, whose role in interpreting Title VII of the Civil Rights Act of 1964 was more formal and direct than that of the Comptroller General, declared the plan to be legal and advised the Secretary of Labor to ignore the Comptroller General's opinion and to continue administration of the plan.[99]

It was hardly anticipated that this exercise would precipitate a near constitutional crisis. However, the Administration quickly found itself in a dispute over the separation of powers.[100] Efforts were made to attach a rider to a supplemental appropriations bill that would have prohibited the utilization of funds for the administration of the Philadelphia Plan. After vigorous debate in which the issue was characterized as a conflict between the

---

[97] For a full discussion of the Philadelphia Plan exercise, see Earl Leiken, "Preferential Treatment in the Skilled Building Trades: An Analysis of the Philadelphia Plan," 56 *Cornell L. Quarterly* 84 (1970); Jones, *supra* note 84; Robert Gosseen and Donald Moss, "The Philadelphia Plan: A Critical Analysis," *New York University, Twenty-third Annual Conference on Labor* (1970), p. 169; Note: "Title VII of the Civil Rights Act of 1964 and Minority Group Entry into the Building Trades Unions," 37 *Univ. of Chicago L. Rev.* 328 (1970); Comment: "The Philadelphia Plan: A Study in the Dynamics of Executive Power," 39 *Univ. of Chicago L. Rev.* 723 (1972).

[98] See 49 Comp. Gen. 59 at 71 (1969).

[99] See 42 Opinions of the Att. Gen. No. 37 (Sept. 22, 1969).

[100] See Hearings on the Philadelphia Plan and Sec. 931 Before the Subcommittee on Separation of Powers, Senate Committee on the Judiciary, 91st Cong., 1st Sess. (1969). See also Comment: "The Philadelphia Plan," *supra* note 97.

President and the Congress, and between the power of the purse on the one hand and civil rights on the other, the appropriations rider was defeated.[101]

The Courts Sustain and Sustain—From Eastern Contractors Association v. Shultz to Associated Contractors of Massachusetts v. Altshuler

I do not believe that the courts' support of the government's revised Philadelphia Plan came as any great surprise to most perceptive labor lawyers. Nor do I find it particularly surprising that so many appellate courts found no difficulty with goals and timetables under appropriate circumstances.[102] The legal basis of this modest use of numbers for law-enforcement purposes rested on sound precedents, albeit borrowed from other fields of law. Applying such theories to a different set of problems seems a rather modest act of creativity. What was surprising was not that the courts sustained the exercise, but that its reception prior to the court confirmation was so unimaginatively negative.[103] The Third Circuit Court of Appeals opinion[104] sustaining the Secretary of Labor followed the most "conservative" theory available to reach its conclusion. Judge Gibbons eschewed reliance upon presidential authority under the Fifth Amendment to the Constitution, and concluded that the plan was within the implied powers of the President, or his designee, unless prohibited by some other act of Congress.

Addressing the issue of conflict between Philadelphia Plan requirements and other statutes, the courts found no violation or conflict with Title VII or Title VI, with the National Labor Relations Act, with the Executive Order itself, or with the Due Process clause of the Fifth Amendment. The Supreme Court declined to review the Third Circuit's decision.[105] This type of administrative program, initiated by executive action, has been

---

[101] Sec. 115 Cong. Rec. 40906 (1969). The vote in the House was 208 to 156; the vote in the Senate was 39 to 29, 115 Cong. Rec. 40749 (1969).

[102] The author, as U.S. Associate Solicitor of Labor, was a principal legal architect of the revised Philadelphia Plan.

[103] See Jones, *supra* note 84, at 373–82, 385, 394.

[104] *Contractors Association of Eastern Pennsylvania* v. *Secretary of Labor,* 442 F.2d 159 (3rd Cir. 1971), *cert. den.* 404 U.S. 854 (1971).

[105] See 404 U.S. 854 (1971).

sustained in other situations.[106] The Supreme Court has suggested that administrative authority may be even broader than the judicial power to devise solutions to social problems.[107]

Although the Philadelphia Plan and its progeny set forth certain principles of law that have proven reliable, it was not until *Associated General Contractors of Massachusetts Inc.* v. *Altshuler*[108] that the issue of race as a constitutionally suspect classification was directly faced in the context of such plans.[109] The court there said:

> This marks for the first time, to our knowledge, that a court has been asked to sanction a plan for hiring a specific percentage of minority workers that requires an employer to take "every possible measure" to reach the goal at each job site, and places upon him the burden of proving compliance, under threat of serious penalties if that burden is not sustained. It is but a short step from these requirements to demand that an employer give an absolute percentage preference to members of a racial minority, regardless of their qualifications and without consideration for their availability within the general population. The Commonwealth's affirmative action plan forces us to address the fundamental question: are there constitutional limits to the means by which racial criteria may be used to remedy the present effects of past discrimination and achieve equal opportunity in the future? . . .
>
> There are good reasons why the use of racial criteria should be strictly scrutinized in giving legal sanction only where a compelling need for remedial action can be shown.[110]

The court went on to determine that there was no question that a "compelling need" existed to remedy serious racial imbalance in the construction trades and that the Commonwealth

---

[106] See *Southern Illinois Builders Assoc.* v. *Ogilvie*, 471 F.2d 680 (7th Cir. 1972) ; *Weiner* v. *Cuyahoga Community College District, supra* note 84; *Joyce* v. *McCrane,* 320 F.Supp. 1284 (D.N.J. 1970) .

[107] *Swann* v. *Charlotte-Mecklenburg Board of Education,* 402 U.S. 1 (1970), at 16; cf., *Katzenbach, Attorney General* v. *Morgan,* 384 U.S. 641 (1966) , at 653.

[108] 490 F.2d 9 (1st Cir. 1973) .

[109] Cf. *Norwalk CORE* v. *Norwalk Redevelopment Agency,* 395 F.2d 921 (1968) .

[110] *Supra* note 108, at 17.

plan was repugnant to neither state law nor the federal constitution.[111] If, as the Supreme Court suggested in *Swann* v. *Charlotte-Mecklenburg*[112] that the public authorities' powers are broader than those of the district courts, and if the executive branch is a "public authority," one wonders if the persistence of the controversy over goals was not misguided.

What was most significant about the Philadelphia Plan revised and the subsequent court litigation in *Eastern Contractors Association* v. *Shultz*[113] is their relevance as conceptual predicates for Order No. 4.[114] Prior to the successful launching of the Philadelphia Plan revised and the subsequent successful defense of it in the Congress and in the courts, little meaningful articulation could be made by government of the affirmative action obligation under the Executive Order. In order to give the concept of a *remedial obligation without guilt* any substantive content, it was apparent that numerical goals and timetables were essential. Without them, affirmative action mandates were hortatory and resulted only in "how to" manuals for contacting the minority communities and stimulating interest in applications and the various and sundry "outreach" programs. Little hard enforcement was possible, nor was the monitoring for progress—that is, real progress—possible.[115]

Once the administration had endorsed the goals and timetables concept, the issue had been joined in the Congress and the concept had survived, and the court decision vindicating the executive exercise of the authority had issued, the Office of Federal Contract Compliance as well as other administrators were emboldened to press forward with further articulation of affirmative-action obligations, including goals and timetables. The very crux

---

[111] See also *Rios* v. *Enterprise Association Steamfitters Local 638 of U.A.*, 501 F.2d 622 (2d Cir. 1974) at 629, for a recitation of circuit courts of appeal decisions that construed the delegation of equitable power as authorizing the district courts to establish goals for the purpose of remedying the effects of past discriminatory conduct.

[112] *Supra* note 107.

[113] *Supra* note 104.

[114] 41 C.F.R. §60–2 (1971).

[115] See, e.g., *In re Allen Bradley Corp.*, supra note 86. The ultimate conclusion of the panel in *Allen Bradley* was that the company failed to carry out its affirmative action obligation with regard to recruitment. The government was hard pressed to articulate the full scope of the affirmative-action obligation at that time, the primary difficulty stemming from the government's inability to handle questions regarding the legality of numbers.

of affirmative action, and of Order No. 4, is the utilization analysis—the determination of underutilization and resort to goals and timetables to insure equality of minority participation. The articulation of these requirements was not possible prior to the Philadelphia Plan exercise.[116]

The Supreme Court so far has declined to review the important cases involving goals and timetables. In the recent opportunity to speak to the affirmative-action concept in general in *Defunis* v. *Odegaard*,[117] the Court found the case to be moot. The Court's avoidance of the issue in *Defunis*, the uncertain pronouncements that emanated from the Nixon White House with regard to affirmative action, and the strident persistence and insistance of respondent groups, both liberal and other, that benign quotas are unconstitutional has placed a cloud upon all affirmative-action thrusts, and those subject thereto seem to have taken a wait-and-see attitude. Violent and near-violent demonstrations against busing in schools in both northern and southern cities[118] and congressional reaction to this resentment of the populace in the enactment of antibusing laws,[119] plus the President's assertion of discomfort with, if not disapproval of, busing,[120] have contributed to a change of climate foreshadowing a marked slowdown, if not a retrenchment, in the equal employment area in the near future.

VIII. The Supreme Court Assists

It should not have been unanticipated that the Supreme Court would be presented with opportunities to be of great assistance, or of great impediment, to the securing of workers' rights under the new equal-employment law soon after the law was enacted. However, important cases under Title VII of the Civil Rights Act of 1964 did not reach the court until 1971, and as of 1975 only a handful of cases of substantive significance have been decided. Surprisingly, however, in 1968 the Court resuscitated the Re-

---

[116] 41 C.F.R. §60-2 (1971).

[117] *Defunis* v. *Odegaard*, 416 U.S. 312 (1974).

[118] *N.Y. Times*, Sept. 14, 1975, §IV at 1, col. 2.

[119] *N.Y .Times*, Sept. 4, 1975, §1 at 19, col. 7; Sept. 7, 1975, §2 at 51, col. 2; Sept. 18, 1975, §1 at 29, col. 7; Sept. 27, 1975, §1 at 10, col. 5.

[120] *N.Y. Times*, Sept. 14, 1975, §1 at 32, col. 5; Sept. 17, 1975, §1 at 1, col. 1.

construction Era's Civil Rights Act,[121] thus providing an additional statutory vehicle for the prohibition of employment discrimination—at least if such discrimination were based on race.[122]

In *Jones* v. *Mayer and Co.*,[123] a housing case, the courts reversed an earlier decision,[124] which had ruled that 42 U.S.C. 1981 did not reach private acts of discrimination that interfered with employment rights of blacks. The *Jones* case thus secured the right to contract for employment from infringement by private individuals, as distinguished from activities that require some kind of state action. The Court held that the power in this regard proceeded from the 13th Amendment of the Constitution, which, contrary to the 14th Amendment, is not limited to prohibiting state governments from engaging in racial discrimination.

Beginning with *Grigg* v. *Duke Power Co.*,[125] the Supreme Court has decided a number of cases that interpret and apply Title VII, as well as some that grapple with the relationships between Title VII and other labor laws. In this seminal decision, the Court enunciated several broad principles that are fundamental to the evolution of Title VII law. Although the specifics of the case involve the legality of paper-and-pencil tests and a high-school education requirement that disproportionately screened out blacks without the justification of business necessity, its principal contribution to the interpretation of the law was of much broader import. The Court declared, "Congress directed the thrust of the Act to the *consequences* of employment practices, not simply the motivation,"[126] and in so declaring created a new concept of discrimination. Expansively, the Court said:

---

[121] 42 U.S.C. 1981. "All persons within the jurisdiction of the United States shall have the same right in every State and Territory to make and enforce contracts, to sue, be parties, give evidence and to the full and equal benefit of all laws and proceedings for the security of persons and property as is enjoyed by white citizens and shall be subject to the punishment, pains, penalties, taxes, licenses and extractions of every kind and to no other."

[122] See *Rackin* v. *University of Pennsylvania*, 386 F.Supp. 992 (E.D.Pa. 1974) ; *Waters* v. *Heublein Inc.*, 9 E.P.D. ¶9522. See also *McDonald* v. *Santa Fe Transportation Co.*, 513 F.2d 90 (5th Cir. 1975) ; *contra, Hollander* v. *Sears Roebuck Co.*, 392 F.Supp. 90 (D.Conn. 1975) ; *WRMA Broadcasting Co.* v. *Hawthorne*, 365 F.Supp. 577 (M.D.Ala. 1973) .

[123] 392 U.S. 409 (1968) .

[124] *Hurd* v. *Hodge*, 334 U.S. 24 (1948) .

[125] 401 U.S. 424 (1971) .

[126] *Id.*, at 432.

> The objective of Congress in the enactment of Title VII is plain from the language of the statute. It was to achieve equality of employment opportunities and remove barriers that have operated in the past to favor an identifiable group of white employees over other employees. Under the Act, practices, procedures, or tests neutral on their face, and even neutral in terms of intent, cannot be maintained if they operate to "freeze" the status quo of prior discriminatory employment practices.[127]

The application of the consequence test is procedural. Once the plaintiffs show a prima facie case of discrimination, which case can be made by statistics demonstrating that the test, policy, or procedure used adversely affects more of the protected class than of other employees, the burden is on the employer to demonstrate the manifest relationship of the screening device to ability to do the job. In short, the respondent must meet the "business necessity" test.

In a second case, *McDonnell Douglas Corp. v. Green*,[128] the Supreme Court had the opportunity to explain its prior interpretation of the requirements of Title VII. In that case, involving an allegation by the plaintiff of discrimination in hiring and the defense by the employer that the refusal to rehire was based on personal misconduct of the individual plaintiff, the Court declared:

> The complainant in a Title VII trial must carry the initial burden under the statute of establishing a prima facie case of racial discrimination. This may be done by showing (i) that he belongs to a racial minority; (ii) that he applied and was disqualified for a job for which the employer was seeking applicants; (iii) that, despite his qualifications, he was rejected; and (iv) that, after his rejection the position remained open and the employer continued to seek applicants from persons of complainant's qualifications.[129]

If the employer then comes forward with a rational and neutral business justification for the refusal to hire, plaintiff might still prevail if he can demonstrate that the reason tendered is pretext.

---

[127] *Id.*, at 429–30.
[128] 411 U.S. 792 (1973).
[129] *Id.*, at 802.

In *Albemarle Paper Co.* v. *Moody,*[130] the Supreme Court again addressed problems related to the application and utilization of paper-and-pencil tests and the technicalities of test validation. Additionally, the Court declared that the full equitable powers of the courts to make the injured party whole for any discrimination suffered are available to vindicate the purposes of Title VII. The Court declared that the measure of relief is to be determined by the extent of the plaintiff's injury. This expansive view of the "make whole" authority could have far-reaching implications if it is ultimately applied to all aspects of Title VII, including those which Congress by language has sought to limit. Of particular significance are Sections 703 (h) and (j),[131] in which a certain protected status is sought to be accorded to seniority systems and certain limitations are placed upon the use of population ratios as a basis for requiring preferential treatment.

The Supreme Court in *Alexander* v. *Gardner-Denver Co.*[132] made it clear that its reading of the Title VII mandate was that

---

[130] —U.S.—, 95 S.Ct. 2362 (1975).

[131] 42 U.S.C. 2000 (c)-2 (h), (j) (1964): "Notwithstanding any other provision of this subchapter, it shall not be an unlawful employment practice for an employer to apply different standards of compensation, or different terms, conditions, or privileges of employment pursuant to a bona fide seniority or merit system, or a system which measures earnings by quantity or quality of production or to employees who work in different locations, provided that such differences are not the result of an intention to discriminate because of race, color, religion, sex, or national origin, nor shall it be an unlawful employment practice for an employer to give and to act upon the result of any professionally developed ability test provided that such test, its administration or action upon the result is not designed, intended or used to discriminate because of race, color, religion, sex or national origin. It shall not be an unlawful employment practice under this subchapter for any employer to differentiate upon the basis of sex in determining the amount of the wages or compensation paid or to be paid to employees of such employer if such differentiation is authorized by the provisions of section 206 (d) of Title 29.

"Nothing contained in this subchapter shall be interpreted to require any employer, employment agency, labor organization, or joint labor-management committee subject to this subchapter to grant preferential treatment to any individual or to any group because of the race, color, religion, sex, or national origin of such individual or group on account of an imbalance which may exist with respect to the total number or percentage of persons of any race, color, religion, sex, or national origin employed by any employer, referred or classified for employment by any employment agency or labor organization, admitted to membership or classified by any labor organization, or admitted to, or employed in, any apprenticeship or other training program, in comparison with the total number or percentage of persons, of such race, color, religion, sex, or national origin in any community, State, section, or other area, or in the available work force in any community, State, section, or other area. (Pub. L. 88-352, title VII, §703, July 2, 1964, 78 Stat. 255.)"

[132] 415 U.S. 36 (1974).

Congress intended to allow an individual to pursue his rights under both Title VII and any other applicable state and federal statutes—that the statute guaranteed any member of the protected classes the right of access to federal courts for vindication, in spite of his having previously resorted to arbitration of his grievance under a collective bargaining agreement.[133]

The Court rejected the assertion that to permit litigation of a Title VII claim previously arbitrated would sound the death knell for arbitration clauses in labor contracts. Whether the future utility of arbitration as a dispute-settlement mechanism will be substantially affected by the ruling, only time will tell.

In *Johnson v. Railway Express Agency*,[134] the Supreme Court started to clarify the relationship between the Reconstruction Era Civil Rights Act and Title VII of the Civil Rights Act of 1964 as amended. After pointing out some of the differences between the two laws, the Court concluded that the remedies available under Title VII and under Section 1981, although related and although directed to most of the same ends, are separate, distinct, and independent.[135]

The Court noted that although it had not previously specifically held that 42 U.S.C. 1981 afforded a federal remedy against discrimination in private employment on the basis of race, it recognized that the courts of appeals had interpreted its decision in *Jones v. Mayer and Co.*[136] in that fashion. In *Johnson,* the Court squarely so held, and additionally declared that "an individual who establishes a cause of action under [Section] 1981 is entitled to both equitable and legal relief, including compensatory and, under certain circumstances, punitive damages."[137]

Johnson v. Railway Express and *Alexander v. Gardner-Denver Co.* together provide a basis for assuring substantial protection for the rights of *minority workers*. This, then, is the law, even if it requires that the will of the majority as expressed in most binding arbitration clauses in collective bargaining agreements be

---

[133] See 415 U.S. 36 at 49, fns. 10, 11, where the Court rejected both the "deferral to arbitration concept" and the so-called doctrines of election of remedies or waiver, and the doctrines of res judicata and collateral estoppel.

[134] —U.S.—, 95 S.Ct. 1716 (1975).

[135] *Id.,* at 1721.

[136] *Supra* note 123.

[137] *Supra* note 134, at 1720.

put aside. Moreover, the limitations in Title VII that purport to protect seniority status and to restrict preferential remedies are no part of Section 1981, and equitable relief under the older statute would not seem to be limited by anything in the new one. If Section 1981 would support claims for compensatory and even punitive damages, then certainly make-whole relief, and even so-called constructive seniority, would be well within the remedial scope of the statute.[138]

In *Emporium Capwell Co. v. Western Addition Community Organization*,[139] the Court returned to the task of attempting to harmonize Title VII of the Civil Rights Act of 1964 and the National Labor Relations Act. This time, however, the concern was not in the overlap between Title VII and arbitration agreements pursuant to labor law, but between concerted activities for the purpose of collective bargaining or other mutual aid or protection under Section 7 of the National Labor Relations Act and protest activities under Title VII.

In *Emporium*, a labor organization, after investigating complaints that the company was violating its collective bargaining agreement by racial discrimination, invoked the grievance procedure and demanded arbitration. Certain employees felt that the procedure was inadequate and refused to participate, preferring direct action. The union, bound by the collective bargaining agreement, which included a no-strike clause, advised against the direct action, but the employees proceeded. The employees continued to work, but they engaged in direct protest activity in their off-hours. When they resumed their protest after a warning from the company, they were discharged. Western Addition Community Organization, a local civil-rights association to which the protesting employees belonged, filed unfair labor practice charges with the National Labor Relations Board. The NLRB found that the employees were discharged for attempting to require the company to bargain with them over employment conditions affecting minorities contrary to the exclusive bargaining status provision. As such conduct was unprotected by the NLRA, the discharges were for just cause. The court of appeals reversed, concluding that

---

[138] Discussed *infra* under "Equal Employment Opportunity in 1975—The Emergent but Unresolved Issues."

[139] 420 U.S. 50 (1975).

the concerted activities protesting racial discrimination enjoyed a unique status under the law, and remanded the case to the Board to determine whether the union was actually trying to remedy the discrimination to the fullest extent possible and by the most expeditious and efficacious means. The Supreme Court, reversing the court of appeals, sustained the National Labor Relations Board.

Although nondiscriminatory employment practices are accorded a high priority in national labor policies, that priority does not justify conduct of this sort to bypass exclusive bargaining representatives. The problem created by the case is that such employee direct action would appear to be protected under Section 704 (a) of Title VII of the Civil Rights Act of 1964. Without prejudging that issue, the Supreme Court suggested that even assuming that Section 704 protected the employees' picketing and the consumer boycott, the same conduct was not necessarily entitled to affirmative protection under the National Labor Relations Act. If the discharge violates Title VII, the remedial provisions of that law provide the procedure whereby the plaintiffs must seek to recover their jobs.

Given the assumption that unfair labor practice jurisdiction for failure in the duty of fair representation rests with the National Labor Relations Board, and given the range of activity that might both breach the duty of fair representation and violate Title VII obligations, concurrent jurisdiction of matters by both the National Labor Relations Board and the Equal Employment Opportunity Commission seems inevitable. If, as appears likely after the *Emporium* case, each agency will independently determine discrimination using different standards, we can anticipate a substantial period of conflict and confusion before the rights, responsibilities, and relief under these two laws are ultimately clarified.

The Court has begun to address a host of other problems, but the current "state of the art" permits little more than our calling attention to a few of them. It has been struggling with the evolution of the constitutional standard whereby protections accorded female workers are to be judged. Differing constitutional standards as between sex and race may create some special problems for cases falling both within and without Title VII prohibitions.[140] As to the protection of workers against religious discrimination, the law is less strictly construed. The need of the employer for efficiency in operating his plant receives greater weight in assessing whether or not there has been religious discrimination than is accorded in cases alleging discrimination on the basis of race or sex.[141] Prohibitions against discrimination on the basis of national origin do not prevent an employer from requiring citizenship as a condition for employment,[142] but beyond this one case there is little law developing the scope of nation-origin discrimination under the modern statutes.

IX. Congress Again—The Equal Employment Opportunity Act of 1972

Those who follow legislative developments at the federal level would not have anticipated that Congress would so quickly return to the drawing board in the equal employment opportunity area. After less than eight years of operation of the Civil Rights Act of 1964, Congress extended and strengthened the Act by passing the Equal Employment Opportunity Act of 1972.[143] It would seem more appropriate to characterize what Congress did in 1972 as repair of obvious defects in its 1964 creation rather than as a radical overhaul. Despite the conventional wisdom that for a Fair Employment Practices Commission to have adequate powers of enforcement, it should be patterned after the NLRB under the National Labor Relations Act,[144] Congress stayed within the ba-

---

[140] See Note: "Preferential Economic Treatment for Women: Some Constitutional and Practical Implications of Kahn v. Shevin," 28 *Vanderbilt L. Rev.* 843 (1975); Julius Getman, "The Emerging Constitutional Principle of Sexual Equality," 1972 *Supreme Court Rev.* 157 (1972); John Johnston, Jr., and Charles Knapp, "Sex Discrimination by Law: A Study in Judicial Perspective," 46 *N.Y.U.L. Rev.* 675 (1971); also, Barbara Brown, Thomas Emerson, Gail Falk, and Ann Freedman, "The Equal Rights Amendment: A Constitutional Basis for Equal Rights for Women," 80 *Yale L. J.* 871 (1971).

[141] See *Dewey* v. *Reynolds Metals Co.*, 429 F.2d 324 (6th Cir. 1970), *aff'd by equally divided court*, 402 U.S. 689 (1971); *Claybaugh* v. *Pacific Northwest Bell Tel. Co.*, 355 F.Supp 1 (D.Ore 1973). See also Harry Edwards and Joel Kaplan, "Religious Discrimination and the Role of Arbitration under Title VII," 69 *Mich. L. Rev.* 599 (1971); Note: "Title VII—Religious Discrimination in Employment," 16 *Wayne L. Rev.* 327 (1969); also Note: "Religious Observance and Discrimination in Employment," 22 *Syracuse L. Rev.* 1019 (1971).

[142] *Espinoza* v. *Farah Manufacturing Co., Inc.*, 414 U.S. 86 (1973).

[143] See George Sape and Thomas Hart, "Title VII Reconsidered: The Equal Employment Opportunity Act of 1972," 40 *Geo. Washington L. Rev.* 824 (1972).

[144] See Sovern, *supra* note 28, at 206-207, and Joseph Witherspoon, *Administrative Implementation of Civil Rights* (Austin: University of Texas Press, 1968).

sic dimensions of the original act and provided enforcement in the federal district courts (by an independent General Counsel). It also retained in the law the right of employees ultimately, by their own attorneys, to go to court to enforce the law. The enforcement aspect was probably the chief among the repair jobs performed. Additionally, protection was provided for employees of state and local governments, of the federal government, and of educational institutions. This coverage expansion, along with extension of the law to private employers and labor organizations with 15 or more full-time employees, substantially expanded the scope of the protection provided by Title VII. At the same time, Congress retained the provisions requiring referral to state agencies with adequate equal-employment laws and increased the status to be accorded disposition of cases by such state agencies. To go along with the maintenance of the plaintiff's right to sue in his own behalf, the provision for attorney's fees was maintained. However, recognizing the economic potential of open-ended back-pay liability, Congress limited back-pay claims to no more than two years prior to the filing of the charge. The Act also gave increased recognition and status to the President's Executive Order program and affirmative action plans prepared pursuant thereto, albeit in a somewhat indirect fashion.[145]

The new Act has created at least one constitutional problem. Recognizing the awkwardness of covering state employees, Congress provided for court enforcement against a state by the Attorney General of the United States rather than by the EEOC. However, the right of action by the plaintiffs by their own attorney is preserved. Moreover, Congress invoked both the Commerce Clause and 14th Amendment as constitutional predicates for the enactment of the 1972 Act. The 11th Amendment of the Constitution denies to the federal courts the power to entertain suits by private citizens against states. Unless the subsequently enacted 14th Amendment, and perhaps the 13th Amendment, authorizes Congress to provide such relief in the federal courts despite the 11th Amendment, imperfect relief may be available to private plaintiffs where the state is the offending party. While

---

[145] See 42 U.S.C. §2000 (c) -15.

legal fictions have managed to avoid this difficulty in the past, where sizable back-pay remedies are involved it is unlikely that suing the agent of the state will be sufficient to avoid the issue.

X. Equal Employment Opportunity in 1975—The Emergent but Unresolved Issues

To a very large degree, most of the law that has been shaped under Title VII of the Civil Rights Act of 1964 and related statutes has dealt with blue-collar employment. Probably more "professional" equal-employment law has been developed in connection with school desegregation cases than in any other area, but school law is not resorted to generally in attempting to evaluate equal-employment law. Recently we have seen a beginning of what may be a proliferation of concern about professional and technical employment in police and fire departments and a fair amount in the air transportation industry. We have also witnessed emerging concern regarding federal employment.

We can anticipate increased attention to these professional and technical areas in the next decade, as well as to the problems of the extent to which principles may be transferred from the blue-collar sector to professional and technical employment. Without doubt, concepts developed with regard to the job-relatedness of tests will be utilized to challenge a host of professional and technical qualifications imposed by licensing mechanisms as well as by employers; also challenged will be requirements of particular diplomas or degrees.

The issue has not been prominent in the blue-collar sector, but in the employment of professionals the question of "qualified" or "best qualified" is likely to surface as a thorny issue in due season—particularly as you approach the academic as well as the civil service community. The question probably will be presented in a variety of situations: (1) Must an employer employ the best qualified by the test measure in order to avoid discrimination charges? And (2) given limited participation in the work force by minorities, *may* an employer be required to skip the best qualified and take only the qualified minority individual?

One of the issues currently pending before the Supreme Court involves the clash between collectively bargained seniority rights and affirmative-action programs.[146] Title VII of the Civil Rights Act contains language that, it is contended, protects seniority systems against affirmative-action relief, and these potential conflicts are unavoidable as the economic down-turn forces job curtailment and last hired/first fired seniority provisions to come into play. Not only must the court grapple with the status of these issues under Title VII, but also under the independently based 42 U.S.C. 1981 that does not contain the Title VII limitations.

Not unrelated to the seniority affirmative action issue is the ever-present problem of goals or quotas—reverse discrimination or remedy. The Supreme Court has not faced squarely the constitutional question of benign employment quotas, absent a history of prior discrimination and an adjudication requiring such a remedy. Since this issue underlies so much of the current conflict and confusion, the Supreme Court must ultimately step in and resolve it. The continued viability of the Executive Order program of the President, as well as many state and local programs, may depend upon early Court resolution of this fundamental issue.

With increasing numbers of individuals being employed by state and local governments, the application of the federal Civil Rights Act to these employees is due for increasing attention. Title VII of the Civil Rights Act provides them with the right to sue their employer for engaging in prohibited acts, but the 11th Amendment of the Constitution restricts the jurisdiction of the federal district courts to entertain such suits. If the real defendant, the state rather than its agent, cannot be sued under the federal law, then the back-pay remedy provided for the state employee may, in fact, be nonexistent, or at least may be made workable only if the Attorney General of the United States steps in to prosecute the matter.

Finally, the clash of labor relations laws with equal employment laws is likely to involve us in the process of harmonizing these national policies for a long time into the future.

---

[146] See, e.g., *Franks* v. *Bowman Transportation Co.*, 495 F.2d 398 (5th Cir. 1974), *cert. granted* 95 S.Ct. 1421 (1975) ; *Watkins* v. *United Steelworkers Local 2369*, 369 F.Supp. 1221 (E.D.La. 1974), *rev'd* 516 F.2d 41 (5th Cir. 1975) ; *Waters* v. *Wisconsin Steel Works*, 502 F.2d 1309 (7th Cir. 1974), pet. for cert. filed Feb. 24, 1975, 43 U.S.L.W. 3505; *Jersey Central Power & Light Co.* v. *Local Unions 327, 749, 1289, 1303, 1309, and 1314 of IBEW*, 508 F.2d 687 (3rd Cir. 1975).

XI. Conclusions—Where Do We Go from Here?

As 1975 comes to a close, the policies and practices to protect workers against invidious job discrimination are about 30 years behind other protective labor and labor relations programs. The requisite priority in national policy was not accorded this problem area until 1965—the year Title VII of the Civil Rights Act of 1964 became effective. Moreover, Congress as recently as 1972 amended its earlier vehicle, providing new coverage and creating new problems. We are, therefore, still in the formative stages of interpreting and applying the new law and the new concepts that necessarily emerge from it. The legal process, motivated by the private attorney's usually representing the plaintiff as well as by the newly armed Commission, will continue to provide further elucidation as the litigation proceeds in the normal course.

Problems already are apparent and others will emerge, the resolution of which will require resort to the congressional drawing board. And there are other matters that may well be sorted out by firm executive or administrative leadership in coordinating and harmonizing the multiplicity of agencies involved in the equal-employment area. Crucial to both the vigorous prosecution of the law as well as to forceful administrative leadership are the future political and economic climates. In my judgment, a sustained period of economic growth would have a favorable impact upon the political climate and would make the accommodation of the various conflicting interests involved in the administration of the protection of workers' rights in the equal-employment area more attainable.

For purposes of comparison with other labor programs, we could conclude that the transformation of fair employment practices policies should only be dated as of 1965. The 30 years preceding were marked by virtual absence of any functional fair employment practices policy. With this more limited view of the historical antecedents, we could conclude that the transformation of fair employment practices policies was on a parity with other labor laws. That is, in 1975 equal employment policies have progressed about as far as labor relations policies had progressed in 1945.

CHAPTER 8

Comprehensive Safety and Health Measures in the Workplace

LEO TEPLOW
Industrial Relations Counselors

Occupational hazards have always characterized occupational effort, just as home hazards and recreation hazards and transportation hazards have characterized human activity off the job. The major difference is that when the average person is off the job, he is on his own and can decide how much risk he wants to assume. On the job, however, he is, to some extent, under economic and social pressure to carry out his duties under conditions which are, in large measure, determined by his employer.

For many years, work hazards were considered an integral part of the job, and it was assumed that he who accepted employment also voluntarily assumed or accepted the risks inherent on the job. Yet there have always been those who made special efforts to reduce the risk entailed in the occupation. As long as 400 years ago, one Domenico Fontana, supervising the work of moving the Obelisk in the courtyard of St. Peter's Cathedral in Rome, anticipated the modern hard hat and had his workmen wear battle helmets to protect their heads.[1]

In the early days of the United States, safety in the workplace was considered a private matter for determination by the employer and his employees, and not appropriate for government concern. It was not until large-scale catastrophes occurred that government was called upon to act.

State Programs

It was because of mine accidents and deaths in Schuylkill County, Pennsylvania, anthracite mines in 1858 that anthracite coal miners asked for official supervision of these mines. When a

---

[1] Brenda McCall, *Safety First—At Last!* (New York: Vantage Press, 1975), p. 16.

bill finally was able to get through the state legislature in 1869, the new law provided for one mine inspector in Schuylkill County. It was not until 1870, after an anthracite mine fire in Luzerne County killed 109 miners that Pennsylvania enacted legislation covering all anthracite miners in the state. Later other states followed Pennsylvania's lead and passed laws dealing with safety in bituminous coal mines.[2]

The relative paucity of legislation in the face of well-publicized catastrophes in the 19th and early 20th centuries is probably attributable to such factors as: (1) the assumption, shared by employers and employees, that hazard was inherent on the job; (2) pride in being able to work in the face of known hazards; (3) the assumption that the constitutional provision of federated states under a central government of limited powers barred federal action, so that when government action appeared to be desirable, it was considered appropriate for the states to act; and (4) the normal diversity of interests and increasing demands on state budgets made the states reluctant to act until major catastrophes galvanized enough public support to make state legislation possible.

With the beginning of the 20th century, it became obvious that occupational hazards were becoming a serious factor in disabling family wage-earners in an increasingly industrialized society. But the political effort was directed mainly at ensuring compensation for the injured rather than at preventing the injury. To overcome the technical obstacles to recovery for injuries—proof of employer negligence, possible negligence of the injured employee or of fellow employees—automatic recovery for employment-related injuries was made possible by widespread state workmen's compensation in the individual states. It is quite possible that the emphasis on workmen's compensation in the decade around 1910 deterred legislation dealing with the causes of occupational injuries. It was hoped, of course, that merit-rated workmen's compensation legislation would provide an incentive to employers to take action to reduce accidents and thereby earn a lower insurance rate for workmen's compensation coverage.

The various states did experiment with safety and health legislation, however, with administrative responsibility frequently divided

---

[2] McCall, p. 38.

between the Commissioner of Labor (safety) and the Commissioner of Health (occupational health). The initial efforts provided for inspection of factories, elevators, and boilers. The emphasis was on investigation and consultation, later supplemented by sanction as a last resort. The authorizing legislation depended in large part upon the degree of industrialization (as in New York), awareness of social progress (Wisconsin), and rapidity of growth (California).

In the period between 1930 and 1970, individual states experimented with safety/health legislation, with occupational safety as the more readily recognized need. Safety engineering had become a recognized profession—the first of the three E's of safety: Engineering, Education, and Enforcement. Various states adopted safety codes, relying heavily on the safety standards promulgated by the various voluntary consensus organizations associated with what is now the American National Standards Institute (ANSI). The sanctions of fines and, in extreme cases, imprisonment were provided under many states laws, but were usually considered as a last resort reserved for cases of highly refractory or reckless employers.

As public concern about occupational safety and health became more evident, so did state legislative activity. In fact, the Bureau of Labor Standards reported in its publication *Safety Standards* (July/August 1970) that state activity in occupational safety and health legislation during the 1967–1968 biennium was "the greatest in 20 years."

As one looks at the entire trend of state action in occupational safety and health, the following characteristics seem to stand out: (1) The original assumption that safety was the employer's sole responsibility was replaced by the attitude that extreme situations required governmental action—even if such action consisted primarily (at first) of no more than inspection and fact-gathering. (2) When and if government action was indicated, the state government was the appropriate level of government to become involved. (3) Government involvement was to be expressed primarily by inspection, education, and counseling, reserving sanctions to be used as a last resort.

The history of state activity and the limited nature of the exercise of state authority serve to explain some of the differing views on the merits of state versus federal administration of occupational safety and health legislation that became evident during congressional consideration of the Occupational Safety and Health Act of 1970 (OSHA), as well as the unique mix of state and federal enforcement provided in the Act.

Voluntary Progress

Americans have a unique genius for voluntary, cooperative action. Nowhere is that trait better illustrated than in what has come to be known as the safety movement. Long before specific legal provisions imposed accountability on employers, individuals in management were investigating the causes of accidents and starting accident-prevention campaigns, undertaking research, and preaching safety with missionary zeal.

In the first decade of this century, the United States Steel Corporation established one of the first formal industrial-safety programs. It might have been anticipated that the steel industry should be a leader in safety, since the making of steel is inherently dangerous and was even more so 70 years ago, before the era of remote controls, automatic strip mills, and air-conditioned crane cabs and control pulpits.

In 1912, the Association of Iron and Steel Electrical Engineers called the first national conference on occupational safety. Out of that conference shortly thereafter developed that extraordinary voluntary, nongovernmental organization—the National Safety Council. It is difficult to summarize the full scope of National Safety Council activities or to measure the results. The Council provided the focus of interest, the leadership, and the information that brought together the enthusiasm of safety missionaries and the discipline of safety engineers and, to a lesser extent, hygienists, to provide inspiration and working tools to thousands in industry. Later the scope of the Council's work was expanded to include not only manufacturing industry (which continues to be its major support), but also agriculture, construction, mining, women's groups, insurance companies, organized labor (the Labor Conference of the Council was formed in 1956), and federal and state governments. Local safety councils have been organized to promote both on-the-job and off-the-job safety on the municipal or area level.

The rate of injuries in companies reporting to the Council decreased sharply. However, during the mid-fifties the various measures of injury-frequency reached a plateau for reasons that are still not clear, although it can be speculated that the dynamics of change of employee personnel, production methods, or new materials, and even the dynamics of rapid growth were important related factors. When the lack of further progress in accident-reduction became evident during the mid-sixties, interest in state and federal action increased.

Another notable example of the American genius for voluntary, cooperative action is represented by the voluntary consensus standards system. To the uninitiated, a standard appears to be a simple matter to develop, adopt, and promulgate. In fact, workable standards, if they are to be national in scope and if they are to be practical enough to be actually applied in the workplace, are extremely difficult to write.

Standards applicable to business must be written by people who understand not only the nature and variety of hazards to be protected against in hundreds of different industries, but also the impact of the standard upon the countless varieties of situations in which that standard is to be applied. A choice of alternatives can be made correctly only by those who understand how the proposed standard would affect choice of production method, capital costs, productivity, and quality of product.

The federated voluntary consensus standards system now operating within the framework of the American National Standards Institute was started about the time of World War I and soon included safety standards (and, to a lesser extent, health standards as well) within its scope. The system provides a mechanism by which volunteers from the various interests likely to be affected by a proposed standard organize standards-writing committees composed of expert and experienced representatives of manufacturers, users, consumers, labor, government, insurance, and independent experts; the committees hammer out standards that would not only provide protection against recognized hazards, but would do so in a manner consistent with the magnitude of the hazard and a practical understanding of the availability of resources. ANSI has developed and is applying elaborate measures to make sure that a true consensus exists before the result can be issued as an American National Standard.

By 1968, when Congress began debating the legislation which

ultimately became OSHA/1970, hundreds of health and safety standards had been issued by ANSI to provide a basis for voluntary adoption by individual companies as well as for state safety codes. These health/safety ANSI standards were written with an understanding that a great deal of discretion would be used in their application to business; both employers and most state governments understood that approach with respect to consensus standards. Discretion and cooperation, rather than confrontation, constituted the hallmark of occupational health programs and progress, and the consensus standards fitted well into that kind of discretionary climate.

Unfortunately, the safety movement and the voluntary consensus standards system maintained a low profile while making important contributions to occupational safety. Consequently, when Congress began to deal with general occupational safety legislation early in 1968, it had no knowledge of the progress made or the existing institutions for dealing with occupational safety and health. Attempts at that late date to educate Congress were likely to be considered as pretexts for deferring congressional action rather than as honest efforts to place the problem and its solution in perspective.

Both the state programs and voluntary efforts and achievements were heavily discounted by those who urged strong measures relying on sanctions rather than cooperation. As late as 1974, a responsible labor spokesman put it this way:

> Well, just for the record and trying honestly to be a reasonably decent and honest historian, I think the record demonstrates beyond any conceivable, rational doubt that for 60 years we have had "education" in the various States of the Union. And for 60 years we were also displeased with that kind of result. . . .[3]

While organized labor has a right to be "displeased with that kind of result," it is nevertheless impossible to estimate the extent of suffering avoided and the thousands of lives saved because hundreds of thousands of employers and their staffs went far beyond what the law then required in contributing to employee

---

[3] Jacob Clayman, secretary-treasurer, Industrial Union Department, AFL-CIO, in *Hearings Before the Subcommittee on Labor of the Committee on Labor and Public Welfare, U.S. Senate,* July 22, 1974, pp. 111–12.

safety and health. Had it not been for all the voluntary effort
and progress over the years, there would not have been a core of
experienced professionals, in or out of government, for OSHA
to draw upon when Congress enacted OSHA/1970;[4] nor would
there have been a substantial number of ready-made standards for
OSHA to use in promulgating its extensive list of mandatory safety
standards.[5]

Speaking at the 17th annual convention of the Idaho State
AFL-CIO at Twin Falls on June 10, 1975, then Assistant Secretary
of Labor John H. Stender said:

> It may surprise you to know that management helped de-
> velop many of the standards that OSHA enforces today.
> These standards came about because conscientious em-
> ployers have understood the need for safety and health
> for many years, and worked with private groups such as
> the American National Standards Institute (ANSI) to
> develop voluntary standards. . . . When OSHA came into
> being four years ago, the Act authorized us to adopt these
> standards as law, and enforce them. . . . That was the
> beginning. . . .

While occupational health had not received as much emphasis
pre-OSHA as had occupational safety, a number of leading companies had established well-rounded occupational health programs
and had carried on a great deal of research, contributing extensively
to available knowledge and literature and eliminating major health
hazards, long before OSHA/1970.[6]

The importance of emphasizing the voluntary progress made pre-
OSHA is this: Many of those who had worked in the occupational
safety/health field for many years before OSHA are convinced that,
had Congress and the public (as well as organized labor) been
better informed concerning the voluntary safety/health movement,
the resulting legislation would have been far more constructive
and less punitive, and would have better served the function of
"[b]uilding upon advances already made through employer and

---

[4] Public Law 91-596, Sec. 3 (9), 6 (a), and 6 (b) (8) (Dec. 29, 1970).

[5] Today, more than five years after OSHA/1970 became law, the national
consensus standards are still the mainstay of OSHA administration of the Act.

[6] Robert E. Eckardt, M.D., "Annals of Industry—Noncasualties of the Work
Place," *Journal of Occupational Medicine*, vol. 16 (July 1974), pp. 472–77.

employee initiative for providing safe and healthful working conditions," as set forth in Sec. 2 (b) (4) of the Act.

Federal Legislation to 1970

The history of federal intervention in occupational safety and health until 1970 reveals not so much a deliberate development of policy as a piecemeal approach to issues as they arose, bearing in mind the constitutional question concerning the permissible role of the federal government in matters originally believed to be within the exclusive domain of the several states. For many decades it had been taken for granted that if any governmental action was warranted, it would have to be at the state level, as described above.

Perhaps the most notable exception occurred in 1910 when President Taft proposed legislation prohibiting the manufacture of phosphorus matches because of the dire health effects on employees working with phosphorus without adequate industrial hygiene controls. That legislation went into effect in 1913 and was the first federal legislation on occupational safety/health. It should be noted, however, that the law did not set standards for safe use; it simply prohibited the manufacture of the matches.

A more typical reaction was that which followed the Triangle Shirtwaist fire in New York City in 1911, when over a hundred women died when a fire in a crowded sewing shop resulted in desperate attempts by employees to flee by jumping out of windows when escape doors were locked or blocked. The public outcry that followed this tragedy resulted in state legislation dealing with fire escapes, fire prevention, and exit doors. At that time it was taken for granted that any needed legislation was within the purview of individual states, just as was the issue of workmen's compensation, then being acted upon by many states.

However, in order to avoid the constitutional issue in another context—that of wage-hour legislation—Congress seized upon a different federal authority (the right to define conditions for the production of goods purchased under federal government contracts) to enact the Walsh-Healey Public Contracts Act[7] on June 30, 1936.

---

[7] U.S. Code 1958, Title 41, Sec. 35–45.

While the basic objective of the Act was to set minimum wages and provide for premium pay for excessive daily or weekly hours for employees of government contractors, almost incidentally (there is no legislative history with respect to the provision) , the Walsh-Healey Act also provided:

> . . . no part of such contract will be performed, nor will any of the materials, supplies or equipment to be manufactured or furnished under said contract be manufactured or fabricated in any plants, factory buildings or surroundings, or under working conditions which are unsanitary or hazardous or dangerous to the health and safety of employees engaged in the performance of said contract. Compliance with the safety, sanitary and factory inspection laws of the State in which the work or part thereof is to be performed shall be prima facie evidence of compliance with this subsection.

It should be noted that even while Congress was then dealing with a subject clearly within the federal jurisdiction, the proviso includes a nod to state interest in occupational safety/health.

Since the thrust of Walsh-Healey was in the direction of wage and hour regulation, relatively little attention was paid to the safety-health proviso at first. Then, slowly, efforts were made to develop some standards to guide the Walsh-Healey safety inspectors. The first guide to basic safety and health requirements for government contractors was not issued until 1942—six years after enactment of Walsh-Healey. Revisions followed in 1951, 1956, and 1960. As government contracts became a more and more significant factor in the national economy, the private sector became more concerned about Walsh-Healey standards. Revisions proposed in 1963 and 1968 were delayed in implementation until January 1969.

Promulgation of the new Walsh-Healey standards on the last business day of the outgoing Johnson Administration in January 1969, to go into effect 30 days thereafter, seemed apparently to be designed to present the incoming Nixon Administration with a fixed set of standards to enforce, although the new Administration had no voice in their development. The new Administration, acting through Labor Secretary George Shultz, delayed the effective date of new standards for 90 days and appointed a tripartite Secretary of Labor's Safety Advisory Committee to review the published standards, particularly those related to noise, coal dust, and air contaminants.[8]

From the time of Walsh-Healey enactment in 1936 to the enactment of OSHA/1970, the U.S. Department of Labor never had more than 23 inspectors at any one time to enforce the Act's safety proviso throughout the country. Congressionally imposed budgetary restraints permitted no more extensive enforcement organization. Those who later gave strong support to federal safety/health enforcement and denigrated the role of state governments apparently had not looked critically at the federal government's 34-year record of Walsh-Healey enforcement.

In general, progress was being made in the private sector, although it was uneven. Some states had effective legislation and enforcement, many of the state standards having been modeled on ANSI or other voluntary consensus standards. These standards, however, were not rigidly enforced (or intended to be rigidly enforced). They were intended to allow for the use of discretion in both application and enforcement. When the consensus standards were later promulgated by OSHA, the discretionary aspect was eliminated, and they became rigid requirements, even though some were primarily statements of good practice with only tangential applicability to employee safety/health.

Another pre-OSHA federal involvement in occupational safety/health resulted from the 1958 amendments of the Longshoremen's and Harbor Workers' Compensation Act. This amendment,[9] enacted August 23, 1958, required covered employers to furnish and maintain employment and places of employment reasonably safe for employees.[10] It was natural that longshoring should have attracted federal action: Accident rates in the industry were ex-

---

[8] It is interesting to note that the standard of occupational noise, which remained in effect throughout OSHA's first five years and was applied to all employments under OSHA's supervision, had actually been adopted for application to government contractors only, with no more public discussion than that involved in two meetings of the Secretary's Advisory Committee. A subsequent economic study commissioned by OSHA concluded that the cost of compliance with this standard alone for 19 industries (not covering the complete OSHA jurisdiction) would amount to many billions of dollars. Bolt, Beranek, and Newman, *Impact of Noise Control at the Work Place,* Rep. No. 2671.

[9] U.S. Code 1958, Title 33, Sec. 941.

[10] Compare this modest objective with the expressed congressional purpose and policy in Sec. 2 (b) in OSHA/1970, "to assure so far as possible every working man and woman in the Nation safe and heathful working conditions. . . ."

tremely high, and maritime activities in navigable waters were clearly within the federal domain.

The Longshoring amendments authorized the Secretary of Labor to promulgate and enforce safety/health regulations, to conduct inspections and investigations, to conduct training, and to collect data on longshoring injuries and illnesses. The regulations and standards adopted by the Secretary for this industry (as well as shipbuilding, ship-repair, and ship-breaking) were promulgated only after extensive consultation with the parties at interest, with the result that they achieved broad voluntary acceptance. While the injury records of the Bureau of Labor Standards indicated a dramatic reduction in accidents following enactment of the Longshoring amendments (frequency of lost-time accidents being reduced from 132 million manhours in 1960 to 79 in 1968), recent research has cast some doubt on the validity of the statistics.[11]

Another major area in which the federal government had become involved in occupational safety and health was mining—especially coal mining. The Federal Coal Mine Safety Act, adopted July 16, 1952 (again dealing with a highly hazardous industry), was amended in 1966 and completely revised and toughened in 1969, providing for mandatory standards and fines for violating them and for violation of orders issued by the Secretary of the Interior. Under that Secretary's jurisdiction also came the Federal Metallic and Non-Metallic Mine Safety Act, adopted in 1966.[12]

Since the Walsh-Healey Act applied only to government contracts (of $10,000 and over) for materials, supplies, articles, equipment, or naval vessels, but not to other government contracts, additional legislation was subsequently enacted to cover government contracts for services and other government purchases. The most important of these was the Construction Safety Act of August 9, 1969, which applied the Walsh-Healey concepts to construction under government contract or financed by the federal government. Among the provisions of the Construction Safety Act was authority for the Secretary of Labor to promulgate safety and health stan-

---

[11] See Carol Sanford, "An Evaluation of OSHA's Impact in the Longshoring Industry," at the U.S. Department of Labor's conference on "Evaluating the Effects of the Occupational Safety and Health Programs," March 18–19, 1975, Annapolis, Md., mimeographed.

[12] The Act authorizes the Secretary of the Interior to promulgate both advisory and mandatory standards and to close a mine in case of imminent danger.

dards in accordance with the requirements of the Administrative Procedures Act and after consultation with the Construction Industry Advisory Committee created by the new law. The Construction Safety Act also provided for programs of safety/health education for employees and employers.

After enactment of OSHA/1970, standards for government contractors under the Walsh-Healey Act and the Construction Safety Act became standards applicable to all activities under OSHA jurisdiction, but many gray areas remain, with employers unclear as to what activities are covered by standards for "general industry" and what activities come under construction standards.

Pressures for Comprehensive Federal Legislation

While questions concerning the constitutionality of extensive federal intervention in the private sector are beyond the scope of this paper, it is enough at this point to note that the question of the propriety of federal action in the general field of occupational safety/health was a serious one in many minds. It is widely believed that OSHA/1970 could not have been enacted without special provisions for limited state administration of the law (under carefully circumscribed circumstances). Aside from the legal or constitutional questions, there was also the conviction that the government closest to the problem could best deal with it, and state governments were closer to most working sites than was Washington.

During the period of 1930–1967, there appeared to be little pressure from labor, management, or the public for general federal legislation relating to occupational safety and health. Each of the federal laws referred to above was considered a special case, designed to solve a special problem.

Labor unions did devote some attention to safety/health issues in collective bargaining, as reflected in various agreements. Many of those dealing with safety simply provided that the employer would continue his existing safety programs. As late as 1970 it was reported that, of 272 agreements covering 500 or more employees, only 71 (or 26 percent) contained provisions for labor-management safety committees, and only 104 made reference to safety equipment.[13] By 1972 (after OSHA/1970), only 124 out of

---

[13] Personal letter from Harry P. Cohany, chief, Division of Industrial Relations, Bureau of Labor Statistics, U.S. Department of Labor, Aug. 17, 1970.

503 selected newly negotiated agreements (24.7 percent) provided
for joint safety committees.[14] While these figures do not point to
a definitive conclusion, since union interest must be balanced
against possible employer opposition, it would appear that safety
and health did not have a high priority in organized labor's collective bargaining strategy, even after allowing for possible employer
opposition based on the theory that safety was considered the sole
responsibility of management.

On the other hand, some industries had substantial records of
labor-management cooperation for safety. In the steel-producing
industry, for example, a 1956 survey by the American Iron and
Steel Institute led to the conclusion that, while such committees
(which had been operating in the steel industry for many years)
had not lived up to their potential, they were helpful in the
promotion of accident-prevention programs.

The prevention of accidents depends on continuing, unrelenting
effort that is often carried out as a matter of faith, since it is
difficult to point out that a program actually prevented someone
from getting hurt. On the other hand, when a union can show
that it has obtained a larger workmen's compensation award for an
employee than what he had previously been offered, it is easy to
demonstrate that the union has rendered him a measurable service.
It is therefore not surprising that, in the days before OSHA/1970
raised everyone's awareness of the importance of safety/health,
unions did not give it a higher priority. The steel industry survey
referred to above disclosed that, in some cases, the meeting of the
joint safety committees became workmen's compensation gripe
sessions rather than vehicles for accident prevention.

Prior to 1970, relatively few international unions followed the
lead of the International Union of Operating Engineers, the United
Auto Workers, the International Union of Carpenters and Joiners,
the International Union of Electrical Workers, and the United
Steelworkers of America in hiring full-time safety directors or safety
and health professionals. While full-time safety directors or hygienists do not necessarily make or break a safety/health program,
the numbers of such people on the staffs of major unions may
properly be regarded as one measure of pre-OSHA priority that
such unions put on occupational safety and health.

---

[14] Winston Tillery, "Safety and Health Provisions Before and After OSHA,"
Monthly Labor Review (Sept. 1975), pp. 40–43.

Shifts in public opinion and the role of consumer organizations may have contributed to changing organized labor's scale of relative priorities. Union spokesmen admitted, during congressional hearings on OSHA, that they had been remiss in failing to exert greater effort for safety. For example, Jack Suarez, health and safety director, IUE, stated at the 1968 hearings before a House committee: "I think a good part of the reason is our fault in labor. I go around speaking on behalf of this. In negotiating a contract, it appears that safety and health clauses come after coffee breaks."[15]

In the years 1968, 1969, and 1970, the following factors combined to assure federal legislation on occupational safety and health: (1) A general trend in the direction of reduction of injury frequency in manufacturing had reached a plateau. (2) The realization grew that not only occupational safety but health as well was being endangered by little-understood air contaminants or other physical or chemical agents in the work environment, including the highly publicized "black lung" in coal mining. (3) The burgeoning consumer movement spilled over into public and occupational safety and health. (4) Labor leadership was embarrassed at having been relatively inactive in the past in an area of employee well-being that was drawing increasing public recognition. (5) The November 1968 Mannington coal mine disaster aroused miners, consumer advocates, and political activists to a new pitch of concern about safety and occupational health, coming as it did at a time of increasing concern about coal-miners' pneumoconiosis (black lung).

The stage was set for lively debate and action on federal safety and health legislation.

Legislative Issues: Labor and Management Positions

Some of the major issues that had to be resolved with reference to safety/health legislation were:

1. What should be the respective roles of state and federal governments?

2. Should there be a "general duty" clause that would make the employer a virtual guarantor of employee safety and health?

3. Should (a) development of safety/health standards, (b) in-

---

[15] *Occupational Safety and Health Act of 1969: Hearings Before the Select Committee on Labor of the Committee on Education and Labor,* U.S. House of Representatives, 91st Cong., 1st Sess., p. 244.

spection, and (c) enforcement and penalty determination all be concentrated within the Department of Labor or divided among separate agencies?

4. Should a special role be assigned to national consensus standards?

5. Should the inspector have the right to close down an operation or order the employees off the job if he found that there existed what he believed to be an imminent danger?

6. Should employees be paid for time lost from work because of hazardous conditions in the workplace (or conditions employees believed to be dangerous)?

As to the first issue—state versus federal responsibility—most employers felt more comfortable with state administration since they were familiar with it from past experience, and they also felt that state administrators might be more realistic. Consequently, the initial testimony of the major business witnesses was to the effect that the states should develop and administer the safety/health standards, with the federal role being limited to assistance in financing, research, education, and training.

Organized labor stoutly opposed state administration as a proven failure, despite the fact that the various states had a total force of about 1600 safety/health inspectors, whereas the U.S. Labor Department had very few (about 20 Walsh-Healey inspectors and possibly 200 maritime inspectors). As the congressional debates continued during 1968, 1969, and 1970, however, all sides agreed that the federal government was to have the major role in standards promulgation and enforcement, but employers insisted that the states also should have a meaningful role.

The issue was resolved by providing that the Secretary of Labor would be primarily responsible, but he was to encourage the states to assume responsibility for enforcement of safety/health standards providing, among other things, that the state's "standards (and the enforcement of which standards) are or will be at least as effective in providing safe and healthful employment and places of employment" as the federal standards.[16] This provided a floor—the standards must be at least as stringent as the federal, and their enforcement must be at least as tough—but no ceiling.

---

[16] Public Law 91-596, Sec. 18 (c) (2).

While the wisdom of utilizing the resources of the states cannot be gainsaid, experience with the varying standards, policies, and methods of enforcement and appeals in the various states has been so difficult for multistate companies to deal with that a substantial number of companies (but not all) have concluded that, with all its faults, centralized federal administration of the law is to be preferred to the variety of administrative problems associated with state administration under federal surveillance.

Some of the states, likewise, have had a change of heart. At one time or another, 50 states and territories had submitted plans for state-administered programs (with the incentive of substantial federal financing of plan development and administration). As of mid-February 1976, 23 states were operating with approved plans, with enabling legislation enacted; 15 additional states had submitted plans which had not yet met with OSHA approval; 11 states had withdrawn their plans (including six that had been approved); one state (Virginia) was involved in a formal rejection proceeding; and six states had failed to submit any plan at all.[17]

If number of inspections is any criterion of program effectiveness (which the author questions), it may be noted that whereas OSHA accounted for 88,801 inspections 1975[18] (an average of 7400 per month), the 22 states with approved programs that made reports for the last quarter of 1975 conducted 33,448 inspections during that period, or an average of 11,149 per month.[19] It is obvious that a very substantial part of the inspection load is being carried by the states—excluding those states in which state inspection had been preempted by OSHA.

With organized labor strongly committed to federal administration and opposed to state administration, and with business views divided, it can be anticipated that, if the law remains unchanged, more states will yield the administration of mandatory health/safety standards to the federal government, contenting themselves with programs of training and consultation under federal subsidies.

The second issue that Congress faced in considering federal legislation—the general duty clause—in its broadest form would

[17] OSHA, "Status of State Plans" (Washington: Feb. 13, 1976), mimeographed.
[18] "OSHA Issues December Figures on Job Safety and Health Inspection," U.S. Department of Labor news release, Feb. 25, 1976.
[19] "Quarterly State Job Safety, Health Inspections Total More Than 33,000," U.S. Department of Labor news release, Feb. 27, 1976.

have meant that any injury or illness attributable to work exposure was evidence of violation of the Act. Labor's attempt to make the employer a virtual guarantor of the employee's safety and health was bound to fail, since in many cases the hazard is caused by the employee's failure to follow specific safety/health rules supplemented by safety/health training. Had the union position prevailed, managements would have been forced to operate with Prussian discipline—which neither employers nor unions could live with.

The general duty clause finally incorporated in the Act requires the employer to furnish each of his employees a place of employment "free from recognized hazards" that could be expected to cause "death or serious physical harm."[20] This is still a heavy responsibility (in addition to a long list of specific standards), but it was a substantial compromise between the respective views. As more safety/health standards are promulgated, it can be anticipated that the general duty clause will be invoked less frequently, since it is intended to cover only those cases in which a recognized hazard is not covered by a specific standard.

The third legislative issue—whether standards development, inspection, and enforcement were to be concentrated in a single agency or divided among two or more agencies—was the focus of much of the debate during the three-year consideration of the Act. Organized labor was all for having all three functions administered by the Secretary of Labor. There was the feeling that the Department of Labor was their department, their champion in the federal establishment, more sensitive to the views of labor, and that they would have more confidence that it would administer the law in the way organized labor felt it should be administered.[21]

Business was quite prepared to have the Department of Labor discharge the duties of inspection, but businessmen felt that the inspector should not set the standards and that it would be better to have the standards developed by an independent board (with

---

[20] Public Law 91-596, Sec. 5 (a) (1).
[21] As reported on p. 641 of *Occupational Safety and Health Act of 1969: Hearings* . . ., Andrew J. Biemiller, AFL-CIO chief legislative representative, stated: "Regardless of what Administration it has been, the experience of the American labor movement is that the Department of Labor has, by and large, tried to do a first-class job in protecting the rights of American workers. We think this is quite true and will continue."

heavy reliance on the voluntary consensus system). Similarly, businessmen preferred that the enforcement function, including the determination of penalties, if any, should be vested in an independent board, court, or commission.

The resolution of this issue was also a compromise: The development of standards was allocated to the Secretary of Labor, with careful direction for the observance of due process (and with a special status provided for national consensus standards). The inspection function was likewise assigned to the Secretary of Labor, but the enforcement (and penalty-setting) function was assigned to a newly created independent Occupational Safety and Health Review Commission.

The half-decade that followed enactment of OSHA/1970 has demonstrated that the development and promulgation of safety/health standards is indeed a difficult, time-consuming task. A limited number of general industry safety standards have been amended, and a very few health standards (initiated as emergency standards) have been promulgated. One wonders whether an independent standards board, freed from other responsibilities, might have done better.

As for the independent Occupational Safety and Health Review Commission, the wisdom of providing an independent agency is demonstrated by the large proportion of contested citations that have been modified or dismissed by the Commission. However, the effectiveness of the Review Commission has been limited by unfortunate and unseemly quarrels among its individual members.

As to the fourth legislative issue—the relationship between OSHA standards and national consensus standards—businessmen were familiar with these standards because, over a period of four or five decades they had been involved in their development (with limited labor participation), and they had learned to live under them when they had been incorporated in a substantial number of state safety codes. They were also somewhat concerned about the kind of standards that might be developed in the Labor Department under pressure from organized labor. Organized labor denigrated consensus standards as representing the "lowest common demoninator" and as being inadequate, and they charged that the consensus organizations, including ANSI, were business-dominated. The latter charge was probably true, since business supported the consensus organizations and took a much more active role than did organized labor in the development of consensus standards, although labor representatives were invited and served on most consensus committees.

To a substantial extent, Congress adopted the business position by providing, in Section 6 (a) of the Act, that during the first two years after the effective date of the Act the Secretary could, by simple rule, promulgate any national consensus safety/ health standard as a standard under the Act. Under another section,[22] the Secretary is required to explain in the Federal Register if he adopts a standard different from an existing applicable consensus standard.

Had there been no provision for the direct adoption of national consensus standards, the first few years of OSHA might have been rather barren. As this chapter is being written five years after OSHA/1970 became law, very few standards other than preexisting consensus (and preexisting government) standards have been adopted. On the other hand, mandatory enforcement of consensus standards has demonstrated that standards designed for discretionary application are not ideally suited for police-type enforcement.

The five-year OSHA experience demonstrated that (1) it is extremely difficult to develop safety/health standards for universal application and enforcement; (2) the consensus system offers unique advantages in bringing together not only diverse viewpoints, but also diverse experiences and, above all, diverse expertise and disciplines; and (3) both the consensus standards and the personnel that brought them into existence might well be considered an OSHA resource in the development and amendment of safety/health standards.

The fifth issue—the right of the inspector to close down an operation and call employees off the job if he believes they are in imminent danger—brought about the most direct confrontation. Some employers, especially those in the petroleum industry, testified that unions had falsely alleged unsafe conditions in an effort to get local, state, or federal officials to close down plants (or refineries) that continued to operate during a strike. They

---

[22] Public Law 91-596, Sec. 6 (b) (8).

pointed to the tremendous pressures that would be brought on OSHA inspectors to find "imminent danger" in such cases. This issue was resolved by requiring the Secretary of Labor to petition a U.S. District Court for a temporary restraining order in case of imminent danger and authorizing the inspector to inform the employer and employees in such cases (Section 13 of the Act).

Although the problem of dealing with an imminent danger was a major issue during congressional debates on the Act, there have been very few incidents in which the imminent-danger provision has been invoked during the first five years of the Act. Although imminent danger is an emotional issue, its existence is not so prevalent or so obvious that an OSHA inspector is very likely to find it in his inspection.

As to the sixth issue—whether employees should be paid for time lost when they are called off the job (or refuse to work on a job) because of alleged danger—businessmen argued that the issue was one which should be left to employer policy or collective bargaining since it was primarily an economic issue. Labor took the position that no one should have to risk his pay in case of a dangerous job situation.

The Act is silent on this issue, and it has become the subject of litigation. At the time of writing this chapter, no court has ordered pay for such time under OSHA/1970. The first of the health standards promulgated by OSHA—the standard on exposure to asbestos—requires that any employee transferred from his regular job because of exposure to asbestos must be given the opportunity to transfer to another job with equal pay, status, and seniority, if such a job is available.[23] OSHA's right to require any rate of pay undoubtedly will be tested. Similar provisions have not been included in subsequent health standards, although they recur in some proposed standards.

The Act is also silent on the related issue of whether an employee representative who accompanies an OSHA inspector on a walk-around is required to be paid by the employer during such time. So far, when the issue has been raised, payment has not been required, although many employers, voluntarily or under a collective bargaining agreement, pay for such time lost from work.

---

[23] 29 C.F.R., Sec. 1910.1001 (d) (2) (iv) (c).

Special Problems

While the legislative battle was joined primarily on the philosophical issues discussed above, the Act as it came out of the congressional conference committee contained other provisions that are likely to make much of the federal program counterproductive. Perhaps the major obstacles to achievement of occupational safety and health under the Act, in the opinion of the author, are (1) its punitive nature, and (2) the difficulty of compliance by small business.

Largely due to pressures from organized labor, which approached the legislation as though it were a collective bargaining confrontation, the Act bears the marks of an attempt to punish an employer rather than to achieve optimum safety/health results. For example, a violator must be caught by surprise, and a $1,000 penalty is provided for giving advance notice of an inspection. This may also deprive the employer of the opportunity to check the measurements being made by an OSHA industrial hygienist, and consequently deprive him of the opportunity to obtain the best possible evidence in his own defense.

For another example, any citation issued by an OSHA inspector must be posted in the workplace immediately upon receipt. The citation is not proof of violation; it merely indicates that the inspector believes that there has been a violation. For instance, a citation for failure to undertake feasible control measures to reduce excessive exposure to noise may be dismissed or vacated later because of lack of feasible control measures. Or, after further clarification, the citation may be withdrawn by OSHA or vacated by the Review Commission. Nevertheless, the citation must be posted upon receipt. The posting of an official federal document charging the employer with violation of federal safety/health standards may damage employee relations. It may also affect the employer's credibility if he has been waging a safety campaign and is now held up as being a violator himself.

For yet another example, no employer may invite an OSHA inspector to look over his plant and advise him of possible hazards without running the risk of citation, penalties, and abatement dates if some standard is, in the opinion of the inspector, being violated. Telephone consultation is possible, however, but it is not nearly as helpful, especially for the small employer. The need for consultation has been recognized with proposals to amend the Act for this purpose. In the meantime, OSHA is seeking arrangements with private consultants to be available for consultation. Steps have also been taken to make some form of consultation available, especially to the small employer, by OSHA's encouragement and financing of state action; such programs are in effect in almost all of the approved state plans. However, the emphasis of the Act is on policing standards rather than promoting safety and health programs.

As for the small employer (however defined), it is extremely difficult for him to become familiar with the complex matrix of standards (let alone their interpretation) which may be applicable to his operation. If he is not familiar with hundreds of pages of safety/health standards, there is no way that he can tell whether he is in compliance, whether an OSHA citation is valid, whether an abatement order is reasonable, and what the results of contesting a citation are likely to be. Since he can hardly be expected to know all the standards, the small businessman just about has to take the risk that he may be inspected and possibly cited. The man from OSHA is not regarded as a friend and counselor; rather, he is an enemy who may require that difficult and incomprehensible changes be made. An OSHA inspection may result in an abatement requirement that the small businessman does not know how to evaluate or to contest.

While there might be some relief for small employers if they would and could contest invalid citations, most of them have no way of determining the validity of citations and are not likely to tangle with "City Hall." They do not generally contest citations, and thus they find themselves involved in difficult, costly, and sometime unproductive abatement procedures. The position of the small employer would become even more difficult if current OSHA proposals for putting on the employer the burden of proving infeasibility are adopted.

Other special problems that OSHA brings in its wake relate to the peculiar difficulties of occupational health—both standards compliance and development; the question, far from answered, as to feasibility; the lack of a statistical base and problems of evaluating OSHA's effectiveness; the dichotomy between compliance with standards and promotion of occupational safety/health programs; the uneasy relationship between state and federal administration of safety/health standards; and the gray area of overlapping jurisdiction between OSHA and other federal agencies such as EPA, MESA, and the Department of Transportation. Another recurring problem is the differing missions given OSHA and the National Institute of Occupational Safety and Health (NIOSH, created by OSHA/1970), and how these missions might be reconciled.

These "special problem" areas require for their adequate consideration more space than is available here. They will be referred to only as they may be germane to OSHA's impact on collective bargaining.

OSHA's Impact on Collective Bargaining

The ultimate impact of OSHA/1970 has hardly been felt. One student, steeped in the history of occupational safety and health, notes: "It is without doubt the most comprehensive industrial safety law ever passed in human history."[24] Of even greater interest, as far as this volume is concerned, is OSHA's impact on industrial relations and collective bargaining.

Spokesmen for both labor and management agree that OSHA's impact on collective bargaining is of major proportions. George Taylor, executive secretary, AFL-CIO Standing Committee on Safety and Occupational Health, has said: ". . . it is my opinion that this Act will have massive implications on the whole field of industrial relations, similar in scope to the changes in labor-management relations after enactment of the Labor Management Act of 1947."[25] Similarly, the author of this chapter has stated: "The Act authorizes the most extensive federal intervention in day-to-day plant operations than any previous legislation— and of a nature that is bound to have substantial employee relations and union relations impact."[26]

The provision of the Act having the most obvious impact on industrial relations is Section 8 (f) (1), which gives any employee (or union) the right to complain to the Secretary of Labor when the employee (or union) believes that a violation of a safety/

---

[24] McCall, p. 201.
[25] *Collective Bargaining: Survival in the 70's* (Philadelphia: Wharton School, University of Pennsylvania, 1972) , p. 394.
[26] *Collective Bargaining . . .*, p. 402.

health standard threatens physical harm or that an imminent danger exists. If the Secretary believes there are reasonable grounds for the complaint, he is required to order a special inspection of the alleged hazard "as soon as possible."

It is not a simple matter for the Secretary to determine whether such a complaint is made in good faith or whether it is made as a result of a collective bargaining dispute or internal union rivalry. In any event, the temptation to resort to a complaint or to threaten a complaint in any dispute between union and management (whether or not safety/health is in issue) is so great that the very existence of this new right can impair union-management relations and make agreement more difficult.

A complaint almost always insures an inspection—an inspection that otherwise might not be made for years, if ever. An inspection is likely to uncover some violations, even though the particular condition complained of may not be a violation. In fact, the author has received reports from companies that many union or employee complaints are found, on Labor Department inspection, not to be violations of standards, but that some other violation is often found in such employee- or union-inspired inspections. Consequently, the implicit or explicit union threat to file a complaint, whatever the subject in dispute, has to be taken seriously. The author is in doubt whether the right to file a complaint with the Secretary of Labor does more to promote safety/health in the workplace or to promote labor relations mischief.

Another obvious labor relations problem springs from the relationship between OSHA violations and Section 502 of the National Labor Relations Act, which provides that the quitting of labor "in good faith because of abnormally dangerous conditions of work at the place of employment" shall not be deemed a strike. Does the violation of an OSHA standard create "abnormally dangerous conditions of work"? It would not seem so, since over 97 percent of all OSHA citations are issued for nonserious violations. However, the temptation is there to use one more lever against the employer if the union is so minded.[27]

These two provisions of the Act—the right to trigger an in-

---

[27] Robert P. Moran, then chairman, Occupational Safety and Health Review Commission, in *Collective Bargaining . . .*, pp. 396–98.

spection and the right to quit work because of an allegedly dangerous condition flowing from possible violation of an OSHA standard—also have the potential for misuse in union organizing campaigns as well as collective bargaining.

While, as pointed out above, the number of safety/health clauses in union contracts apparently has not grown at a rapid pace, the nature of such provisions has changed, especially in major industry negotiations. Safety/health provisions have become much more sophisticated, and the operation of joint committees, where they exist, has become more far-reaching. In the petroleum industry, for example, an industry negotiation (on an individual-company basis) that included a lengthy strike against one major company resulted in substantial elements of the industry agreeing to a form of joint safety/health committee operation which, in the view of many industry observers, ceded some management functions to the joint committees and to the international union.

A joint safety (or safety/health) committee has definite advantages, in appropriate cases, from the viewpoint of the employer. It provides at least some employees with an opportunity for personal involvement that can make a positive contribution to the safety/health program. It can be a good forum for the discussion of pending changes in programs or rules or anticipated new hazards. It can encourage employees to communicate to management safety/health problems that bother them, and to do so in a nonadversary climate.

On the other hand, when labor members of a joint committee seek to have the committee empowered with authority to operate the safety/health program, most managements are likely to oppose it because they feel they cannot fulfill their legal (and moral) obligations if someone else—the joint committee—has the power to manage the program. This is the issue at the bottom of much management opposition to joint committees, despite the potential contributions they might make to safety/health programs under favorable conditions.

One of the more promising new directions, in the author's opinion, is in the agreements negotiated in 1970 between the major rubber companies and the Rubber Workers union, as an effort to approach the safeguarding of employee health in a rational manner. These agreements provided for joint committees to over-see extensive research programs conducted by two of the better known graduate schools of public health and designed to identify work-related causes of death or disease in that industry. That kind of research is likely to lead to constructive steps to solve any health problems that the research may uncover.

The Steelworkers and the major steel-producing companies have agreed upon extensive safety/health provisions that range from joint committees to treatment of alcoholics. Safety and health are matters that have long been recognized by the parties in the steel industry as deserving urgent consideration of both parties and it would be expected that their approach would be constructive. (So mature is the relationship between the parties in that industry that when OSHA was considering the promulgation of a coke-oven emission standard in 1975–1976, public hearings on the proposed standard were recessed to give the parties an opportunity to make a joint recommendation. Unfortunately, the negotiations were un-successful.)

The automobile industry, likewise, has developed its unique collective bargaining solution in agreements with the United Auto Workers. Here the outstanding features include company-paid and company-trained union safety representatives, who can subsequently play a more knowledgeable role in helping to improve plant safety/health programs.

Coming OSHA health standards pose difficult problems for both management and unions. Almost every aspect of an occupational health standard now being developed by OSHA raises labor rela-tions issues. Should unions support a zero-level for contaminants in the workplace when the cost of achieving an aseptic atmosphere may limit funds available for wages or raise prices enough to reduce demand for the company's product, or when the cost contributes to inflation or to driving manufacturing plants overseas? Should unions pursue the purist philosophy that all contaminants (or physical agents such as noise) must be engineered out, rather than use alternative protective methods such as ear-protectors or employee rotation? When there is a choice of alternative methods to protect employees—ear protection or engineering controls, for example—are costs of alternative methods a valid criterion to consider in standard-setting and enforcement?

How much education or training about the effect of contaminants needs to be given to employees who may be exposed? How
often must employees be informed if the "safe" level (as identified by the standard) proves unattainable, and the employees
are otherwise protected? Should not every major union as well
as every major company have a competent industrial hygienist
on its staff in order to help eliminate disputes as to the effect
of recognized hazards? When considering various ways of protecting employees against contaminants, should not both technical and
economic feasibility be considered? Should not the measures required to protect against a hazard have some relationship to the
seriousness of the hazard?

The law clothes employees and their representatives with extensive rights and opportunities with respect to the development
of safety/health standards. Decisions in these areas may result
in the incurrence of heavy costs, although some of the standards
have little or nothing to do with safety or health experience.
Consequently, the positions taken by unions and employees may
substantially affect employers' ability to compete, especially with
respect to their foreign competitors. Some employers have already
been accused of establishing "runaway" plants abroad to escape
onerous regulation at home.

A common provision in safety/health clauses in collective bargaining agreements is one in which the employer agrees to conform to existing law (including OSHA/1970). There were 259
such clauses among the 503 selected contracts analyzed by BLS.[28]
The clause appears to be a harmless employer concession, since
most of them expect to live up to legal requirements in any
event, but there is some question whether employers who have
agreed to such a provision recognize that it may result in having
questions of OSHA violations decided by an arbitrator rather than
by the Review Commission or the courts.

One little-noted aspect of OSHA's impact on collective bargaining concerns the largest employer in the United States—the
U.S. government. Since OSHA standards are not applied by mandate to federal establishments, and since unions negotiating with
federal agencies are limited in their wage bargaining, safety/

---

[28] See Tillery, pp. 40–43.

health offers a particularly inviting field for negotiations.[29] The Chairman of the Civil Service Commission recently reported that there were provisions for joint safety or safety/health committees in 1,015 agreements, covering a half-million federal employees and representing 39 percent of all federal contracts (exclusive of Postal Service employees).[30]

One aspect of industrial relations that merits union policy reconsideration pertains to the virtually automatic grievance filing and appeal when an employee is disciplined. The Act provides, in Section 5(b), that each employee shall comply with occupational safety and health standards that are applicable to his actions and conduct, but there are no sanctions if the employee fails to live up to this obligation. The employer is the only one who can enforce it. Since the employer may be cited for a standards violation even when that violation resulted solely from an employee's failure to follow specific instructions, it can be anticipated that employers may have to resort to stricter discipline than before, when other measures fail. Can a union then maintain its posture of championing employee safety/health if, at the same time, it should grieve over employee discipline for repeated violation of safety/health rules or work practices?

The labor relations problems that can arise are well illustrated in the *Weyerhaeuser* case,[31] in which the employer, cited for failure to have his employees wear life-jackets when working over water, defended on the ground that the employees had struck when he had previously tried to enforce the requirement. The employer, in desperation, asked that a cease-and-desist order be issued to Local 3-107, International Woodworkers of America, AFL-CIO.

For both unions and managements, occupational safety and health have been given a much higher priority than they pre-

---

[29] A bizarre example of the tendency to seize upon safety/health issues in government union relations occurred in October 1975 when Local 12 of the American Federation of Government Employees called on the Federal Mediation and Conciliation Service for assistance in negotiations with the U.S. Department of Labor about alleged unsafe working conditions in the Department's new $92,000,000 building. *Occupational Safety and Health Reporter,* Oct. 16, 1975, p. 651.

[30] *Occupational Safety and Health Reporter,* Oct. 2, 1975, p. 54.

[31] *Secretary of Labor* v. *Weyerhaeuser Co.,* Docket 624, 3 OSHC 1107 (April 24, 1975).

viously had had as a result of OSHA/1970 and by the conditions that brought about the law. That higher priority will make occupational safety/health a major issue for years to come, not only in the negotiation of new agreements but in day-to-day relations as well. It will be a disservice to employees if either side uses occupational safety/health as a strategic instrument in negotiations rather than as a valid, desirable objective. It can be anticipated that safety/health will continue to be used as an instrument in union organizing efforts.

Evaluation of OSHA's Effectiveness

After five years of operation, neither proponent nor opponent can say how much good OSHA has done. The Act itself defined occupational injuries in a way that made it impossible to use the pre-OSHA statistics as a base of comparison. Statistics on state workmen's compensation are not very helpful since these past five years have seen dynamic changes in the compensation laws in almost all states. Furthermore, there is no way to determine how many injuries or illnesses would have been avoided had there been complete compliance with OSHA standards. As pointed out above, even where a consistent set of statistics over a 10-year period was available, as in the maritime industry, recent research casts doubt on their validity. Nor does 100 percent inspection appear to make any substantial difference.[32]

The proponents of more, and more pervasive, inspections and more policing of business operations have so far been unable to demonstrate the validity of the assumption that punitive programs make for improved occupational safety/health. This is not surprising since compliance with safety/health standards is but one element—and not necessarily the most important one—of a safety/health program. There is reason to believe that compliance with applicable safety standards would prevent at most only 20–25 percent of all occupational injuries.[33] The vast bulk of injuries results in whole or in part because of employee action or inaction, and can be prevented only by a rounded employee safety/health program that includes not only engineering but also

---

[32] Robert Stewart Smith, "The Estimated Impact on Injuries of OSHA's Target Industry Program," at the USDL conference on "Evaluating the Effects of the Occupational Safety and Health Program," 1975.

[33] Smith p. 13.

education, training, enthusiasm, motivation, self-enforcement, and self-auditing of the program's operation.

In view of the massive governmental and private resources that are being and will be invested in occupational safety and health, it is essential that serious efforts be made to discover the best way of evaluating OSHA's effectiveness.

Prospects for Change in National Policy

Undoubtedly the greatest need today in determining which way the nation should go in improving national policy on occupational health and safety is to find an adequate system for evaluating the merits and shortcomings of the present program. While interesting research is going forward, no method of evaluating the effectiveness of OSHA is presently available. Until we find and use an evaluation system, our efforts toward improving the present program will have to be based on instinct—or on the wisdom and experience of those who have spent years or decades in the promotion of safety before it became a popular issue.

In the absence of reliable objective measures, the following proposals for change spring from whatever reasoning and experience the author has been able to bring to bear on a subject that has long occupied his interest:

To begin with, it should be recognized that *the policing of hundreds of mechanical (or chemical) standards in the millions of mines, mills, construction sites, manufacturing plants, farms, and other places of business is a task of such enormous proportions that no central government will ever have either the manpower or the funds to do it.* While standards are useful as guides or indexes of a part of a safety (or safety/health) program, a far better guide of effectiveness is an audit of the entire safety/health program, combined with a company's record of occupational injuries and illnesses. A health program is more than concern about a contaminant in the workplace. A safety program is more than engineering. Overconcentration on safety/health standards can and does detract from other essential elements of effective safety/health programs. The law should reflect the importance of education, motivation, and self-enforcement rather than concentrating on engineering as the guarantee of safety/health.

The law should be designed to encourage promotion of complete safety/health rather than policing "go–no-go" standards. The OSHA inspector should have as his first priority the task of helping employers and employees to achieve a more effective overall program, reserving sanctions for refractory delinquents. In that way the law would come closer to achieving its fourth policy objective, set forth in Section 2 (b) (4): ". . . building upon advances already made through employer and employee initiative for providing safe and heathful working conditions." The state governments should also be encouraged to play a significant and constructive role in promoting more effective safety/health programs.

Second, *there needs to be a mechanism for developing a labor-management dialogue, at all levels, with the objective of generating policies leading to standards that are practical as well as effective.* This is especially important with respect to health standards. It is difficult to set standards for many air contaminants because the level at which a contaminant becomes a threat to health is not known. Two approaches are possible: (1) reduce all known contaminants and other health-affecting physical agents (heat, cold, dust, radiation) to a zero- or comfort-level, resulting in an aseptic workplace; or (2) utilize the known harmful levels, with an appropriate factor of safety. It is the author's conviction that labor-management dialogue, removed from the adversary proceedings of a public hearing, can result in a much more realistic and practical standard than those now issuing and proposed in the health area. The cost of overregulation is more than a matter of money. Overregulation means that resources that might be used for constructive correction of real hazards or for research on health hazards are being wasted.

Third, *there needs to be built into the law a broad discretion as to the means by which an employer may meet the promulgated standard.* Once a noise level is set by a standard, for example, the employer, by policy decision or through collective bargaining, should be in a position to decide how the standard is to be met—through engineering, limitation on the period of exposure, personal protection, or a combination of all three. The variety of circumstances and conditions throughout American business is too great to permit any single solution to be right in all cases.

Those on the job are uniquely qualified to make that decision. Any other solution is procrustean.

Fourth, *there needs to be built into the law and its administration a greater recognition of economic realities.* The sorry travails of New York City remind us that there is no bottomless well of wealth, even for tax-supported institutions, to meet all socially desirable goals. That recognition should be expressed in terms of requiring careful consideration of the extent to which standards are made applicable to existing facilities (retroactive effect of standards), requiring technical and economic feasibility to be taken into account in both standards development and enforcement, and requiring that costs be taken into consideration in setting abatement dates.

The emphasis on economic realities raises the question of whether the author is putting dollars ahead of human life and health. Almost every decision we make is a choice among options or alternatives. Occupational safety and health is no exception, since it can be promoted in a variety of ways. Economic considerations must be taken into account in any effort to achieve socially desirable goals.

> Even such a liberal senator as William Proxmire (D. Wis.) said last month: "We have to recognize that when we put some of these laws into effect, they had an inflationary impact. We didn't recognize that at the time. We should in the future.
>
> Proxmire called for cost-benefit analysis of environmental and safety measures to insure that "in doing these things that are so desirable, we do them in such a way that it is not going to destroy the economy."[34]

Fifth, *there needs to be some built-in unity and stability about the OSHA operation.* While regional autonomy was inevitable in OSHA's early days before overall policy could be put in place, it is now time for greater central control so that administration may be uniform.

Ever since OSHA came into being, it has been in a constant state of flux. Reorganizations, changes in direction, revisions in priorities, and other discontinuities have been the order of the

---

[34] *Business Week,* Sept. 14, 1974.

day—for five years. Promulgation of emergency standards (with attendant six-month limits on the development of consequent permanent standards) has absorbed so much of OSHA's resources that other functions were mired down. There is need to develop a long-range program and a stable organization to carry it out. No less than three Assistant Secretaries have headed the agency within its first five years, making stable organization and policy impossible. In this connection, it might also be noted that congressional oversight committee hearings, reports, inquiries, and responses have also absorbed many of OSHA's resources that might have been deployed more effectively in carrying out its safety/ health mission.

The Occupational Safety and Health Administration has more than its share of highly competent, devoted, knowledgeable public servants. With lesser sanctions, longer range plans, and a stable management organization, it could make a far greater contribution to the goal of achieving optimum occupational safety and health.

CHAPTER 9

Wage-Price Policy

D. QUINN MILLS
Massachusetts Institute of Technology

Identification of Wage-Price Policy

Wage-price policy is one of a group of governmental policies in the United States that are directed toward economic and industrial relations behavior. Wage-price policy is ordinarily a short-run effort, which is conducted within the context of the continuing development of economic and industrial relations policy generally. Because of its erratic and discontinuous applications, it is more difficult to characterize than other types of federal policy. Even the name given this policy changes over time. During various periods of our history, for example, we have referred to wage-price policy as direct controls, wage and price stabilization policies, and, more recently, as incomes policies.[1]

In the economic sphere, wage-price policy must be distinguished from the fiscal and monetary policies of government. Certainly fiscal and monetary policies are directed at public objectives which include in a substantial way wage and price stability. Indeed, fiscal and monetary policy may be said to carry the weight of stabilization objectives at all times. In some circumstances, however, these macroeconomic policies are supplemented by more direct intervention by the government with the purpose of limiting wage and price inflation. These supplemental efforts are distinguishable from fiscal and monetary policy in that they involve government regulation of particular wage rates and prices, rather than the direct regulation of individual wage rates and prices. Second, wage-price policy has not ordinarily been the sort of unilaterally determined and executed governmental economic policy that fiscal or monetary policy is. Rather, wage-price policy is more akin to public policy with respect to industrial relations in which a legal framework has been

---

[1] A complete presentation of experience with wage controls in the United States may be found in D. Q. Mills, *Government, Labor and Inflation* (Chicago: University of Chicago Press, 1975).

constructed and applied by the government to regulate the relationships of private organizations and individuals. Industrial relations policy was developed with substantial impacts from labor and management and depends to a very large degree for its operation on their cooperation or acquiescence. This pattern of development is very unlike that of fiscal and monetary policy, but is quite analogous to that of wage-price policy. Too often in public discussion of wage-price policy, there emerges a conception of a stabilization program as a set of governmental regulations established to govern the rate of increase of compensation and prices. In this conception, wage-price policy is a unilateral act of the government in pursuit of its economic policy objectives, and the stabilization program involves only the drafting of regulations and perhaps their enforcement by the executive branch of government or the courts. This is, however, too limited a view.

We may characterize wage-price policy as having two major aspects. The first is an arrangement between the government and private groups as to how each will contribute to national economic policy. The second aspect is the administration of the wage-price program itself. The two are different because an agreement among groups in society that a wage-price program is necessary does not automatically insure that machinery can be established that will effectively administer the program.

This article will proceed to a brief historical review of wage-price policy in the United States. Thereafter, we will examine a series of issues arising in the context of a wage-price program, including the overall arrangement of elements of society, administrative arrangements, wage criteria, dispute settlement, and congressional and judicial review. Our emphasis will be on the wage side of wage-price policy, as appropriate to the audience of this volume.[2] A final section suggests some general lessons about wage-price policy.

History and Record of Wage Restraint Programs

The United States has a substantial history of experience with programs embodying a national wage policy. Table 1 lists nine specific programs, beginning with the National War Labor Board

---

[2] For an analysis of price controls, see D. Q. Mills, "Some Lessons of Price Control, 1971–73," *Bell Journal of Economics*, vol. 6 (Spring 1975), pp. 3–49.

TABLE 1

Programs Involving a National Wage Policy in the United States

Period of Military Conflict	Dates	Agency
World War I	1918–1919	National War Labor Board
World War II	1941–1945	National War Labor Board
Reconversion	1946	National Wage Stabilization Board
Korean War	1951–1953	Wage Stabilization Board
	1962–1965	Council of Economic Advisers ("Guideposts")
Vietnam	1966–1971	None
Vietnam	1971–1972	Pay Board
Vietnam	1973–1974	Cost of Living Council
Vietnam	1974–	Council on Wage and Price Stability

of World War I and ending in the current operations of the Council on Wage and Price Stability. What is perhaps most interesting in this historical review is that each of the programs differed from the others in important respects.

For example, the program in the first world war had no explicit wage-stabilization responsibility, but served ostensibly as a device for the settlement of labor disputes. However, disputes could not be settled without the Board's making awards on economic issues, so that a wage policy was introduced, so to speak, through the back door. In contrast, the controls program in 1971–1973 involved only a stated wage policy, with no disputes-settling mechanism associated with the wage policy. Alternatively, some of the programs possessed a statutory basis (including, for example, the Pay Board) ; others, however, did not (including the World War I program and the Guideposts program). Some programs involved the participation of business and labor; others did not. Finally, the standards applied for compensation increases varied considerably from program to program. If one catalogues the various programs listed in Table 1 along the five dimensions mentioned above, no two programs are identical.

It is tempting to explain the variations that have existed among programs as the result of the conscious adaptation of policy elements to the economic, industrial relations, and political environments of the various periods in which the programs have operated. Unfortunately, there is little evidence that policy-makers have generally behaved in this manner. Rather, program characteristics have generally resulted from a variety of influences, only some of which have been the needs of the wage policy itself. Program characteristics have too often been established by government officials with little or no experience or knowledge of the requirements of a national wage policy. Unfortunate consequences have often resulted from the imperfect match of program structure and the economic and industrial relations environment in a particular period. These unhappy experiences have later become a primary factor in causing the reintroduction of program elements in later periods. Thus, a peculiar form of cycle in program design has developed, in which attempts to adjust for previous mistakes cause different errors at a later period. As a single example, the government's frustration at its inability to enforce the Guideposts of the 1960s caused it, in 1971–1972, to develop an excessively legalistic program.

National wage policy in the United States was originally associated with periods of major military conflict. The rampant inflation of the Civil War period (1861–1865) caused concern about inflation during World War I. The Civil War experience and that of Europe in the 1920s generated even greater concern about inflation at the outset of the World War II, so that a wage-price stabilization program was relatively quickly put into place. The World War II experience was drawn on to establish the Korean program in 1951. But, in a major departure from previous experience, the major escalation of the Vietnam War in the mid-1960s was not accompanied by the establishment of a wage-price policy.[3] In retrospect, this appears to have been a major failure of national economic policy. But not only had the government departed from its practice of imposing controls during a major military conflict, it had adopted previously a new policy of experimenting with a wage-price policy in peace time. Thus, from 1962 until 1966, the Council of Economic Advisers conducted what one participant has called "an exercise in Presidential staff initiative,"[4] (the Guide-

---

[3] Michael V. diSalle reported that on the day President Johnson announced a large-scale escalation in Vietnam, he said that he had almost instituted controls that morning. DiSalle, who had been director of the Office of Price Stabilization during the Korean war, added, "Definitely, they should have had price and wage controls that same day." "Full-Scale Wage-Price Controls?" *Nations Business,* vol. 59 (October 1971) , p. 34.

[4] Joseph J. Walka, "The Origins of the Wage-Price Guideposts," *Public Policy,* vol. 16 (1967) , pp. 293–315.

TABLE 2
Increases in Earnings and Consumer Prices in Major Inflationary Periods

	Percentage Change In Average Hourly Earnings in Nonagricultural Industries	Cost of Living
Civil War (1861–1865)	54.4	149.3
First World War (1917–1920)	72.9	48.4
Second World War (1941–1945)	40.2	22.5
Korean War (1951–1953)	11.3	3.0
1962–1966	15.3	7.3
1971–1974	23.0	21.7

Sources: Data for Civil War, World War I, and World War II are from John T. Dunlop, "An Appraisal of Wage Stabilization Policies," in *Problems and Policies of Dispute Settlement and Wage Stabilization During World War II,* BLS Bull. No. 1009 (Washington: U.S. Government Printing Office, 1950), p. 170. Other data (including Consumer Price Index) are from various issues of the *Monthly Labor Review.* Data are compiled from comparisons of annual average figures.

posts) to attempt to constrain wage-price behavior. Unfortunately, the exercise collapsed in a series of labor disputes just as the major impact of the Vietnam War on the economy occurred. And in the aftermath of the main period of the war, President Nixon imposed a comprehensive wage and price control program, again in essentially a peace-time economy.

What has been the record of these efforts to implement a national wage-price policy? A comprehensive econometric review is beyond the scope of this paper, but even a cursory examination of wage and price data reveals some things of interest. Most importantly, major inflationary periods since the Civil War have not involved a decline in real average hourly earnings (see Table 2). This is somewhat surprising, since substantial declines in real hourly earnings were sometimes expected to occur, especially during World War II.[5] Further, it suggests that despite heated charges in all stabilization periods, wage controls have not ordinarily resulted in declining real earnings. This is not to say, of course, that it is not possible to identify periods during which prices rose faster than did earnings, nor that the record might not have been different without the vigilance of labor leaders. Still, it does suggest that we

---

[5] For example, President Roosevelt in an April 27, 1942, message to Congress stated, "We can face the fact that there must be a drastic reduction in our standard of living."

have done a better job managing the inflationary pressures of war-time in the 20th century than we did in the 19th.

Cooperation from Management and Labor

In the United States it has been customary for the leaders of private economic interests to be consulted about the design and development of wage-price programs. In part, this has occurred in order to secure the cooperation of management and labor in assuring the success of the program. Cooperation from the private parties is required primarily because there are many avenues through which management or labor can move to bring about the demise of a wage-price policy that they oppose. Among these avenues are work-stoppages (strikes or lockouts), challenges in Congress, and litigation in the courts. Work stoppages may topple a program dramatically. Congressional challenges may effectively get the program on issues which may be made to seem to legislators to be highly technical, inoffensive matters. Finally, litigation by either management or labor can so delay and place into question key elements of the wage-price program that it is rendered suspect and largely ineffectual for long periods. Thus, the operations of wage- and price-control machinery are predicated to a great degree on voluntary compliance by local unions and employers with the regulations, procedures, and decisions of the program.

In consequence, there is a need for cooperation by private organizations with the government in order to make a wage-price program effective. But what does the requisite "cooperation" entail? It need not involve overt and active support of the program. Historically, few wage-price programs have had overt support from either management or labor, although some have had for brief periods the overt support of one or the other. This situation is readily understandable and can be expected to recur in the future, should the occasion arise. Unions are, after all, less than enthusiastic about wage controls, and employers normally oppose controls as an unwarranted interference with the operation of the private economy.

What then does "cooperation" mean? There are two aspects: what the private parties must do, and what they must not do. The latter is the more important. The effective functioning of a wage-price program requires that the parties not seek actively to undermine it, whether by work-stoppages, lobbying, litigation, or simply ignoring the program's existence. The affirmative cooperation of the parties is less critical to the program, but nonetheless can be of major value. Positive cooperation entails the willingness of the representatives of both sides to advise their constituents to comply with the program's procedures and decisions.

How is such cooperation obtained by the government? Ordinarily, federal officials consult business and labor leaders quietly. In some instances, however, formal labor-management conferences have been held at the President's request. The Labor-Management Conference of December 1941 resulted in labor's giving a no-strike pledge for the duration of the war, in return for the establishment of a tripartite National War Labor Board. Thus, the 1941 conference laid the foundations of the World War II wage-price program. At the end of the war, President Truman convened another labor-management conference and sought authority to continue a wage-price program during reconversion. The conference failed to agree on such a program. The result on the wage side was a largely unilateral federal initiative, the National Wage Stabilization Board, which virtually collapsed early in 1946 and was officially dissolved in February 1947. The formal conference has not been used since as a device to initiate a program. But in 1971 the President, after having announced the structure of the wage-price control machinery, was obliged, in order to secure union acquiescence, to initial a memo granting "autonomy" within the stabilization program to the Pay Board. This recent experience, and that in the Guidepost period, cannot suggest confidence in the ability of the government to conduct successfully the negotiations with business and labor necessary to the firm foundation of a wage-price policy.

When the government explores with private parties the advisability and form of a wage-price program, what areas of concern do the private parties ordinarily express? The unions are generally concerned about three issues. First, they insist that consumer prices as well as wages be restrained. But the degree of restraint on prices, and particularly the question of the expected course of real wages, depend upon the circumstances of the time. In periods of major military conflict, declining real earnings may be acceptable; whereas in peace-time periods, even a limited constraint on real wages may be unacceptable. Second, the unions will ask that profits be restrained. Third, if the government wishes to minimize work stoppages, the unions will insist on a tripartite mechanism to provide a forum for the resolution of disputes.

Business will also emphasize three major concerns. First, it will suggest that the degree of wage and price restraint be commensurate, so that profits are not unduly squeezed. Second, any disputes-settling mechanism will be required to refrain from intervening, as much as possible, in the noneconomic aspects of their relationships with the unions. In part, this position of the business community arises from experience with the War Labor Board during World War II, especially with respect to the issue of union security. Third, in order to avoid government involvement in noneconomic issues, business has normally opposed a disputes function for a stabilization board, and in the Korean War period and also in 1971–1974 the business community largely prevailed in its insistence that there be no disputes machinery as part of the wage-price program.

Finally, a key to the World War II program was the involvement of the agricultural sector in the general arrangement on wage-price policy. Agriculture was not included in the reconversion program, an omission which contributed to its failure.[6] Nor has the agricultural sector been involved in subsequent stabilization efforts; and in 1973–1974, when agricultural prices rose dramatically, that sector contributed substantially to the collapse of the wage-price stabilization policy.

Administrative Arrangements

A wage-price policy, if pursued on a basis involving more than mere exhortation, is a complex undertaking involving the coordination of many separate elements. Several of the elements of a program are central to its overall performance. Analytically, a program may be thought of as analogous to a set of tools designed and employed by the government in an attempt to influence the behavior

---

[6] John T. Dunlop, "The Decontrol of Wages and Prices," in *Labor in Post-war America,* ed. Colston E. Warne (New York: Remson Press, 1949), pp. 3–24

of employers and employees in directions that will contribute to wage-price stability. This section is concerned with several administrative instruments that are necessary to a successful wage-price control program.

Tripartitism

Wage control in the United States has generally been performed by a tripartite board of management, labor, and the government. In part, this has been because labor insisted upon a role in the administration of wage controls as part of the general stabilization arrangement. But there has long been a controversy regarding the appropriateness of tripartite wage boards. Opponents of tripartitism have argued that involvement of business and labor representatives in the decision-making process of a government agency is inappropriate. During World War II, George Taylor, an advocate of tripartitism, occasionally answered the critics of the National War Labor Board (NWLB) by pointing out that the board had been neither an ineffectual debating society nor a dictatorial regulator.[7] But not all were convinced, so that at the advent of the Korean War a bitter battle was waged within the Administration as to the advisability and/or functions of a tripartite board.[8] The performance of the tripartite Wage Stabilization Board during the Korean period did little to convert the critics of tripartitism, and a similar dispute over tripartitism occurred with the Nixon Administration in 1971. The Pay Board was established as tripartite, but soon, due to the labor members' withdrawal, was converted to an all-public board.

The position of the proponents of an all-public wage-stabilization agency was well summarized by the authors of the report on the Wage Stabilization Board. Since the arguments on either side change little with passing decades, it is useful to quote their description here:

> Proponents of an all-public board argue that there are general public values distinct from, conflicting with, and

---

[7] George Taylor, "The War Labor Board's Role in the Democratic Process," address at Swarthmore College, Dec. 6, 1942; text in *Termination Report* of the National War Labor Board, vol. 2, p. 502.

[8] See U.S. Wage Stabilization Board, *Wage Stabilization Program, 1950–53*, vol. 1 (1953), pp. 74–75, mimeo (hereafter WSB).

offsetting the value of responsible participation of collective bargaining parties. They would rather see public representatives make and promulgate wage policy, taking technical advice from interested parties but precluding the latter from voting authority. To some extent this view may represent a belief that private party representatives cannot, in the nature of their allegiances, take responsibility for necessary restraint and regulation but will promote joint interests against the general public and carry public members as mediators along with them. On disputed issues, it represents the contrary complaint that the public members of a tripartite board will take a "pro-labor" or "pro-industry" position rather than voting the "center" or otherwise on the merits of the case.[9]

The case for a tripartite wage board includes the following arguments: First, since a wage-control program cannot be effectively pursued over a prolonged period without the cooperation of management and labor, and since their cooperation (especially labor's) includes the demand to participate in the administration of wage controls, there are no viable alternatives to tripartitism. Second, tripartite boards are better informed and tend to develop more practical and effective policies by virtue of the interchange among the three parties. Third, tripartite boards may obtain a degree of general compliance with the stabilization program that a purely governmental body cannot obtain.

Selective Controls in Construction

Often in the United States it has been urged that controls be applied only in certain industries or to certain employers and unions. The advantages of partial controls are argued to be several, including simplicity in application and minimization of administrative machinery, costs, and delays. Two particular forms of selective controls have occasioned most experimentation: controls by industry, and controls by size of employer. Arguments for selective controls by industry have generally been unavailing, with two exceptions: in the construction industry and, more generally, among industries in a period of gradual decontrol.

---

[9] WSB, vol. 1, p. 20.

The economic and institutional peculiarities of the construction industry have required special treatment in periods of direct wage controls.[10] Inflationary pressures in construction both prior to World War II and in the early 1970s were so acute as to result in the imposition of controls in construction well in advance of those in the economy generally. Also, special wage-control boards have been established for construction in each period of controls, and special policies have been applied. Problems have arisen because some feared that special treatment would be a special license for construction to ignore general stabilization regulations, and because the existence of a construction board created coordination problems with the general stabilization machinery. Yet there can be little doubt that these special arrangements strengthened the overall stabilization policy. Those familiar with construction have been agreed in all periods of controls that the application to construction of policies developed for industry generally would have resulted in chaos.

The record of the Construction Industry Stabilization Committee (CISC) in 1971–1974 deserves special mention. The committee was a tripartite body established in March 1971, five months prior to the wage-price freeze which initiated controls in the economy generally. During the period of operation of the CISC, the total first-year compensation increase in newly negotiated collective bargaining agreements in construction fell from 17 percent in 1970, to 11 percent in 1971, to 6.0 percent in 1972, and to 5.4 percent in 1973. Construction moved from substantially above the overall average of the economy in 1970 to below the overall average in 1973. The CISC was not alone responsible for this moderation, but it was a major contributing factor.[11]

---

[10] D. Q. Mills, "Construction Wage Stabilization: An Historical Perspective," (in *Proceedings* of the IRRA Spring Meeting, 1972), *Labor Law Journal*, vol. 23 (August 1972), pp. 462–67.

[11] See D. Q. Mills, "Explaining Pay Increases in Construction: 1953–1972," *Industrial Relations*, vol. 13 (May 1974), pp. 196–201. The data cited are CISC data and include wage and fringe benefit adjustment. Much of the data published by the Bureau of Labor Statistics are roughly comparable, but are less comprehensive in coverage and in many instances fail to take full account of fringe benefit changes. For an analysis based on BLS data, which charts roughly the same path for construction wages, see Michael L. Wachter, "The Wage Process: An Analysis of the Early 1970s," *Brookings Papers on Economic Activity* (2: 1974), p. 511.

In both World War II and the current period, construction wage-stabilization programs have had important long-range objectives that have not characterized stabilization efforts in the rest of the economy. During World War II, the administration of the no-strike pledge involved the settlement of jurisdictional disputes as well as disputes over wages and conditions of work. "The experience in industry-wide responsibility represented by the Wage Adjustment Board . . . was to provide (personal) associations which were to seek more effective settlement of wage contract disputes and machinery for the problem of jurisdictional work stoppages in the post-war era."[12] The CISC attempted to emphasize the development of institutional arrangements that would improve collective bargaining in the future, the most important such arrangements being bipartite boards in each craft for dispute settlement. Stabilization authorities, of course, hoped to assure the continued existence and effectiveness of the craft boards after the stabilization machinery was abolished; thus they attempted to establish as firm a foundation for the future of the boards as possible.[13]

Case-by-Case versus Regulatory Approach

At the risk of some oversimplification, a contrast may be drawn between two approaches to administration of a wage-stabilization program: a case-by-case approach versus a regulatory approach. To a degree, stabilization authorities must choose between the two in establishing whatever mix of procedures is desired. The case-by-case approach may be characeirzed as eschewing the establishment of specific rules or principles except in the most general sense and placing reliance instead on the adjudication of individual cases on their merits. Out of the accumulation of decisions in specific cases are developed policies applicable in other instances. Potential issues which do not come before the board in specific cases are not decided. Precedents may be utilized by the board, or, as experience accumulates, discarded. The regulatory approach, in contrast, in-

---

[12] John T. Dunlop and Arthur Hill, *The Wage Adjustment Board: Wartime Stabilization in the Building and Construction Industry* (Cambridge, Mass.: Harvard University Press, 1950), p. vii. The National Joint Board for the Settlement of Jurisdictional Disputes was established in 1948 with John T. Dunlop as its first impartial chairman.

[13] See a speech by Secretary of Labor James Hodgson to the craft boards, Jan. 13, 1972, in Washington.

volves the preparation of general rules designed to cover most or all foreseeable situations and the minimization of consideration of particular cases. A stabilization program necessarily involves application of both procedures, so that the choice between the two approaches is primarily one of degree of emphasis.

The major advantages of a case-by-case approach are five in number. First, considering the full record of cases which come before a board provides an unequaled opportunity for education of the members of the board and its staff in the complexities of wage patterns, practices, and interrelationships. No individual or small group of individuals in this country possesses a comprehensive understanding of existing patterns of wage relationships and the changes occurring therein, particularly in the absence of continual direct involvement in wage-setting. Further, since wage determination is only one aspect of the economic decisions confronting management and labor (changes in working rules are fully as significant to cost increases and potential impact on prices, and working-rules changes are often intimately related to wage adjustments), only a review of the entire context of wage adjustments in individual situations can convey the full range of the economic factors involved in a wage decision. Second, as a corollary of the first characteristic, a case-by-case approach allows decisions on wage adjustments to be made in the context of a full understanding of the implications of wage behavior for other economic variables, such as employment, prices, and so on. The likelihood is that the overall purpose of economic stabilization is best served by such a comprehensive review. Third, a case-by-case approach supports tripartitism. As Archibald Cox has pointed out, "Partisan [i.e., labor and management] members of a tripartite board can acquiesce in a policy developed through a series of specific decisions, some of which are favorable to one side and some to the other, even though they are unwilling to give express approval to the same policy when stated in a single document."[14]

Fourth, a case-by-case approach permits subtle shifts in policy when they become necessary, without the elaborate and often controversial task of revising or enlarging detailed regulations.

---

[14] John T. Dunlop and Archibald Cox, "The Bituminous Coal Case," unpublished manuscript, 1954, p. 13.

This capacity of a board to shift policy is increasingly advantageous the more extended the period of controls.[15] Finally, the most often used (historically) advantage of a case-by-case approach is the capacity it affords to depart from general rules when the peculiar conditions of a specific situation require it. "The National War Labor Board," wrote public member Edwin E. Witte, "decides every case on its own facts." In consequence, Witte added, the board may abandon what seems general policy because of the peculiar circumstances of an individual case.[16] In more recent years, both the Wage Stabilization Board and the Pay Board similarly retained the discretion to handle some individual cases outside the automatic application of general regulations.

The advantages claimed for the regulatory approach are in some instances the reverse of those claimed for the case-by-case method—so that advantages of the one are perceived as disadvantages of the other. Four supposed advantages may be listed for the regulatory approach. First, this approach minimizes the substantial administrative task of voluminous processing.[17] Even where a board desires to proceed on a case-by-case basis, it cannot do so in a comprehensive fashion but must utilize individual cases to establish or modify policy for application to other cases. The volume of wage applications always threatens to engulf a wage board, so that a definite requirement for a substantial reliance on a regulatory approach is inevitable. Second, a regulatory procedure permits a stabilization board to avail itself of the advantage of a formal rule-making procedure which may involve a review process (e.g., including hearings) prior to the establishment of individual regulations. In contrast, a case-by-case approach is subject to the objection that, if case decisions are intended to be precedent-setting, they should be based on a survey of the problem area generally, not on the merits of a particular, perhaps unusual,

---

[15] John T. Dunlop, "An Appraisal of Wage Stabilization Policies," in *Problems and Policies of Dispute Settlement and Wage Stabilization During World War II*, BLS Bull. No. 1009 (Washington: U.S. Government Printing Office, 1950), p. 160.

[16] Supplementary opinion of Edwin E. Witte, public member, in the case of *Melville Shoe Corporation*, NWLB No. 111-6642D (Aug. 23, 1945); text in *Termination Report*, vol. 2, p. 401.

[17] "Only enough of a bureaucracy is needed," opined Federal Reserve Board member Sherman Maisel, "to devise reasonably equitable rules of the game, keep them current, and explain them." *New York Times*, Nov. 24, 1971, p. 57.

single case. Third, the regulatory approach tends to create a relatively legalistic atmosphere in the administration of a stabilization program, as opposed to a bargaining or problem-solving approach. To some, the de jure approach is preferable. For one thing, in such an approach the cooperation among public, employer, and labor members characteristic of a tripartite board is minimized in favor of a more technical application of specific rules. For public members adverse to the difficulties of a tripartite structure, or for an administration opposed to tripartitism, a regulatory approach seems most desirable.

Fourth, a regulatory approach tends to minimize the time, effort, and specialized knowledge required of the public members of a board and its staff, as compared to a case-by-case approach. Under a regulatory procedure, decisions may be more easily delegated to staff, with decisions of policy reserved for the board; such decisions will be made in the rarefied atmosphere of abstractions, without the complexities and ambiguities of real-world situations introduced by specific cases. The demands made by such a mode of operation on the board members are reduced from a form of problem-solving in the interest of economic stabilization to one of interpretation and application of rules. Fifth, a regulatory approach tends to relieve a board of any responsibility for dispute settlement by making violation of stabilization policy a matter for after-the-fact enforcement and litigation rather than a matter of assisting collective bargaining and personnel administration to operate in a stabilizing fashion.

Historically, there has been from World War II to the present a steadily increasing reliance on comprehensive regulations as the preferred method of administering stabilization and a consequent reduction of the case-by-case procedure to the handling of exceptions only. What can be offered as an evaluation of the trend toward regulations as the primary focus of stabilization policy? The advantages of the regulatory approach have just been described. But has the increasing use of regulations in wage control uncovered any serious limitations on the method? There are, perhaps, two such limitations apparent in the experience of 1971–1972. First, the regulatory approach engenders an excessive degree of legalism in the stabilization program. Second, regulations and the ensuing legalism become handicaps to actually affecting the decisions of employers and unions in the wage-stabilization area.

Standards for Wage Rates and Fringe Benefits

A General Standard

Standards for compensation increases under a wage-stabilization program have taken many forms. At the extreme, two different approaches may be identified. One approach attempts to establish an employer cost-based standard for the increase in total compensation. The alternative approach establishes separate standards for wage rates and each type of fringe benefit. In general, the proponents of the single-standard approach argue that it is the most simple administratively, and is most intelligible to the public. The proponents of the detailed standards argue their method to be more comprehensive and complete and, therefore, more likely to be successful in restraining compensation increases.

Historically, the National War Labor Board of World War II developed the most comprehensive and complete set of detailed compensation standards in our history. And the Pay Board, in 1971–1972, attempted to carry the single-standard approach to its furthest developments. Yet, even the National War Labor Board found a use for a general standard in the form of the Little Steel Formula. And the Pay Board could not avoid, in part because of congressional action, establishing a long list of exceptions to its general pay standard and special regulations covering certain types of fringe benefits. In general, therefore, one may conclude that the debate between proponents of a single standard and its opponent is one of degree as much as one of principle.[18]

The criteria for establishing or modifying a general pay standard ordinarily occasion considerable public debate, for more, for example, than the equally or more important administrative matters discussed above. The criteria ordinarily proposed as the basis for a general standard are increases in the cost of living or in labor productivity, or both. However, because a discussion of the alternative bases of a general standard would require several pages at the least, and because I have elsewhere examined this topic in a publi-

---

[18] See, for example, John T. Dunlop, "Inflation and Incomes Policies," Eighth Monash Economic Lecture, Monash University, Clayton, Victoria, Australia, 1974.

cation of the Industrial Relations Research Association,[19] there will be no further discussion of these matters here.

Exceptions

Stabilization boards have always provided exceptions of many sorts to a general wage standard. Provisions for exceptions serve several purposes, some of which are integral to the operation of a stabilization program and others of which are somewhat incidental (although not necessarily unimportant) to its operations. Among the various purposes for exceptions that are integral to a stabilization program, five of considerable importance may be distinguished. First, exceptions are necessary to prevent undue hardships to groups of workers or employers which might arise from the application of general standards. A common exception for this purpose has been the special treatment awarded proposed increases for low-paid workers (the substandards exceptions). Second, exceptions may be necessary to permit needed reallocations of manpower. This exception has been especially important in wartime. Third, exceptions may be provided in order to further objectives of public policy not narrowly related to stabilization itself. For example, adjustments in wages necessary to eliminate discrimination by race or sex in compensation (to establish "equal pay for equal work") may be permitted regardless of general standards. Fourth, provisions for the establishment of exceptions provide an important degree of flexibility in a program. For example, the establishment of certain exceptions may be necessary to lessen anomalies created in unusual circumstances by the application of general policies to unforeseen circumstances. Fifth, and perhaps most important quantitatively, exceptions to a general standard are necessary to adjust wage relationships.

Standards for Fringe Benefits

In the years during and since World War II, fringe benefits have become an important element of employee compensation in American industry. Fringe benefits have, therefore, been of in-

---

[19] D. Q. Mills, "The Problem of Setting General Pay Standards: An Historical Review," in *Proceedings of the 26th Annual Winter Meeting*, Industrial Relations Research Association (Madison, Wis.: IRRA, 1973), pp. 9–16.

creasing concern to stabilization authorities. But, if anything, the difficulties of regulating fringe benefits are growing and pose a special problem of great importance for the future. In some important instances fringe benefits have become a virtually uncontrollable engine for inflationary pressures. The inflationary impact of fringes on total compensation increases can be seen in aggregate statistics. In the late 1960s and early 1970s, for example, increases negotiated in fringe benefits exceeded those in wages, causing the package increase (wages plus benefits) to be above that in wages, even at the high rates of wage increase occurring those years.

Two main types of fringe benefits can be distinguished, and these types should be discussed separately.[20] There are, on the one hand, provisions for health care and pensions normally provided through insurance funds. On the other hand, there are benefits such as paid holidays, paid vacations, sick leave, maternity benefits, overtime premiums, shift premiums, and so on. Because of the peculiar circumstances which attend the operation and cost of insurance plans, these two types of benefits have for many years been distinguished in public discussion and in stabilization policies. In general, the relative importance of both types of fringes has been increasing in the total compensation package. For example, the cost of health, welfare, pension, and similar benefits (excluding social security and other payments required by law) in a sample of 146 companies in the United States rose from 6.5 percent of total payroll in 1949 to 10.9 percent in 1969. Payments for time not worked (e.g., overtime premiums, vacations, holidays, paid lunch periods, and so on) rose from 5.8 percent in 1949 to 10.6 percent in 1969.[21]

Health, Welfare, and Pension Plans: There is a long-standing myth that employer contributions to social-welfare plans such as health-insurance or pension plans are not inflationary and therefore are of no interest to stabilization authorities. During the Korean period, when fringes were of less relative significance as an element of compensation than they were later, this view was expressed even

---

[20] The introduction of the term "fringe benefits" has been attributed to a regional chairman of the NWLB. See James C. Hill, "Stabilization of Fringe Benefits," *Industrial and Labor Relations Review*, vol. 7 (January 1954), p. 221.

[21] U.S. Chamber of Commerce, *Employee Benefits*, 1969.

by representatives of government. This argument, that insurance (and pension) plans do not add to purchasing power and therefore cannot be inflationary, is deficient in several respects because it ignores other economic consequences of increases in nonwage compensation. First, increases in prices may be required because of increased employer expenses for insurance programs. Second, inflationary pressures may be exerted in the medical industry by increased health-insurance programs.[22] Third, the impact of an increase in insurance costs on the total compensation package of one group of workers may be transmitted by earnings comparisons to other workers, and translated into either increased fringe benefits or higher wages. Thus, regardless of the impact of insurance programs on purchasing power, other potential consequences of their increase require the attention of stabilization authorities.

History suggests three methods of regulating plans in a period of stabilization: blanket approval, flexible and broad general standards of both benefit and cost nature, and a formula approach to costs exclusively. None is satisfactory with respect to insurance plans in 1970s. Perhaps in no other area of compensation does past experience provide so little guidance for the future. What explains this unusual situation? The fundamental cause is that insurance plans have become, in important instances, highly complex features of the economic environment. There has developed a bewildering variety of plans, benefits, costs, and administrative devices,[23] so that characteristics of a plan may serve as a target for other groups of workers, contributing thereby to economic instability. Several examples may help to clarify the point. First, the cost of maintaining benefit levels has in some circumstances become so high as to exert a destabilizing influence on other wage and benefit packages. This has been especially important in industries characterized by numerous small employee units and multiple employers, where the costs of maintaining pension coverage comparable to that provided in plans covering many workers has sometimes become very expensive. Second, in some instances, benefit

---

[22] Joseph W. Garbarino, *Health Plans and Collective Bargaining* (Berkeley: University of California Press, 1960).

[23] Bureau of Labor Statistics, *Administration of Negotiated Pension, Health and Insurance Plans,* Bull. No. 1425-12 (Washington: U.S. Government Printing Office, May 1970).

levels have been negotiated which both parties know will have extreme cost consequences in the future. Such plans are potentially unstabilizing in their effect on costs and prices in the establishments directly involved and, through comparisons in bargaining, exert unstabilizing influences on compensation in other employee units. A stabilization program which allows cost increases in this situation simply because benefits were previously agreed to by the parties is also an inadequate stabilization effort.

Other Fringe Benefits: Noninsurance fringes, like insurance plans, may be regulated either through the benefits provided or the costs incurred (or both). Past stabilization boards have attempted one or the other method, not both. Control of benefits is, generally, the more complicated and administratively difficult method, but is also potentially the more effective contribution to stabilization objectives. Regulation of both benefits and costs, a yet more difficult and potentially more effective approach, may be required in the future, as is the case with respect to insurance plans. What has been the historical experience with respect to noninsurance fringes? During World War II, these fringes were reviewed on a case-by-case basis, resulting in the establishment of standards for the level of benefits, especially with respect to overtime premiums and shift differentials. In the case of other fringes, the board would permit establishment or improvement, if justified by area or industry practice, but would not award them in disputes cases. During the Korean period the Wage Stabilization Board, following an abortive attempt to include all fringes on a cost basis in the general wage standard, adopted a special policy applicable initially to five types of noninsurance fringes: paid vacations, premium pay for days and hours of work, paid holidays, shift differentials, and call-in (or reporting) pay. These so-called "major" fringes were to be approved by the board on the basis of area or industry practice.

The Pay Board in 1971 abandoned all efforts to regulate benefits. Rather, the board shifted to a totally cost-oriented standard, effectively including noninsurance fringes in the general pay standard. The logic of the board's shift in policy from previous periods was twofold. First, it wished to control total compensation with a view toward constraining unit labor costs of production; there are often substantial secondary (as well as direct) impacts on employer costs occasioned through existing levels of fringes. Second, the Pay Board wished to grant as much flexibility as possible to local parties in the allocation of the permissible pay increases among wage and fringes. No comparative standards for benefits were included, therefore, except insofar as a catch-up exception was permissible— but here again the standard was a percentage increase in cost.

Was Pay Board practice an improvement on past stabilization policies? Probably not. Yet, the consequences of an exclusively cost-based policy for fringe benefits depend on the economic environment and the duration of the stabilization program. In an expansive economy it invites the building of substantial distortions in the benefits provided to different groups of workers. By ignoring comparative factors, the cost-oriented policy invites great difficulties for stabilization authorities in the second and third years of a stabilization program. Furthermore, at the expiration of a stabilization program, the distortion of comparative relationships invites a surge of bargaining to obtain for some workers what others have already received. That is, the same sort of leapfrog bargaining which has become familiar in wage negotiations can operate equally well with respect to fringes. The advantage of comparative benefit standards for fringes is that they provide a method of constraining the possibility of this form of distortion and readjustment of the structure of fringe benefits.

Dispute Settlement

The settlement of labor disputes is a matter both critical to the success of a stabilization program, yet also tangential. Dispute settlement does not involve the structure of a program, or its administration, or the standards for wage adjustments—matters which have been the topic of earlier chapters. Rather, dispute settlement involves the protection of the program from assaults upon it. Yet, this matter is of as great importance as any other, for the effort expended upon the development and administration of a wage-stabilization program is futile unless the program can be defended from those who seek to disrupt it. Since a program that involves significant wage restraint is almost certain to invite challenges, the importance of a method or methods of response to challenges can hardly be overrated. The fundamental problem is to find a method of settling labor disputes within the context of the stabilization policy. Since it is unlikely that overt challenges (such as a strike against the program) can be entirely avoided, a secondary objective is to minimize challenges, so that the government has a chance to confront successfully those that do occur. An important aspect of defeating overt challenges is for the government to mobilize, in advance, support which will deter some adversaries and be effective in constraining others.

The lessons of history are very important in this area. During World War II strikes in the bituminous coal industry and on the railways repeatedly challenged the National War Labor Board, with some success for the unions involved, but they did not destroy the program. In retrospect, the unions' no-strike pledge of December 1941 has been adjudged the single major factor in preserving the stabilization effort. In contrast, the stabilization board of the reconversion period disappeared in a wave of strikes in 1946. During the Korean period, a nationwide steel strike in 1952 seriously undermined the entire stabilization program (both wages and prices) and prepared the way for a bituminous coal dispute to topple the Wage Stabilization Board in the fall of 1952. In 1966, the Machinists (IAM), in a dispute wtih major airlines, administered the coup de grace to the Guideposts. In 1971–1972, the Pay Board avoided a serious threat to the controls program by two stratagems: first, by establishing controls after the major negotiations of 1971 were completed and, second, by administering a very flexible program of limited wage restraint. But, faced with a number of negotiations in 1973, the board's lack of any disputes-settlement machinery became a causal factor in its abolition.

The variations that may occur in the relationships between a wage board and a labor dispute are many, each involving peculiar problems for a stabilization program. In some instances the problem is to achieve settlements within the criteria propounded by the board. In other instances the problem is to prevent a union from compelling an employer to disregard a stabilization board's directives. In yet other circumstances, a board may be required to assist in the resolution of a dispute occasioned by the application of its policies. It is characteristic of industrial disputes, however, that any strike involving the policies of a board, no matter what the strike's origin, may become profoundly threatening to the existence of a wage-stabilization program if the dispute cannot somehow be resolved.

Congressional and Judicial Review

No aspect of the environment of a stabilization program is of greater potential importance to a wage-stabilization board than the opinion of Congress. At any moment Congress is capable of restraining, harassing, or altering a wage-control program. The means at the disposal of Congress are several, including hearings, budgetary limitations, and enactment of legislation. Because of the importance of Congress, the public members of a stabilization board have a special responsibility to keep careful watch on congressional opinion. And since Congress has a long record of generally unfortunate interventions into the operations of stabilization programs, stabilization authorities have every reason to be wary of congressional opinion.

The overt and detailed intervention of Congress in the administration of a wage-control program, which had increased from World War II to the Korean period, increased further in 1971. So substantial did this intervention become in December 1971 that it is important to recount it briefly here. As the Pay Board met to develop policies for application upon expiration of the freeze (November 15, 1971), Congress was considering extension of the Economic Stabilization Act of 1970 beyond its two-year period. On four major issues, Congress wrote into the extension reversals of Pay Board policy. First, it separated certain major fringe benefits from the 5.5 percent general pay standard of the board, which had included them.[24] Second, Congress allowed, generally, retroactive payment of wage increases due during the freeze. Third, Congress established standards for the substandards exemptions which, though not setting a cents-per-hour figure, did permit legal suits to overturn the standard that was established by the Cost of Living Council. Fourth, Congress mandated, in the amendments to the Act, a 5.5 percent pay increase for many federal employees on

---

[24] The Internal Revenue Service, acting as the Pay Board's agent, was ruling in 1971 that all fringe benefits were included in the general standard of 5.5 percent. See, for example, an arbitration award in which Pay Board standards were an issue: *Daily Labor Report*, No. 79 (April 21, 1972), p. A-1.

January 1, 1972, not July 1972, as requested by the President.[25] This was the second major increase for federal employees within a period of less than one year. When the Pay Board hesitated to revise its regulations to reflect these amendments, Chairman Patman of the House Banking and Currency Committee threatened to hold oversight hearings. On March 3, 1972, the Pay Board announced it had completed the revision of its regulations to reflect the congressional actions.

There was little in this conflict between the stabilization authorities and Congress to reflect credit on either party. The wage-stabilization authorities had developed a program with insufficient flexibility and so opaque a group of regulations as to be unintelligible to most persons. Congress, however, did not direct its attention to the real shortcomings of the program, but rather developed a statute which made all but impossible even a far better structured program than that which had been developed.

Stabilization policies may also be challenged in the courts, often successfully. In some instances a successful challenge may be the result of procedures or decisions of a board which are indeed inappropriate under the regulations or policies of the program. In other instances, however, successful challenges may result from the imperfect understanding which federal judges and the Justice Department (which must represent the stabilization program in court) possess of the economic and industrial relations factors that affect a stabilization program. Generally, labor and management have access to a greater fund of knowledge and experience respecting economic and industrial relations matters than does the government, so that a contest in court is often extremely hazardous for stabilization authorities. Furthermore, the most significantly disadvantageous aspects of a legal challenge to an action of a stabilization board may not be the danger of an unfavorable decision but the delays involved in litigation. Pending cases which challenge major policies or decisions of a board may as effectively limit its activities as an unfavorable decision by causing other elements of management and labor not party to the suit to arrange their own behavior to be consistent with the possibility of the government's loss in the decision of the court.

---

[25] *Washington Post*, Dec. 23, 1972, p. 1.

Concluding Comments

1. The single most important element in the success of a wage-price policy is that there be some understanding between management, labor, and the government regarding the form, content, and environment in which the program will operate. No particular type of arrangement is required. Rather, the understanding may be made to fit the circumstances of the moment. At one extreme, a national emergency may require a vigorous program of wage restraint, necessitating an extensive and specific understanding among management, labor, and the government. At the other extreme, a program of moderate restraint in a peacetime economy may require only limited arrangements developed on an ad hoc basis. In this situation, the contribution to the success of a stabilization effort of limited arrangements may be important even when there is conflict among the various groups on most economic and political matters.

2. The interest or involvement of management and labor cannot be long retained by a stabilization program that is narrowly restricted to limiting wage increases. Union leadership cannot justify to its membership participation in such a program, nor can management afford to ignore other aspects of industrial relations by a narrow pursuit of wage restraint. Elements of a stabilization program in addition to wage restraint may include, for example, procedures for dispute settlement, attempts to improve the functioning of collective bargaining in various sectors or industries, and concern for the long-run improvement of industrial relations. A wage-stabilization agency may deeply involve business and labor representatives in the stabilization effort in individual situations through devoting attention to problems at the workplace which may have been translated into requests for economic adjustments before the stabilization program began. In general, what is required of a stabilization agency is that it provide management and labor with an opportunity to address their common problems, which are generally broader than stabilization issues, through the mechanism of the stabilization program. This attention to the broader context of problems within a stabilization framework involves the potential for engaging substantial support of business and labor for the stabilization effort and for continuing that support over a period

of several years, to a degree which a narrow attention to wage restraint alone cannot accomplish.

3. The importance of interrelationships in compensation patterns and practices is an argument against too great reliance in a stabilization effort on formulas or other types of overly generalized wage regulations. The complexity of the economy is such that a stabilization board cannot know in advance what anomalies in individual situations may result from the application of formulas or specific rules. Too often a formula will permit different rates of compensation increase within a closely interrelated system. In such a circumstance a stabilization board is not normally able to resist pressures to permit all units in the group to obtain whatever level of increase has been allowed to other units. In practice, stabilization authorities are generally confronted with an unpalatable choice: allowing all units the highest increase permitted for any of their group, or attempting to maintain differentials which the industry does not desire or, in some cases, will not tolerate. Minimizing the frequency of such situations requires a stabilization program involving qualitative standards, with considerable latitude for flexibility in application to particular instances. And there is required an understanding of the most important interrelationships in the economy.

4. It has often been alleged that the primary effect of the various periods of stabilization policy in the United States has not been to restrain inflationary pressures but merely to postpone their impact. Unfortunately, there is evidence to support this conclusion, especially from the experience of the aftermath of the World War II program. But there is no inherent reason why a wage-stabilization effort must be followed by a surge of wage adjustments, if attention is provided by stabilization authorities to the potential long-run impact of stabilization policies and to the form and timing of the transition from controls to an uncontrolled economy.

A major source of problems for stabilization policy in the long run is the tendency of government officials, stabilization authorities, and the public generally to view a program of controls exclusively as a device to restrain immediate or short-term increases in compensation. In consequence, rarely is any thought given to the implications of a program's policies for the future. Not only is this disregard of future consequences unfortunate in the later instability it invites, but it also represents a default of government leadership. For a stabilization program provides the opportunity for government to encourage the development of better compensation practices, improved means of dispute settlement, and generally improved industrial relations. Were stabilization authorities to seize these opportunities by emphasizing the longer run implications of their policies, then the aftermath of a stabilization program need not be made unstable as a consequence of the previous controls.